KAMILAROI AND KURNAI

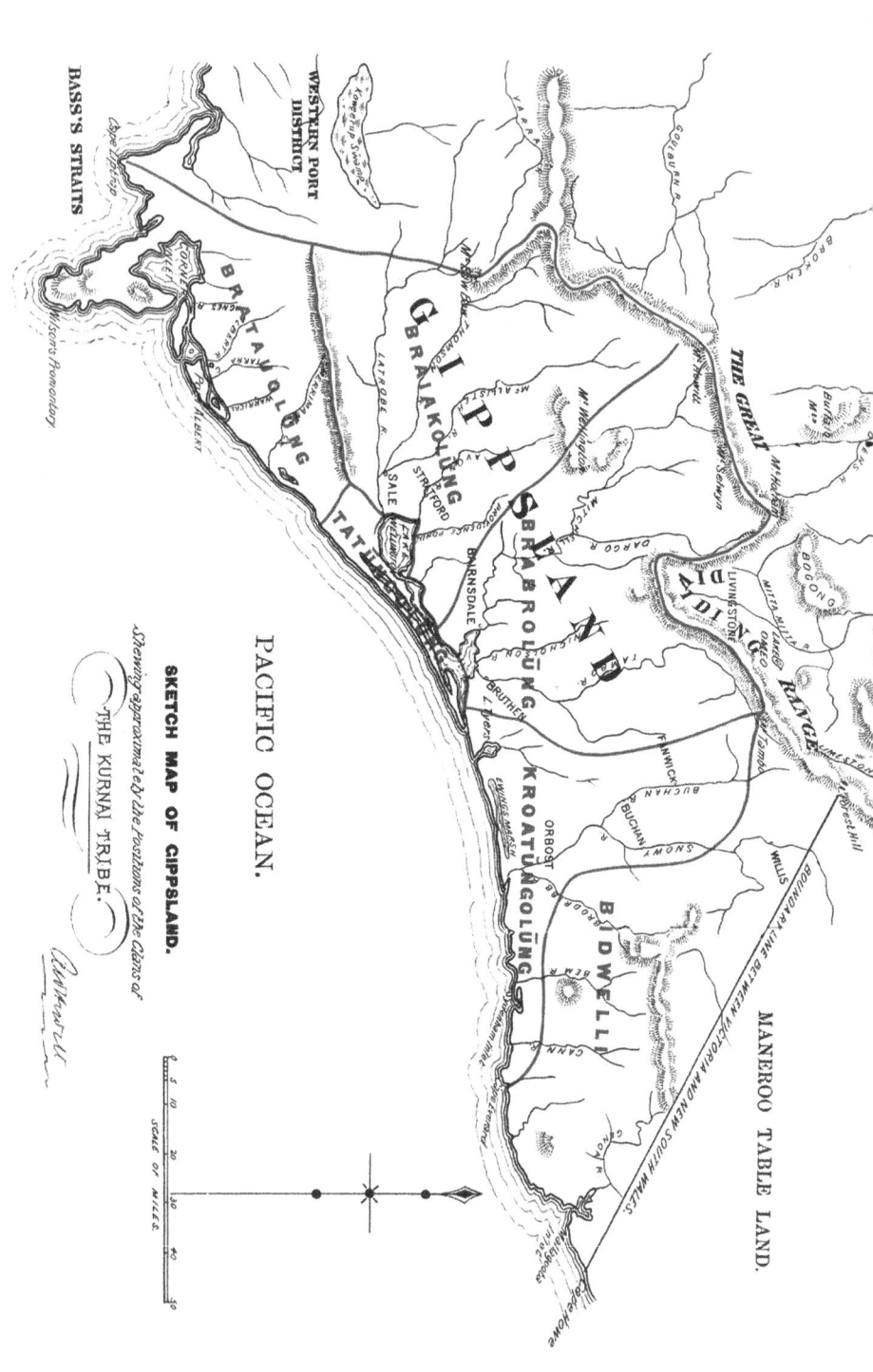

KAMILAROI AND KURNAI

GROUP-MARRIAGE AND RELATIONSHIP, AND
MARRIAGE BY ELOPEMENT

Drawn chiefly from the usage of the Australian Aborigines

ALSO

THE KURNAI TRIBE

Their customs in Peace and War

BY

LORIMER FISON, M.A., AND A. W. HOWITT, F.G.S.

WITH AN INTRODUCTION BY

LEWIS H. MORGAN, LL.D.

AUTHOR OF "SYSTEMS OF CONSANGUINITY," "ANCIENT SOCIETY," &c.

"*Indiciis monstrare recentibus abdita rerum.*"—HOR.

GEORGE ROBERTSON
MELBOURNE, SYDNEY, ADELAIDE, AND BRISBANE
MDCCCLXXX

[*All rights reserved*]

FACSIMILE EDITION PUBLISHED IN 1991 BY
Aboriginal Studies Press
for the Australian Institute of Aboriginal and
Torres Strait Islander Studies, GPO Box 553, Canberra,
ACT 2601 Australia

The views expressed in this publication are not
necessarily those of the Australian Institute of Aboriginal
and Torres Strait Islander Studies

THIS EDITION © AUSTRALIAN INSTITUTE OF ABORIGINAL AND TORRES
STRAIT ISLANDER STUDIES, 1991

Apart from any fair dealing for the purpose of private
study, research, criticism or review, as permitted under
the Copyright Act, no part of this publication may be
reproduced by any process whatsoever without the
written permission of the publisher

NATIONAL LIBRARY CATALOGUING-IN-PUBLICATION DATA

Fison, Lorimer, 1832–1907.
Kamilaroi and Kurnai: group marriage and
relationship, and marriage by elopement drawn chiefly
from the usage of the Australian Aborigines .
Facsimi ed
Includes index.
ISBN 0 85575 222 X.

[1] Aborigines, Australian — Marriage customs and
rites [2] Aborigines, Australian — Kinship
[3]. Jamilaraay (Australian people) — Rites and
ceremonies 4. Kurnai (Australian people) — Rites and
ceremonies. 5. Consanguinity — Australia. I Howitt,
A. W (Alfred William), 1830-1908 II. Title

306 0899915

PUBLISHER'S NOTE: *Kamilaroi and Kurnai* was first published in
1880 by George Robertson, Melbourne, Sydney, Adelaide and
Brisbane, and printed by Walker, May and Co, Melbourne
Apart from this page, this volume is a faithful photographic
reproduction of an original copy held in the Library of the
Australian Institute of Aboriginal and Torres Strait Islander
Studies This facsimile edition was printed in Australia by the
Australian Print Group, Maryborough, Victoria

TO THE HONOURABLE

LEWIS H. MORGAN, LL.D.,

THIS VOLUME

IS

𝔇𝔢𝔡𝔦𝔠𝔞𝔱𝔢𝔡,

AS A TOKEN OF ESTEEM,

BY THE AUTHORS

CONTENTS.

PREFATORY NOTE .. 1

KAMILAROI MARRIAGE, DESCENT, AND RELATIONSHIP 21

GROUP MARRIAGE AND RELATIONSHIP 97

THE KURNAI, THEIR CUSTOMS IN PEACE AND WAR .. 177

THEORY OF THE KURNAI SYSTEM . 293

SUMMARY AND GENERAL CONCLUSIONS . 315

ERRATA.

P. 44. The following statement, which occurs here, requires correction:—
"The two sets of gentes are conterminous with the original classes; and, descent being through the mother, they alternate between those classes in alternate generations

Ipai-Kumbu (Yungaru) = Kangaroo-Opossum-Iguana.
Muri-Kubi (Wutaru) = Emu-Bandicoot-Blacksnake.

In the next generation :—

Ipai-Kumbu = Emu-Bandicoot-Blacksnake.
Muri-Kubi = Kangaroo-Opossum-Iguana "

This is incorrect Ipai-Kumbu always = Emu-Bandicoot-Blacksnake and Muri-Kubi always = Kangaroo-Opossum-Iguana The gentes, therefore, do not "alternate between the original classes in alternate generations."

P. 52, line 2 of Latin quotation from "Eyre's Discoveries," *for* "*præbet*" *read* "*praebet*."

P. 59, line 29, *for* "kinship," *read* "kinsfolk."

P. 72, line 4, *for* "Gurgela-Burbia," *read* "Wungo-Kuberu."

P. 121, in the diagram of "Descent through males," *for* "n^1" *read* "m^1."

P. 140, line 10, *for* "Derbet and (Torgot or Tchoro)," *read* "Derbet (or Tchoro) and Torgot."

PREFATORY NOTE.

THE following memoirs—the first by the Rev. Lorimer Fison, and the second by Mr. Alfred W. Howitt, F.G.S.—were sent by these gentlemen to the undersigned, and they very kindly requested me to add an introduction, and such footnotes as the text might suggest; but the facts are so carefully and plainly presented that nothing seems left for me to do, except to call attention to the value of the materials contained in these memoirs, and to their bearing upon the early history of mankind.

While collecting materials for my work on "Consanguinity," which forms the seventeenth volume of the "Smithsonian Contributions to Knowledge," it was my good fortune to interest, as a co-labourer, Mr. Fison, then resident in the Fiji Islands. He became a direct contributor to that work, as will be seen by consulting the same, pp. 573–583. Soon afterwards, he removed to Australia, where he entered upon a wider series of investigations into the social organization of the Australian tribes, their customs in respect to marriage and descents, the form of the family, and the systems of consanguinity and affinity pertaining to the same. These researches, which extended over a period of several years, are in part embodied in the first of the memoirs named. It is proper to add that the late Professor Joseph Henry was acquainted with Mr. Fison's work, and that he addressed him a letter, in which he commended his labours, and encouraged him to continue their prosecution. Mr. Fison found an efficient fellow-labourer in the Australian field in Mr. A. W. Howitt, whose memoir is also attached. Although engaged in arduous official duties, he has found time to do excellent ethnological work, as his memoir will show. These gentlemen united in a list of printed questions touching organization, kinship, and consanguinity among the Australian blacks, which they distributed widely in the principal settlements of that country, inviting correspondence, as well as prompting inquiries. They also held personal intercourse with the natives as far as possible. From a number of original sources, they have accumulated a large body of facts, illustrating phases of savage life, and exhibiting the principal institutions, and some of the customs of the Australian aborigines.

In this connection I cannot forbear to remark, to the lasting credit of these gentlemen, that, while charged with weighty professional avocations, they have felt it their duty to stretch forth a timely, as well as an active, hand to save from oblivion the facts embodied in these memoirs.

The Australian tribes are melting away before the touch of civilization, even more rapidly than the American aborigines. In a lower ethnical condition than the latter, they have displayed less power of resistance. They now represent the condition of mankind in savagery better than it is elsewhere represented on the earth—a condition now rapidly passing away, through the destructive influence of superior races. Moreover, it is a condition of society which has not hitherto been thought worthy of special scientific investigation, although it is one of the stages of progress through which the more advanced tribes and nations of mankind have passed in their early history, and although some of the more important institutions of civilized states must be sought, in their rudimentary forms, in this very condition of savagery in which they originated. In a few years nothing will be known of the arts, institutions, manners, customs, and plan of life of savage man, except as they are preserved in memoirs like the present.

Part First of the following contribution to Australian ethnology is by Mr. Fison, on the origin and development of the classificatory system of kinship. It treats of the Australian class divisions organized upon the basis of sex, together with their laws of marriage and descent, and their system of consanguinity and affinity, in a clear, precise, and exhaustive manner. I shall limit this notice of Mr. Fison's important memoir to the following subjects:—

I.—The Mŭrdu-Legend.
II.—The extent of the distribution of the organization upon the basis of sex among the Australian aborigines.
III.—The organization into gentes or clans, with a rule prohibiting intermarriage in the gens.
IV.—Marriage in the Group.
V.—The Turanian character of Kamilaroi kinship, resulting from the class organization and from the prohibition named.
VI.—Severe penalties for violating the rule in respect to marriage—*i.e*, marrying into a prohibited class.
VII.—Mr. Fison's explanation of the classical legend concerning the trial and acquittal of Orestes by the gods, as presented by Æschylus.

These several topics by no means reach all the important questions presented and discussed in this memoir, a careful study of which will amply repay the reader.

I.—The Mŭrdu-Legend.

Mr. Fison introduces the first chapter with the very striking legend named, which recognizes a state of society in certain Australian tribes, at some early period in their history, in which the consanguine family existed. This family, the probable existence of which has been denied by a limited number of authors,[*] has been deduced theoretically from the Malayan system of consanguinity and affinity, and from the facts of the social condition of the Polynesian tribes. It is not claimed that this family exists at the present time. That state of society has passed away. This legend opens with the following paragraph, which is borne out as to its truthfulness by what is now known of Australian society :—

"After the creation, brothers and sisters, and others of the closest kin, intermarried promiscuously, until the evil effects of these alliances becoming manifest, a council of the chiefs was assembled to consider in what way they might be averted."

There we have the testimony of an accepted and perpetuated native legend, which gives to the consanguine family a basis of probability. It has more weight than mere negative assertions, which are necessarily incapable of proof. It is also a plain statement of facts as they appeared to the native mind, familiar with their present, and, to some extent, with their anterior condition. The Australians and Polynesians are alike in the condition of savagery, in which state alone the consanguine family was possible. Until their social condition and sexual relations are more thoroughly investigated, the existence of a consanguine family among them, at some early period, is

---

[*] See Address of Mr. C Staniland Wake before the London Archæological Institute (Journal for November, 1878), which seems to have received the entire concurrence of the members of the institute.

an unavoidable conclusion. It is rendered so far probable by existing knowledge that the probability can only be set aside by actual facts to the contrary.

The movement referred to—the legend goes on to say—resulted in the establishment of the Australian class system, with such an arrangement in respect to marriage that own brothers and sisters were thereafter excluded from the marriage relation. This legend not only admits consanguine marriages as previously real, but also treats the establishment of the classes on the basis of sex, with the prohibition named, as designed by its authors to avert a recognized evil. Evolutionists are slow to ascribe to savages any conscious desire for reformatory measures They concede that they try different measures by accident, and that when they discover a practical benefit, they adopt the means by which the benefit was gained. It is not supposable that savages design, consciously, reformatory measures, in the strict sense of the term; but that they are without intelligence in their action and aims, cannot be truthfully spoken. "The thoughtless brain of a savage" will answer as a poetical phrase, but it cannot be accepted as literally true. If the brain of the savage had always remained thoughtless, mankind throughout the earth would have remained savages to the present hour.

II.—The distribution of the organization on the basis of sex among the Australian aborigines.

This memoir settles the question of the wide prevalence of this most archaic organization among the Australian tribes. It was not the mere fancy of the tribes speaking the Hawaiian language, among whom it was first discovered; but it has been found in a large number of tribes scattered over immense areas in Australia. The names for the classes of males and of females, in some of the tribes, are changed dialectically beyond identification, thus showing that these classes have existed among them from a very early period. The memoir is valuable for this fact alone, and Mr. Fison is entitled to the thanks of ethnologists for ascertaining and verifying the facts contained in this table.

III.—The organization into Gentes or Clans, with the rule prohibiting marriage in the Gens.

This remarkable organization on the basis of kin, with descent in the female line universal in the early period, and in the male line universal in the later—which was retained among the Greeks and Romans until civilization was reached, when gentile society was superseded by political society, on the modern basis of territory and of property—is one of the striking facts in the history of the human mind, and of human institutions of government. A comparison of the several forms of the gentile organization among different races, leaves no doubt that it is the same organization wherever found, but in different stages of development. The Gens of the Greek and Roman peoples, the Gens of the Iroquois, the Scottish Clan, the Irish Sept, the Phratria of the Athenians, the Thum of the Mayars of India, the Kinships of the Tribes of Siberia and of Africa, and the Divisions of Kin in Australia, named after animals, are unquestionably the same organization, whatever may be asserted to the contrary.* It is shown by the composition of the group, by the mutual obligations of its members, by the rules in respect to marriage, descent, and inheritance, and of the character and tenure of the office of chief, in which there is a substantial concurrence among them all, with narrow limits of variation. It shows that the principal races of mankind, white, red, yellow, and black, derived this organ-

* See a review of "Ancient Society," in the *Academy* of 20th July, 1878, by E. B. Tylor, where the contrary is maintained.

ization from their ancestors in a far anterior condition of the respective societies which gave it birth, and that the organization was transmitted to their several descendants, who are now found upon all the continents. We are thus enabled to trace, by its uniformity, the operations of the human mind, in its upward progress from savagery to civilization, far back of the period of recorded history into the dim twilight of far-distant periods of time, with the means of reconstructing a portion of the institutional history of mankind upon evidence of the highest character.

We may now turn to one of the aspects of the Australian class divisions, which I will venture to preface with a quotation from "Ancient Society":—

"From the preceding statements, the composition of the gentes will be understood when placed in their relations to the classes. The latter are in pairs of brothers and sisters derived from each other, and the gentes themselves, through the classes, are in pairs as follows:—

Gentes.	Male.	Female.	Male.	Female.
1. IGUANA.	All are Murri and	Mata or	Kubbi and	Kapota.
2 EMU.	,, Kumbo ,,	Buta ,,	Ippai ,,	Ippata.
3. KANGAROO.	,, Murri ,,	Mata ,,	Kubbi ,,	Kapota.
4 BANDICOOT.	,, Kumbo ,,	Buta ,,	Ippai ,,	Ippata.
5. OPOSSUM	,, Murri ,,	Mata ,,	Kubbi ,,	Kapota.
6. BLACKSNAKE.	,, Kumbo ,,	Buta ,,	Ippai ,,	Ippata.

"The connection of children with a particular gens is proved by the law of marriage. Thus Iguana-Mata must marry Kumbo; her children are Kubbi and Kapota, and necessarily Iguana in gens, because descent is in the female line. Iguana-Kapota must marry Ippai; her children are Murri and Mata, and also Iguana in gens, for the same reason. In like manner Emu-Buta must marry Murri; her children are Ippai and Ippata, and of the Emu gens. So Emu-Ippata must marry Kubbi; her children are Kumbo and Buta, and also of the Emu gens. In this manner the gens is maintained by keeping in its membership the children of all its female members. The same is true in all respects of each of the remaining gentes. It will be noticed that each gens is made up, theoretically, of the descendants of two supposed female ancestors, and contains four of the eight classes It seems probable that originally there were but two male and two female classes, which were set opposite to each other in respect to the right of marriage, and

8 PREFATORY NOTE.

that the four afterwards subdivided into eight. The classes, as an anterior organization, were evidently arranged among the gentes, and not formed by the subdivision of the latter.

"Moreover, since the Iguana, Kangaroo, and Opossum gentes are found to be counterparts of each other, in the classes they contain, it follows that they are subdivisions of an original gens. Precisely the same is true of Emu, Bandicoot, and Blacksnake, in both particulars; thus reducing the six to two original gentes, with the right in each to marry into the other, but not into itself. It is confirmed by the fact that the members of the first three gentes could not originally intermarry; neither could the members of the last three. The reason which prevented intermarriage in the gens, when the three were one, would follow the subdivisions because they were of the same descent, although under different gentile names. Exactly the same thing is found among the Seneca Iroquois."*

There is an entire concurrence between the views presented by Mr. Fison, and those in the above paragraph —with, perhaps, a slight difference of opinion as to the manner in which the number of classes were evolved. If we suppose Iguana and Emu are a pair of original gentes, the eight classes are divided between them, four in each. Since Mata is the mother of Kubbi and Kapota, and Kapota is the mother of Murri and Mata, the four classes are in reality but one, with a male and female branch. They form one kinship, with descent in the female line. It is the same with the Emu gens. It would seem, therefore, more proper to say that the two original intermarrying classes in the two gentes subdivided by segmentation into eight, independently of gens, rather than that each gens subdivided into four classes, with the right to intermarry into the four classes of the other gens. The two organizations of gens and class are independent entities, of which the class is oldest in time, and the original unit of the system. The unit of organization cannot be subdivided from a greater whole,

* "Ancient Society," p. 56.

because it is necessarily an original growth. The same argument holds with respect to the four remaining gentes. Three of the six are counterparts of each other in the classes they contain, and altogether consist of but two intermarrying classes in each pair of gentes. It seems here also more proper to say that Kangaroo and Opossum were formed by the segmentation of Iguana, and that Bandicoot and Blacksnake are segments of Emu; supposing in both cases that Iguana and Emu were the first two gentes formed. It may as well have been either of the other two pairs, for aught that is known; but as there are reasons for believing that in the beginning of this organization gentes began in pairs, it may be concluded that it was the same among the Kamilaroi.

Nothing is stated showing the existence of the phratric organization among them. It may never have appeared as a definite and higher organization of two or more gentes for certain common objects. But from the form of their social system, as it appears in Mr. Fison's memoir, the basis of two phratries is found in the relation of the gentes to each other. Thus Iguana, Kangaroo, and Opossum would naturally form one phratry, composed of gentes having the same class, all the members of which are of the same lineage; Emu, Bandicoot, and Blacksnake a second phratry— they also have identical classes. Although we have here the gentile organization in its lowest, and, in some respects, in an archaic form, there is a theoretical probability that they possessed the phratric organization in its simplest form, which time and experience would have developed into a positive form. These views of the evolution of the system are merely opinions; and those of Mr. Fison, where any degree of opinion exists, are entitled to as much, and, perhaps, to greater weight than my own. They are submitted with the greatest deference to Mr. Fison's views.

IV.—Marriage in the Group.

It is very difficult for the men of our times to understand marriage in the group, which is something new, even in ethnology. Marriage among civilized races is so entirely different from this, that it is not easy for us to recognize marriage in the group as a form of the marriage relation. A part of the embarrassment arises from the use of the term marriage to express relation of the sexes so peculiar; but with this qualification the use of the term is justified, because it is a form of marriage followed by cohabitation. Among the Australian savages, as this memoir fully shows, groups of males are found united to groups of females—not by any ceremony of a formal marriage to which the groups were parties, but by an organic law, respected by tribal usage, recognized over large areas, and followed in actual practice by the cohabitation of the parties. A woman is found one day living with one man in the marriage relation, and on the next day with another man of the same group in the same relation, and perhaps several men with several women at the same time. In Chapter III., to which attention is invited, the subject of marriage and descents is treated. Marriage in the group is presented and explained. A group of males, distinguished by the same class name, are the born husbands of a group of females bearing another class name; and whenever a male of this class meets a female of the other class, they recognize each other as husband and wife, and their right to live in this relation is recognized by the tribe to which they belong. Mr. Fison remarks, upon this subject, that "this seems to be the most extensive system of communal marriage the world has ever known. . . . It is an arrangement extending across a continent (see Table B), which divides very widely-scattered tribes into intermarrying classes, and gives a man of one class marital rights over women of another class in a tribe a thousand miles away, and speaking a language other than his own." Near the end of this chapter, while commenting upon descent in the female line, which is the general rule in Australian tribes, he observes that "when a woman is married to a thousand miles of husbands, then it is evident that paternity must be, to say the least of it, somewhat doubtful." The facts presented in this memoir shed a new light upon this singular relation of the sexes low down in savagery.

> V.—The Turanian character of Kamilaroi kinship, resulting from the class organization, with the prohibition of marriage in the Gens.

The main difference between the Malayan and the Turanian systems of consanguinity is in those relationships which depend upon the intermarriage or the non-intermarriage of own brothers and sisters. As among the Australian tribes, divided into male and female classes, such marriages are prohibited by an organic law, the Turanian system of consanguinity would be expected to exist, unless it was superseded by a system in principle like the Aryan; for but three systems have as yet been found among the tribes and nations of mankind. In chapter IV. Mr. Fison shows, among the Australian tribes organized in classes, the presence of the Turanian system. His general discussion of the subject of consanguinity, in this and the succeeding chapter, is deserving of the attention of the reader. It is done with thoroughness, and with a profound understanding of the elements of a difficult subject.

> VI.—Severe penalties for violating the rule in respect to marriage—*i.e.*, for marrying into a prohibited class.

Marriage in the group is a practice seemingly so singular and extraordinary that it would be natural to explain it as a custom originating in laxity of morals, and in low views of the relations of the sexes among savages. Under such usages, no restraints whatever upon the passions of the sexes would be expected to exist. But such a hypothesis is met by the fact that this usage is upheld by public sentiment and organic law, which condemns and punishes every infringement of prohibitions in the relations of the sexes which forms a part of a general system. Accordingly, we find that any attempt to take a wife from a prohibited class in the same tribe, or even from a distant and hostile tribe, having a similar class organization, is at once resisted, and punished with severity by the tribe itself. A number of illustrations are given in Chapter III., of which the following is one:—

"If a warrior took to himself a captive who belonged to a forbidden class, he would be hunted down like a wild beast; and, unless he managed to keep out of the way until the hot wrath of the tribe had cooled down, he would be killed, and his captive with him. This is a strong statement, but it rests on strong evidence."

It thus appears that low down in savage society, where usages and customs exhibit the lowest possible views of the relations of the sexes, restraints exist; and these restraints are upheld and maintained by custom and by public opinion with vigour and persistency. It exhibits, dimly, a type of that moral sense which binds together the elements of civilized society, and refutes the fallacious proposition stereotyped in the phrase, "the thoughtless brain of a savage." The thoughts of a savage are feeble in degree, and limited in range, of which Mr. Howitt's monograph furnishes a number of examples; but the principle of intelligence, though infantile, is ever present and ever active.

VII.—Mr. Fison's explanation of the classical legend of the trial and acquittal of Orestes by the gods, as presented by Æschylus.

In an appendix to his memoir, Mr. Fison re-examines the celebrated trial of Orestes, who is pursued by the furies for the murder of his mother. Sir John Lubbock and others have essayed explanations of this case of some ingenuity, but that of Mr. Fison seems to be as conclusive as it is original and complete.*

The monograph of the Kŭrnai, by Mr. Howitt, is also a contribution to ethnology of exceptional value. The Kŭrnai tribe inhabit Gippsland, Victoria, in the south-east part of Australia—an area which is separated from the remainder of the continent by natural barriers, more or less formidable. This insulation was favourable to their progress. In the arts of life, they are not specially advanced beyond the other Australian tribes; but in their social relations, particularly in their usages in respect to marriage, and in the form of the family, they show a marked advance beyond other Australian tribes. This memoir is based upon a personal knowledge of the usages and customs of the Kŭrnai, gained by direct personal intercourse with the remnant of this once large tribe, through a long residence in their country. For ascertaining and verifying the facts embodied in this memoir, Mr. Howitt possessed peculiar facilities. It presents a fresh and vivid picture of aboriginal life, and has the merits of an original and intelligent investigation of the usages and customs of savages.

In speaking of the special subjects treated in this memoir, I propose to confine myself to a brief notice of the following :—

    I.—Infanticide.
    II.—Marriage between single pairs by mutual consent, followed by elopement.

* This appendix has now been incorporated with the memoir.—L F.

III.—Non-intercourse between son-in-law and mother-in-law.

IV.—Previous marriage in the Group, and with it a punaluan family, and back of that a consanguine family, among the Kŭrnai, deduced by Mr. Howitt as necessary antecedents of their present marriage customs, and of their system of consanguinity.

V.—The Kŭrnai belief that death is not the natural termination of life, but a consequence of accident, open violence, or necromancy.

VI.—Insecurity of life among savages.

While these topics give an imperfect conception of the contents of this memoir, they will serve to illustrate its general character.

I.—Infanticide.

The subject of infanticide, which has been so often exaggerated, is presented by Mr. Howitt in a plain manner, with the native reasons alleged for the practice. The main fact is made to appear that it is limited to families overburdened with children, and thus is of very limited practice, which is most likely the case. As a general rule, wherever infanticide prevails, or has prevailed in the past, Mr. Howitt observes—

"On speaking to a number of the Kŭrnai upon this subject, they gave me the following explanation. It is often difficult to carry about young children, particularly where there are several. Their wandering life renders this very difficult. It sometimes happened that when a child was about to be born, its father would say to his wife, 'We have too many children to carry about—best leave this one, when it is born, behind in the camp.' On this, the new-born child was left lying in the camp, and the family moved elsewhere. The infant, of course, soon perished. The Kŭrnai drew this singular distinction, that they never knew an instance of parents killing their children—but, only of *leaving behind* new-born infants. The aboriginal mind does not seem to perceive the horrid idea of leaving an unfortunate baby to die miserably in a deserted camp. . . . It may be that the feelings of affection arising from association and dependence have not, in such a case, been aroused, and the natural parental feelings seem to be overborne by what they conceive to be the exigencies of their circumstances."

In such a case, the term infanticide, which implies an act of direct personal violence by the parents, producing death, is hardly appropriate. Desertion, or exposure of infants to perish, expresses the act more accurately, while it mitigates, in some degree, the deep atrocity of the crime.

II.—Marriage between single pairs by mutual consent, followed by elopement.

Among the Kŭrnai is found the extraordinary usage that marriage by the consent and procurement of parents, so universal in barbarous society, is the exception, while marriage by consent of the parties to be married, independently of parents, is the rule, followed by elopement to escape the violence of parents and kindred. Such a custom as that here indicated is unusual in the tribes of mankind, whether savage or barbarous, and I am not aware that anything precisely like it has elsewhere been observed.

"The young Kŭrnai," Mr Howitt remarks, "can, as a rule, acquire a wife in one way only. He must run away with her. Native marriage may be brought about in various ways If the young man is so fortunate as to have an unmarried sister, and to have a friend who also has an unmarried sister, they may arrange with the girls to run off together; or he may make his arrangement with some eligible girl whom he fancies, and who fancies him; or a girl, if she fancies a young man, may send him a secret message, asking—'Will you find me some food?' and this is understood to be a proposal. But in every such case it is essential to success that the parents of the bride should be utterly ignorant of what is about to take place. It is no use his asking a wife excepting under most exceptional circumstances, for he can only acquire one in the usual manner, and that by running off with her."

The father, brothers, and kindred pursue the runaways,

and, if they find them, they are cruelly treated, and punished as for an actual offence.

"Her father perhaps spears her through the leg, or both feet, and her mother and brothers may severely beat her. As for the husband, when he returns, he has to fight her male relatives. . . . At length, the family becoming tired of objecting, the mother may say—'Oh! it's all right, better let him have her'"

The form of the family resulting from these unions is called by Mr. Howitt the Pairing Family, which is entirely accurate, from what is elsewhere stated of their social condition. As this custom must have commenced as an accidental practice, it seems singular that it should have ripened into a permanent tribal usage.

III.—Non-intercourse between son-in-law and mother-in-law.

This singular custom, which has been found so widely prevalent among the lower races of mankind, is found in an equally positive form among the Kŭrnai, and seemingly with reasons for the practice. Mr. Howitt gives the following illustration :—

"A Brabrolūng, who is a member of the Church of England, was one day talking to me. His wife's mother was passing at some little distance, and I called to her. Suffering at the time from a cold, I could not make her hear, and said to the Brabrolūng—'Call Mary, I want to speak to her.' He took no notice whatever, but looked vacantly on the ground. I spoke to him again sharply, but still no answer. I then said—'What do you mean by taking no notice of me?' He thereupon called to his wife's brother, who was at a little distance, 'Tell Mary Mr. Howitt wants her,' and turning to me, continued, reproachfully, 'You know very well I could not do that ; you know I cannot speak to that old woman.'"

It seems not unlikely that the hostile feelings aroused against him in the mind of her mother in consequence of his elopement with her daughter, which must be supposed real, received a continued expression from the mother through

PREFATORY NOTE. 17

this refusal of all intercourse with her son-in-law. An occasional occurrence at first, ripened in time into a settled custom.

IV.—Previous marriage in the Group, and with it a punaluan family, and back of that a consanguine family, among the Kŭrnai, deduced by Mr. Howitt as necessary antecedents of their present marriage customs, and of their system of consanguinity.

Passing over Mr. Howitt's discussion of the office of elder or of chief, of blood feud, and of their organization into kinships or clans (Table A), I will next refer to his remarks upon their system of consanguinity, as presented in Tables B and C, with his inferences therefrom. Premising that the existence of the consanguine family, so named, is proved mainly by the Malayan system of consanguinity and affinity, which gives the relationships that would actually exist in such a family, and that the existence of the punaluan family, so called, is mainly proved by the Turanian system of consanguinity and affinity still prevalent in Asia, and by the Ganowanian system still prevalent in America, which gives the relationships that would actually exist in a punaluan family, Mr. Howitt finds evidence, in their present terms of relationship, that the Kŭrnai must have had both the punaluan and the consanguine families at some anterior periods. He remarks that—

"The inter-relations of this group are, I think, strictly Malayan in theory, for they are all regarded as brothers and sisters to each other. This is further carried out in their relations towards each other, except when they stand in the relation of *Mŭmmŭng* [father's sister] and *Babŭk* [mother's brother] * It is highly significant that, in these instances, as in others which may be perceived on examining the Table B, the secondary relations—if I may so term them—are such as should

* In order that Dr Morgan's meaning may not be misunderstood, see the group referred to—Nos. 12, 13, 14, 15.

3

be indicated logically by the primary terms themselves. It lends much strength to the belief that they have arisen at first through adaptation of language to existing relationships, and not as mere terms of personal address. For comparison I give, in Table C, the principal Kŭrnai terms, together with analogous ones used by two far-distant tribes. The comparative simplicity of the former will be apparent. These terms suggest a family in which a group of brothers had their wives in common, or in which a group of sisters had their husbands in common, but in which it did not perhaps necessarily follow that the brother's children were the husbands and wives of the sister's children. [This gives the punaluan family] They also, I think, strongly suggest a more archaic form of family, in which marriage was consanguine."

This inference of Mr. Howitt is important. His familiarity with the condition of the Australian tribes gives weight to his opinions; and it seems to the writer that they are fully warranted by the native system of consanguinity.

V.—The Kŭrnai belief that death is not the natural termination of life, but a consequence of accident, open violence, or necromancy.

Among the curious beliefs of the Australian blacks, two may be here repeated. "It is not difficult," says Mr. Howitt, "to see how, among savages, who have no knowledge of the real causes of diseases which are the common lot of humanity, the very suspicion even of such a thing as death from disease should be unknown. Death by accident they can imagine—death by violence they can imagine—but I question if they can, in their savage condition, imagine death by mere disease. . . . Thus the belief arises that death occurs only from accident, open violence, or secret magic; and, naturally, that the latter can only be met by counter-charms." And, of a like belief in ghosts, he gives the following instance of a native mistaking a living European for a ghost:—"A Brabrolūng told me that, when he was a little boy, near the Tambo river, and he saw a white man for the first time, he felt sure that it was a *mrart* [ghost], and he ran away. He said he was sure it was a *mrart*, because 'it was so very pale.'" These, and a number of other beliefs, usages and customs presented in these memoirs, give a new insight into the life of savages, and show the feebleness of their mental powers in comparison with those of civilized men. Some realization of this great difference between the savage and the civilized man may be gained from this contribution to Australian ethnology. It indicates the low place from which the human race started on its upward career.

VI.—Insecurity of life among savages.

One of the greatest results of civilization is the security it gives to individuals and to families except in time of actual war; and now even the approach of war has ceased to be sudden. Among barbarians, and especially among savages who occupy limited areas, they are constantly exposed to sudden and stealthy attack. A family retires to rest at night without any assurance they may not be attacked before the morning comes, or that the day will pass without the sudden appearance of an enemy. It is one of the dangers of their condition, as well as obstacles to their progress. The Kŭrnai are no exception to the rule. "In one aspect," Mr. Howitt remarks, "the life of the Kŭrnai is a life of dread. He lives in fear of the visible and the invisible. He never knew the moment when the lurking Brajerak might not spear him from behind; and he never knew the moment when some secret foe among the Kŭrnai might not succeed in passing over him some spell against which he could not struggle, or from which even the most potent counter-charm given him by his ancestors could not free him."

The distribution of food among the Kŭrnai, discussed at the end of the memoir, and the character of the Kŭrnai for intelligence, also discussed at its close, are interesting and suggestive subjects, but the unexpected length of this note precludes their consideration. Ethnologists will read this contribution to Australian ethnology with pleasure, and with a sense of grateful obligation to its authors. It is an attempt to fill up some of the great deficiencies in our knowledge of the condition of savage tribes, a knowledge which necessarily lies at the foundation of an intelligent scheme of human history and development.

I am compelled also to omit any notice of Mr. Fison's brief discussion of the theory of the Kŭrnai system, which forms the third part of these memoirs. It forms a necessary and important sequel to Mr. Howitt's monograph.

LEWIS H. MORGAN.

ROCHESTER, New York, *May*, 1879.

NOTE.—This introduction was written by Dr. Morgan after a perusal of the MSS , the concluding portion of which was sent to him in February, 1879. Since that time the entire work has been carefully revised, much additional matter has been put in, and the arrangement has been considerably altered.

The Committee of the Smithsonian Institution did the authors the honour of accepting their memoirs, but they had so many works already in hand that a very long delay before publication was unavoidable. The authors were consequently compelled reluctantly to forego the great advantage of having their memoirs issued from the Smithsonian press.

KAMILAROI MARRIAGE, DESCENT, AND RELATIONSHIP:

An Attempt to Trace the Origin and Development of the Turanian System of Kinship, as shown in the Class Divisions of the Australian Aborigines, with their Laws of Marriage and Descent.

BY

LORIMER FISON.

PREFACE TO KAMILAROI MARRIAGE, &c.

THE chief object of this memoir is to trace the formation of the exogamous intermarrying divisions which have been found among so many savage and barbaric tribes of the present day, and to show that what the Hon. Lewis H. Morgan calls the Punaluan family, with the Turanian system of kinship, logically results from them. The Australian classes are especially valuable for this purpose, because they give us what seem to be the earliest stages of development.

To the gentlemen who were good enough to furnish me with information concerning the tribes whose customs are within their knowledge, I am under deep obligation. Their names will be found in connection with such of the facts supplied by them as I have had occasion to use.

My special thanks are due to the courteous editor of the *Australasian*, who published several of my letters of inquiry in that ably-conducted journal, and thereby gained for me some of my most valued correspondents. Above all, it is to the publication of those letters that I owe the help of my friend and fellow-worker, Mr. Alfred W. Howitt, F.G.S.

As it has come in my way to question more than one of the views advanced by Sir John Lubbock in his "Origin of Civilization," it is only fair to call attention to the fact that my remarks are based upon the second edition of that work. It would be inexcusable on the part of one who has easy access to books to deal solely with so early an issue of a work which has passed through several subsequent editions. My excuse is, that a mission station in Fiji affords no such access, even now that the group forms a part of the British empire, and that, until within the last two or three years, we were almost entirely excluded from the outer world. The second edition of the "Origin of Civilization" was the latest issue I could procure when I visited Australia in 1871.

With reference to the spelling of Australian words, I have endeavoured to follow a uniform plan, by sounding the consonants as in English, and giving the vowels their proper sounds. My difficulty here has been to find out what sounds our correspondents intended to express, and I cannot suppose that I have overcome this difficulty in every case.

I have used the word "class" in preference to tribe, sept, or clan, because each of these words is apt to have a sort of confused meaning to the reader which might tend to produce a wrong impression. The Greek "phratria" would be the most correct term; but, for several reasons, "class" seemed to be the more convenient for the special purposes of this memoir, to designate the primary divisions of a community, and their first subdivisions.

LORIMER FISON.

FIJI, *August*, 1878.

CHAPTER I.

INTRODUCTORY.

MURDU-LEGEND—M'Lennan's Theory of Kinship Terms—The Three Kinds of Class Divisions—Object of the Treatise—Explanatory Remarks.

IN a valuable pamphlet on the Dieyeri (Cooper's Creek) tribe of Australian aborigines, Mr. Samuel Gason tells us the following legend with regard to the custom called Mŭrdu:—

"After the creation, brothers, sisters, and others of the closest kin, intermarried promiscuously, until—the evil effects of these alliances becoming manifest—a council of the chiefs was assembled to consider in what way they might be averted, the result of their deliberations being a petition to the Muramura (Good Spirit), in answer to which he ordered that the tribe should be divided into branches, and distinguished one from another by different names, after objects animate and inanimate, such as dogs, mice, emu, rain, iguana, and so forth; the members of any such branch not to intermarry, but with permission for one branch to mingle with another. Thus, the son of a dog might not marry the daughter of a dog, but either might form an alliance with a mouse, rat, or other family. This custom is still observed, and the first question asked of a stranger is, 'What murdoo?'—*i.e.*, 'Of what family are you?'" ("Gason's Dieyeri Tribe," p. 13. Cox: Adelaide, South Australia, 1874.)

There can be no doubt that this is a genuine Australian legend. Mr. Gason is well known as a trustworthy person. He has an intimate acquaintance with the people of whom he writes, and he speaks their language fluently. But, whatever may be thought of the legend itself, or of its value as evidence with regard to the state of society to which it points, it is certain that divisions similar to those which it mentions are found throughout the length and breadth of the Australian continent, as well as in many other parts of the world, and that from these divisions, with their intersexual arrangements, flows the entire system of kinship called the Turanian* by Mr. Lewis H. Morgan, in his work on "Systems of Consanguinity and Affinity of the Human Family," and in his more recent work entitled "Ancient Society."

Mr. J. F. M'Lennan refuses to accept the terms of kinship common to the numerous tribes whose system is the Turanian, as expressing either consanguinity or affinity. He looks upon them as forming a mere "system of addresses," and disposes of Mr. Morgan's theory as to the origin of the classificatory system of kinship in the following words:—

"The space I have devoted to the consideration of the solution may seem disproportioned to its importance; but, issuing from the press of the Smithsonian Institution, and its preparation having been aided by the United States Government, Mr. Morgan's work has been very generally quoted as a work of authority, and it seemed worth while to take the trouble necessary to show its utterly unscientific character."†

This is certainly a somewhat high-handed manner of setting aside as worthless a most painstaking and accurate

---

* "Turanian." This term of Mr. Morgan's has been objected to by some of his English critics as inappropriate; but we may as well use it until a better be provided. Mr. Morgan is doubtless more concerned to establish his facts than to insist upon his nomenclature. It should be noted that, strictly speaking, the "Kamilaroi system" is what he calls the Ganowanian, as distinguished from the Turanian. The distinction between the two is in the line of descent, which is through females in the former, and through males in the latter. But, as the line of descent does not affect personal relationship, it did not seem worth while to trouble the reader with more than one term in this memoir. I have, therefore, used Turanian as applying to both lines.

† "Studies in Ancient History," quoted by Morgan, "Ancient Society," p. 509.

INTRODUCTORY. 27

summary of the result of researches carried on for more than twenty years in almost every part of the world; and, even if we do not take into account the value of the facts collected and collated by Mr. Morgan, we may perhaps do well to hesitate before we cast aside as utterly worthless the theory which he has founded on the facts. His theory certainly finds strong confirmation in the evidence afforded by the Australian classes, and it seems to be the only reasonable explanation of those divisions.

They are of three kinds, arising from—

1. The division of a tribe into two exogamous intermarrying classes—the word *tribe* being used as synonymous with *community*.

2. The subdivision of these two classes into four.

3. Their subdivision into gentes distinguished by totems, which are generally, though not invariably, the names of animals.

One set of these classes—viz., that with the class names Ipai, Muri, Kubi, and Kumbu—has been briefly noticed in M'Lennan's "Primitive Marriage," Tylor's "Early History of Mankind," Bonwick's "Tasmanians," and other works. A memorandum upon it, and its totemic subdivisions, by the Rev. W. Ridley, M A., was printed in the journal of the Anthropological Society, and it has also been carefully examined by Morgan in his "Ancient Society."

My present object is to trace the formation and the gradual development of the classes in the order already stated, to set forth their laws of marriage and descent, and to show that the terms of kinship peculiar to the Turanian system necessarily arise from class divisions, which are governed by such laws. If this can be shown, it will be difficult to maintain Mr. M'Lennan's theory that those terms represent nothing more than a system of addresses, unless we suppose that the Australians and American Indians, as well

28   KAMILAROI MARRIAGE.

as the numerous Asiatic and African tribes—who have similar divisions governed by similar inter-sexual laws—invented those divisions and founded those laws by a sort of common inspiration, for no other purpose than that individuals might be enabled to call one another by fictitious terms of kinship instead of by their own proper names. Mr. M'Lennan seems not to have been aware that there are tribes—the Friendly Islanders, for instance—whose system of kinship is the Turanian, who use all the terms peculiar to that system, but who never employ them in addressing one another.

A few words of preliminary explanation may be useful here. It must be distinctly understood, and borne in mind, that the laws of marriage and descent which I shall endeavour to set forth can be said to prevail in Australia among those tribes only which have the organization hereinafter described. We have found many such tribes, but there are very many others yet unreached by our inquiries, and there are others again concerning which our information is imperfect. Some of these appear not to fall in with the system which we may call the Kamilaroi,* and much work yet remains to be done in order to ascertain their regulations.

In the following pages the words *marriage, husband, wife,* and indeed all the terms of kinship, are used in a certain accommodated sense. Husband and wife are not

---

* Some of the South Australian tribes in particular appear to differ widely from the Kamilaroi. They are divided into clans distinguished by totems, but they seem not to have the class organization, and their line of descent is said to be through males. Further investigation may, perhaps, connect their present regulations with the Kamilaroi system, as in the case of the Kŭrnai (*See* Theory of the Kŭrnai System, &c.), but the information available concerning them is not sufficient to warrant anything more than a bare conjecture. There are also tribes which have the two primary classes, but which do not appear to have adopted the four classes with the peculiar marriage arrangements.

necessarily man and wife according to our ideas. "My husband," for instance, among tribes such as the Australian, does not necessarily single out any one man in particular. A woman may apply it to any one of a group of tribal brothers who have the right of taking her to wife.

The word *tribe*, also, is a very misleading term, and requires careful definition. In these pages it will never be used (unless in quotation) to denote any division within a community. Where used, it will denote the entire community—*e.g.*, by "the Larakia tribe" will be meant "the community of Australian aborigines calling themselves the Larakia."

It must also be borne in mind that present usage is not to the full extent that set forth by the class divisions. It is founded upon them, and is conformable to them, but the present inter-sexual arrangements are those of an extremely loose form of polygamy rather than those of what may be called group marriage—*i.e.*, communal marriage. Every marriage at the present day among the Australian blacks who have the Kamilaroi system—giving to the word *marriage* a very wide meaning—is necessarily regulated by the classes; but certain modifications as to the extent of the matrimonial privilege have been introduced. Here, as elsewhere, present usage is in advance of the ancient rules. But those rules underlie it, and are felt through it; and the underlying strata crop up in many places.

By present usage, I mean that which has been developed by the natives themselves, not that which has resulted from their contact with the white men. This is a factor which must be altogether cast out of the calculation, and an investigator on this line of research needs to be continually on the watch against it. Even now the information supplied by the few aborigines who remain near our more populous settlements has to be received with caution, and probably in a few years it will be only in the far interior that inquirers will find trustworthy evidence concerning the Australian classes. Most of the tribes within easy reach are already so reduced in number that they cannot observe the class regulations. Clan after clan has died out, and the few wretched survivors are obliged to take such mates as death has left them, whether they be of the right classes or not. The rum-saturated natives in the neighbourhood of our towns long ago so far profited by the teaching of the higher civilization as to make money by the prostitution of their women. No wonder that the inter-sexual rules, which were held as sacred obligations by their fathers, should be well-nigh forgotten by them. The black mounted police, and natives who take service with the owners of cattle or sheep stations, learn from the white men to disregard native customs; and that which is disregarded soon drops out of the aboriginal mind. The old people may remember the old rules, but the young folks grow up in ignorance of them, and in a few years there will be none of those elders left.

"I regret," writes one of our informants,[*] "that my attention was not directed to this matter ten years ago, when the natives were numerous, when there were old people of intelligence to be found among them, when one might, without hesitation, accept their ideas and expressions as original. . . . You remark truly that now is the time to gather information. A year or two hence, and it will be too late. The tribe with which I identified myself was 900 strong twenty-eight years ago, when I first began to study their habits. Now they number only seventeen!"

[*] Mr. D. S. Stewart, to whom we are indebted for much valuable help.

CHAPTER II.

THE CLASS DIVISIONS.

Wide-spread prevalence of the Class Divisions—Division of a Tribe into Two Classes—Subdivision into Four Classes—Subdivisions distinguished by Totems—Kamilaroi Marriage with the Half-sister.

A FEW quotations from the letters of gentlemen who have furnished information to Mr. Howitt and myself will be sufficient to show that the class division is no mere local institution as far as Australia is concerned. It extends across the continent from east to west, and from north to south, and it has been traced far among the islands also. But I do not mean to assert that it takes in every tribe some one of the forms which I am about to describe. It may, however, be safely asserted that these forms are of wide prevalence.

Mr. Lionel H. Gould writes from Nicol Bay, West Australia :—

"In this district I include the country—say from 100 miles east of the De Grey River to the North-west Cape, and inland—say 150 miles. Throughout this extent of country, although dialects differ every fifty or sixty miles, the same class distinctions are observed."

Mr. G. F. Bridgman, Mackay, Queensland, writes as follows :—

"I have a Brisbane black with me who has been over nearly all Australia, the Kamilaroi country among other places. He tells me the divisions are nearly the same over all the continent, though the names (*i e.*, the class names) are different. One term here represents another in another place."

Mr. William Reeve, jun., says :—

"My informant, Dora, a native of the Herbert River (Queensland) tribe, says all the tribes round—say within a radius of 100 miles—are bound by the same laws as her own, though the actual names indicating particular relationships are often different"

The next words of Mr. Reeve's letter show that, by "the names indicating particular relationships," he means, not specific terms of kinship, but names indicating class divisions.

"For instance," he continues, "a Tarawangan is called a Kolelangan in a neighbouring tribe, and she cannot marry a Tarawang in Dora's tribe, or in any other tribe." (Mr. Reeve uses *tribe* as equivalent to *community*)

Similar testimony concerning the usage in South Australia, the Darling River country, and many other districts, might be quoted here.

The Rev. R. H. Codrington, M.A., of the Melanesian Mission, writes :—

"I have ascertained that they (the class divisions) are identical as far south as the north of Pentecost at any rate ; that a Banks Islander knows, or easily learns, which is his 'side of the house' (*i e.*, class) in all that group, and that Star Island people know theirs in Aurora. The Aurora people know theirs in Leper's Island, and the people of Leper's know theirs in Espiritu Santo"

The Rev. George Brown, F.R.G S., of the Wesleyan Mission, tells me that he has found the divisions at New Britain also ; and all our informants agree in stating that the rules of marriage and descent are substantially uniform throughout the districts within their knowledge. It will be seen that, *mutatis mutandis*, they coincide with the rules of the exogamous intermarrying tribal divisions which have been observed in so many other parts of the world.

THE CLASS DIVISIONS.

DIVISION OF A TRIBE INTO TWO CLASSES.

The simplest, and probably the earliest, form of the class division among the Australian aborigines is the separation of a community into two intermarrying classes, each having a distinctive title, which is taken by every one of its members.

This form has been found from South Australia to Northern Queensland, as well as among the islands.

The Mount Gambier (South Australia) tribe divides into two classes, called respectively Kumite and Krokī. The females are called Kumitegor and Krokigor. (Informant, Mr. D. S. Stewart, Mount Gambier.)

The Lower Darling tribe divides into Kilparas and Mukwaras. There is a tradition that the Darling River Adam had two wives with those names. Kilpara's descendants are called Kilpara; Mukwara's descendants are called Mukwara. (Informant, Mr. Charles G. N. Lockhart, Wentworth, New South Wales. Other informants write Maguara for Mukwara.)

A Queensland tribe divides into Yūngarū and Wūtarū. The feminine forms are Yungaruan and Wutaruan. (Informant, Mr. G. F. Bridgman, Mackay, Queensland.)

Similar divisions of a tribe, or community, into two intermarrying classes, are found among the Banks Islanders and others, who separate into two Veve. Veve = Mother. (Informant, the Rev. R. H. Codrington, M.A., Norfolk Island.)

At New Britain, the two intermarrying classes are called Pikalába and Mŭramŭra. (Informant, Rev. G. Brown.)

Charles New, Burton, Du Chaillu, and others, mention similar divisions into two classes among the Gallas and other African tribes. It is well worth while to inquire whether to these we may not add the ancient Sun and Moon divisions of India.

The laws of marriage and descent connected with these divisions will appear from the following table and diagram :—

TABLE A.

Tribe and Informant	Class	The Male Marries	Children
Mount Gambier, S A :— Mr D. S Stewart.	Kumite. Kroki.	Krokigor. Kumitegor.	Kroki-gor Kumite-gor.
Darling River :— Mr C G N Lockhart.	Kilpara Mukwara.	Mukwara Kilpara.	Mukwara. Kilpara.
Mackay, Queensland :— Mr G. F. Bridgman	Yungaru. Wutaru	Wutaruan Yungaruan	Wutaru-an Yungaru-an.
Mota, Banks Islands:— Rev R H Codrington.	Veve A Veve B	Veve B Veve A	Veve B Veve A.
New Britain :— Rev G. Brown	Pikalaba Muramura	Muramura Pikalaba	Muramura. Pikalaba.

The regulations of these classes being the same in every case, as is manifest from the foregoing table, a diagram showing the descents to grandchildren in any one tribe will suffice for all :—

DIAGRAM No. 1.

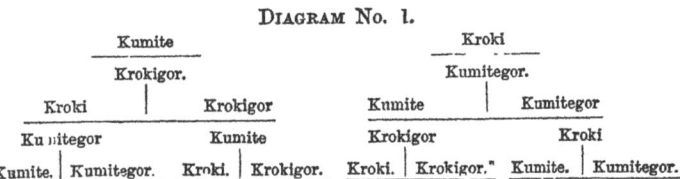

Allowing to each marriage a son and a daughter, we have in the second descent two males and two females of each class. Let this be kept in mind for comparison with the descents in tribes whose class divisions take other forms.

Mr Howitt has found two tribes—the Ngarego of Carawong, Maneroo, New South Wales, and the Wakeruk, an East Gippsland tribe—which have the two divisions, but their regulations are seemingly anomalous. These require investigation, as pointing to a system differing from that hereinafter described. Indications of such a system are found elsewhere in Australia.

DIVISION OF A TRIBE INTO FOUR CLASSES.

In many Australian tribes we find four classes, which can be shown to be subdivisions of two primary classes.*

A selection of class names, indicating the four divisions, is given in the following table. Others might be inserted, but these will amply suffice to show the laws of marriage and descent, as well as to indicate the wide-spread prevalence of these class divisions.

---

* It is possible that the four classes may have been formed by the amalgamation of two tribes, each of which was divided into two classes. See p. 70 for a detailed statement of this hypothesis.

TABLE B.*

Tribe and Informants.	Class Name.		The Male Marries.	Children.	
	Male.	Female.		Male.	Female.
Kamilaroi :— Mr. T. E. Lance. Rev. W. Ridley. †	Ipai. Kumbu. Muri. Kubi.	Ipatha. Butha. Matha. Kubitha. ‡	Kubitha. Matha. Butha. Ipatha.	Muri. Kubi. Ipai. Kumbu.	Matha. Kubitha. Ipatha. Butha.
Antakerinya Tribe, Central Australia.— Mr. C. Giles, jun.	Bultara. Parula. Panangka. Kumira.	The same. ,, ,, ,,	Kumura. Panangka. Parula. Bultara.	Panangka. Kumura. Bultara. Parula.	The same. ,, ,, ,,
Herbert River, Queensland : Mr. W. Reeve, jun.	Tarawang. Bunda. Barang. Bulgowang.	Tarawangan. Bundagan. Barangan. Bulgowangan.	Bulgowangan. Barangan. Bundagan. Tarawangan.	Barang. Bulgowang. Tarawang. Bunda.	Barangan. Bulgowangan. Tarawangan. Bundagan.
West Australia :— Mr. L. H. Gould.	Paliali. Poronga. Banaka. Kimera.	The same. ,, ,, ,,	Kimera. Banaka. Poronga. Paliali.	Banaka. Kimera. Paliali. Poronga.	The same. ,, ,, ,,
Mackay, Queensland.— Mr. G. F. Brdgman.	Gurgela. Burbia. Wungo. Kuberu.	Gurgelan. Burbian. Wungoan. Kuberuan.	Kuberuan. Wungoan. Burbian. Gurgelan.	Wungo. Kuberu. Gurgela. Burbia.	Wungoan. Kuberuan. Gurgelan. Burbian.

THE CLASS DIVISIONS. 37

We might reasonably conclude that these four classes were formed by subdividing two primary classes, from the fact that they are composed of two pairs of non-intermarrying classes, each pair corresponding to one of the original classes, and intermarrying with the other pair, as shown in the foregoing table.

Thus Ipai does not intermarry with Kumbu, nor does Muri intermarry with Kubi; but the Ipai-Kumbu pair intermarries with the Muri-Kubi pair. These pairs represent the original classes.

So also with all the other sets. Bultara, for instance, does not intermarry with Parula, nor does Panangka intermarry with Kumura; but Bultara-Parula intermarries with Panangka-Kumura; and, even if there were no other evidence, we might take it for granted that these pairs represent the original classes.

* Since Table B was prepared, Mr Howitt received the following information from the Rev R H Codrington:—"At Florida, one of the Solomon Islands, there are four *Kema* (divisions for marriage) They are exogamous, and the child follows the mother" These Kema are subdivided, and it appears that the subdivisions are distinguished by totems

† Kubitha, Table B—The Kamilaroi class names were first published, I believe, by the Rev. W Ridley, M A, whose attention had been called to them by Mr. T. E Lance. Mr Ridley pointed them out to me in 1871, and I sent a memorandum on them to Mr. Morgan, following Mr. Ridley's method of spelling, and in that guise they appear in Mr. Morgan's "Ancient Society." Subsequently Mr Lance informed me that the spelling aforesaid did not correctly represent the sound of the words. After a careful inquiry from several competent informants, I altered the spelling to that given in the table, which, to my ear, comes as nearly as possible to their pronunciation, the vowels, of course, having their proper sounds.

I am careful to give this explanation minutely, because there hangs to it something more than a mere question of orthography. Kubi s sister is called Kápŏta by Mr. Ridley, and the fact is thereby concealed that this class name is simply Kubi with the feminine termination *tha*, just as Tarawangan is the feminine form of Tarawang From the spelling given in the table, it is seen at a glance that, in the Kamilaroi language, the feminine names are formed from the masculine by adding *tha*, as they are formed elsewhere by adding *an*, *gan*, or *gor*. Matha and Butha are evidently contractions of Muritha and Kumbutha.

This inference, which naturally suggests itself from the inter-sexual arrangements shown in the table, is strengthened into certainty by the fact that in some tribes the class names of the primary divisions are still found side by side with those of the four classes.* Thus it is known that the four classes of the Mackay tribe are subdivisions of the two classes, Yungaru and Wutaru, already given in Table A. The class names Yungaru and Wutaru are still used.

Yungaru includes Gurgela and Burbia.

Wutaru includes Wungo and Kuberu.

Elsewhere the names of the original classes may have dropped out of use, but their subdivisions are still recognized as "brother" classes, and, consequently, do not intermarry. It may be that they have escaped the notice of our informants, whose attention was fixed upon the four classes by our inquiries. Mr. Bridgman, before-mentioned, states, on the authority of an intelligent aborigine of the Yungaru class who visited the Kamilaroi people, that those tribes have a division corresponding to Yungaru—that is to say, a class composed of Ipai and Kumbu; and if so, they must have the other class, composed of Muri and Kubi.

It will be seen from the following table and diagram that, though the range of matrimonial choice is reduced by the subdivision of the two primary classes into four, the laws of marriage and descent remain unaltered as far as their fundamental principles are concerned. Marriage is still forbidden within the class, and descent is still reckoned through the mother.

* *See* p. 69.

THE CLASS DIVISIONS.

TABLE C

Primary Class	Subdivision	The Male Marries	Children
Yungaru Yungaru	Gurgela. Burbia.	Wutaru-Kuberuan Wutaru-Wungoan	Wutaru-Wungo-an. Wutaru-Kuberu-an.
Wutaru Wutaru	Wungo. Kuberu.	Yungaru-Burbian. Yungaru-Gurgelan.	Yungaru-Gurgela-n. Yungaru-Burbia-n.

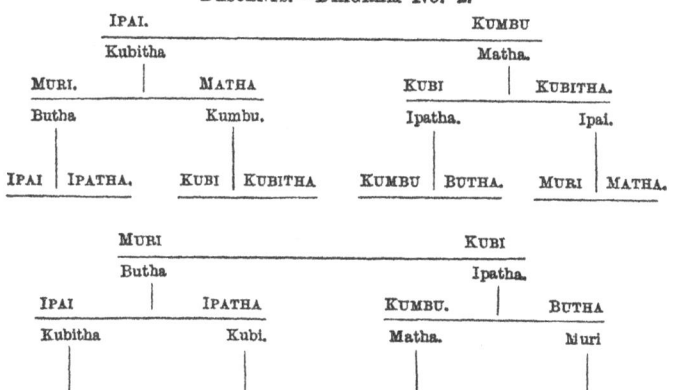

DESCENTS.—DIAGRAM No. 2.

If this diagram be compared with Diagram No. 1, showing the descents in the classes Kumite and Kroki, it will be seen that the results are precisely the same in both cases.

In the first descent one class produces the other. Ipai-Kumbu produces Muri-Kubi, and Muri-Kubi produces Ipai-Kumbu, just as Kumite produces Kroki and Kroki, Kumite.

The second descent gives a male and a female of each of the four classes as the grandchildren of Ipai and Kumbu; and, again, a male and a female of each of the four classes as the grandchildren of Muri and Kubi. In other words, the second descent gives two males and two females of each class, as with Kumite and Kroki. (*See* Diagram No. 1.)

Hence it is manifest that the laws of marriage and

descent are not affected by the subdivision of the two original classes into four, save as to the range of marriage selection. A man who, under the two classes, had matrimonial rights over the women of half the tribe, is now restricted to one-fourth. Ipai-Kumbu could marry any Matha-Kubitha. Ipai can marry Kubitha only. Kumbu can marry Matha only. But marriage must still be without the class, and descent is still reckoned in the female line.

SUBDIVISIONS OF THE TWO CLASSES DISTINGUISHED BY TOTEMS.

It is, perhaps, not too much to say that every tribe of the Australian aborigines has subdivisions distinguished by totems, which are generally the names of animals. It is certain that some of these contract the range of matrimonial selection, but our information is not sufficiently complete to enable us to assert that this is always the case. In some places the primary divisions are distinguished by totems at the present day. Probably they were so distinguished everywhere in ancient times. "The symbol of the Yoongaroo division," says Mr. Bridgman, "is the alligator, and of the Wootaroo the kangaroo." Mr. A. S. P. Cameron gives the following list of class names used by the Queensland natives, who speak the Unghi language, as the equivalents of the Kamilaroi, Ipai, &c.:—

Kamilaroi.	*Unghi* [*]
Ipai.	Oorgilla
Cubby.	Uberoo.
Combo.	Nganbay
Murri.	Woongoo.

[*] With the exception of Nganbay, these are evidently the Mackay class names given by Mr Bridgman. Oorgilla is undoubtedly Gurgela (which probably should have been written Gurjela); Nganbay is Burbia; Woongoo is Wungo (which ought perhaps to be written Wungu); and Uberoo is Kuberu. The dropping of the letter K is of frequent occurrence. Several Fijian tribes drop it from every word in which it occurs, a curious break,

THE CLASS DIVISIONS.

And Mr. William Chatfield, of Bowen, Queensland, informs us that each class has "a distinguishing animal—a sort of heraldic crest—viz.:—

"Utheroo has emu, or carpet snake.
Mulleroo ,, iguana
Yungaroo ,, opossum
Goorjilla ,, kangaroo, or scrub turkey."

Whence it appears that Ipai, &c., can be identified with class names elsewhere which have distinguishing totems. But for all practical purposes we may take the totems as indicating subdivisions of the classes, at least among the tribes who have the class divisions already described

Mr. Lockhart writes concerning the Darling tribe, who are divided into Kilpara and Mukwara:—

"There is a further division into tribes or families, such as the Emu, Wildduck, and Kangaroo tribes, but the main division is by no means thereby affected. . . . The females of the Wildduck, we shall say, are all Kilparas, and they take Mookwara men of the Emu. The children remain Kilparas and Wildducks No Kilpara man can approach these Kilpara women, and the Kilpara Wildduck boys look out for, say, Mookwara Emu girls. The children and the pedigree always run through the woman."

These totems affect the inter-sexual regulations only as the development of the four classes from the original two affects them—*i.e.*, no otherwise than by narrowing the range of matrimonial selection. They do not touch "the main division," as Mr. Lockhart justly observes. They are, in fact, subdivisions of the Kilpara and Mukwara classes, analogous to the Ipai, Kumbu, &c., of the Kamilaroi. Given two Kilpara totems, the Wildduck and the Kangaroo, and two Mukwara totems, the Emu and the Hawk,

or catch, being heard in the hiatus. Thus Katakata is pronounced 'ata 'ata, the apostrophe representing the break Other Fijian tribes drop T in like manner The language has a word, *Ngato*, for this letter-dropping; and the Rev R. H. Codrington informs me that in Mota (Banks Islands) Gato means "to speak like a foreigner," "to speak in a foreign tongue."

42   KAMILAROI MARRIAGE.

and we have the four classes as we have them in the subdivisions of the Queensland Yungaru and Wutaru. Mr. Stewart, however, who has been for nearly thirty years in close intercourse with the Mount Gambier tribe, assures us that the numerous totems used by that people do not in any way restrict matrimonial selection.* "A Kumite can take any Krokeegor : a Krokee any Kumitegor," he wrote in reply to a specific inquiry as to whether the totems affect the marriage regulations. But it may be that the old rule differed from this. Mr. Stewart's words refer to present usage; and this, in the case of the Mount Gambier blacks, cannot be taken as conclusive. A tribe, which in less than 30 years has been reduced from 900 souls to 17, is compelled to make such matrimonial arrangements as it can, whether they be according to ancient law or not. †

The Kamilaroi totems are peculiar. At least, they have a peculiarity attached to them which calls for special attention. Unlike the Darling totems, at first sight they appear to affect "the main division" by legalizing to a certain limited extent marriage with the half-sister by the father's side. This is *marriage within the class*, an utter abomination to all, or nearly all, the other tribes. It will be seen, however, that the totems are not answerable for this. It is an innovation, and an overriding of their rules.

The Kamilaroi totemic divisions will be most easily made intelligible by reverting to the two primary classes, which have been shown to be Ipai-Kumbu and Muri-Kubi. In one generation—the order is reversed in the next—Ipai-Kumbu divides into Kangaroo, Opossum, and Iguana; Muri-Kubi divides into Emu, Bandicoot, and Blacksnake.

* *See* also the Gournditch-Mara tribe of Western Victoria—Part II., Appendix F.
† *See* Mr. Stewart's noteworthy remarks quoted at the conclusion of the introductory chapter.

THE CLASS DIVISIONS.

For the sake of distinction, let us call these subdivisions *gentes*,* which is the term most appropriate to them.

The following table shows the marriages and descents of the Kamilaroi gentes, or totemic subdivisions, so called for the sake of convenience to distinguish them from the classes:—

TABLE D. (Informant, Rev. W. Ridley, M.A.)

Gens.	Marries.	Children.
1. Ipai ... ... Of any gens, when Ipai — Kumbu = Emu —Bandicoot — Blacksnake.*	Kubitha—Kangaroo. Kubitha—Opossum. Kubitha—Iguana.	Muri and Matha—Kangaroo. Muri and Matha—Opossum. Muri and Matha—Iguana.
2. Kumbu ... ... Of any gens, when, &c.	Matha—Kangaroo. Matha—Opossum. Matha—Iguana.	Kubi and Kubitha—Kangaroo. Kubi and Kubitha—Opossum. Kubi and Kubitha—Iguana.
3. Muri ... ... Of any gens, when Muri — Kubi = Kangaroo — Opossum — Iguana.	Butha—Emu. Butha—Bandicoot. Butha—Blacksnake.	Ipai and Ipatha—Emu. Ipai and Ipatha—Bandicoot. Ipai and Ipatha—Blacksnake.
4. Kubi ... ... Of any gens, when, &c.	Ipatha—Emu. Ipatha—Bandicoot. Ipatha—Blacksnake.	Kumbu and Butha—Emu. Kumbu and Butha—Bandicoot. Kumbu and Butha—Blacksnake.

* Where Ipai-Kumbu = Kangaroo-Opossum-Iguana, then Ipai marries Kubitha-Emu, and so on.

* The use of this term must not be taken as implying that these gentes are identical with the Roman gens They have uterine succession, whereas its succession was agnatic—to use a term which, if not strictly correct, is so extremely convenient that even the sternest precisian may wink at its employment.

KAMILAROI MARRIAGE.

That these gentes are subdivisions of the original classes Ipai-Kumbu and Muri-Kubi (= the Queensland Yungaru and Wutaru) is manifest from the fact pointed out by Mr. Morgan,* that they subdivide those classes into two non-intermarrying triplets (if this convenient term may be allowed), each of which intermarries with the other. Thus, the Emu gens cannot intermarry with the Bandicoot or the Blacksnake, but it can intermarry with the Kangaroo, Opossum, or Iguana. Emu, Bandicoot, and Blacksnake are "brother" gentes, and, therefore, cannot intermarry. So, also, are the other three. The two sets of gentes are conterminous with the original classes, and descent being through the mother, they alternate between those classes in alternate generations.

Ipai-Kumbu (Yungaru) = Kangaroo-Opossum-Iguana.
Muri-Kubi (Wutaru) = Emu-Bandicoot-Blacksnake.

In the next generation—

Ipai-Kumbu = Emu-Bandicoot-Blacksnake.
Muri-Kubi = Kangaroo-Opossum-Iguana.

But it does not follow from this that the gentes are older than the four classes. It is but another proof that the two primary classes were not discarded when they were subdivided. Their laws still ruled the tribe. The old form was not broken up to be re-cast into a new shape. The four classes, and the gentes also, were looked upon as subdivisions *within two still-existing classes*, whose regulations they must still obey. To use a homely illustration, the construction of the four classes and the gentes was like the succession to their father's business of two sons in the one case and three in the other. These are partners in the firm now, and each takes his own share of the proceeds, but the old firm is the old firm still.

* "Ancient Society," page 51.

THE CLASS DIVISIONS. 45

Hitherto, as is manifest from the foregoing table, the laws of marriage and descent are in nowise affected by the Kamilaroi gentes. They are identical with those found in Table B. But we now come to the innovation which legalizes marriage with the half-sister. This, together with its descents, is shown by the following table, wherein are stated certain marriages additional to those already given in Table D.

TABLE E. (Informant, Rev. W. Ridley, M.A.)*

Gens.	Marries.	Children.
Ipai—Emu	Ipatha—Blacksnake.	Kumbu and Butha—Blacksnake.
Ipai—Bandicoot	Ipatha—Blacksnake.	Kumbu and Butha—Blacksnake.
Ipai—Blacksnake	Ipatha—Emu.	Kumbu and Butha—Emu.
Kumbu—Emu	Butha—Blacksnake.	Ipai and Ipatha—Blacksnake.
Kumbu—Bandicoot	Butha—Blacksnake.	Ipai and Ipatha—Blacksnake.
Kumbu—Blacksnake	Butha—Emu.	Ipai and Ipatha—Emu.
Muri—Kangaroo	Matha—Iguana.	Kubi and Kubitha—Iguana.
Muri—Opossum	Matha—Iguana.	Kubi and Kubitha—Iguana.
Muri—Iguana	Matha—Kangaroo.	Kubi and Kubitha—Kangaroo.
Kubi—Kangaroo	Kubitha—Iguana.	Muri and Matha—Iguana.
Kubi—Opossum	Kubitha—Iguana.	Muri and Matha—Iguana.
Kubi—Iguana	Kubitha—Kangaroo.	Muri and Matha—Kangaroo.

* Mr. Ridley's list of these marriages was incomplete. Those which he had not been able to ascertain were collected by subsequent inquiry.

Hence, it is manifest that—

1. The gentes are strictly exogamous. No marriage can take place between a male and a female of the same totem.

2. Two of the gentes—the Bandicoots and the Opossums—though they take the extended matrimonial privilege for their men, refuse it to their women.

According to the regulations shown in the table, no Bandicoot or Opossum woman can marry a man of her own class. If the arrangement had been that Emu married Bandicoot, Bandicoot married Blacksnake, and Blacksnake married Emu, with a like arrangement for the other class, all would have shared alike in the extended privilege. But since Emu and Blacksnake intermarry with one another, the Bandicoot women are necessarily excluded. They cannot marry Bandicoot men, for this would be marriage within a gens, which is strictly forbidden. So also with the Opossums. I can offer no explanation of this other than the conjecture that the innovation was begun by the Emus and Blacksnakes in the one class, and the Kangaroos and Iguanas in the other, intermarrying one with another. These, it will be observed, are corresponding gentes.

3. This extension of the matrimonial privilege, while it allows marriage with the paternal half-sister, does not permit marriage with the uterine half-sister.

A man's uterine half-sister bears her mother's totem, which is his also (Tables D and E); and, therefore, they cannot marry. They are of the same gens.

4. The extended privilege does not include all the half-sisters by the father's side. A man's paternal half-sisters may be found in two gentes; but he may take them to wife from one only of those gentes. Thus, Ipai-Emu's half-sisters by the father's side may be either Ipatha-Bandicoot or Ipatha-Blacksnake (Table D); but he can have the Blacksnake only

5. The law of descent is in nowise affected by the marriage with the paternal half-sister.

The children of these marriages with the half-sister take the class name and totem of their mother's children by the man who may be called her proper husband (*see* Table D). The mother alone is looked to, as far as descent is concerned: the father is utterly ignored. This will be seen in the following diagram:—

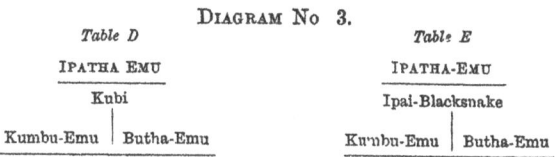

This partial breach of the general rule which forbids marriage within the class seems to be peculiar to the Kamilaroi, and it is even doubtful whether it prevails among all the tribes included under that name *

A letter of inquiry concerning it called forth a number of replies from correspondents in various parts of Australia, who expressed surprise at the statement concerning marriage with the paternal half-sister, and assured us that it was unknown to the natives with whom they were acquainted. Some of these gentlemen had lived for many years in the country occupied by the Kamilaroi blacks. Mr A S. P. Cameron wrote as follows:—

"In your letter, published in the *Australasian*, it is asserted that in some instances Ipai marries Ipatha In any district where I have been Ipai marries Cubetha, and no other; and yet there are the same subdivisions, such as Emu, Kangaroo, Snake, &c "

* *Kamilaroi* —Strictly speaking, this is a name of a language, not of a tribe It is derived from the negative "Kamil," which some of our correspondents give as Kumil, and the language as Kumilrai The Kamilaroi are the people who say "Kamil " Under this term are included quite a number of tribes

The materials gathered by Mr. Howitt and myself are insufficient for a satisfactory settlement of this matter; but it seems almost certain that the half-sister marriage is only a local infringement of a class law which is looked upon as of universal obligation by all the other tribes who have the class organization, and we may therefore set it aside for the present. Not, however, because it is of little worth. At first sight, apparently, a retrograde movement, a more careful inspection shows it to be a most important forward step in the direct line of advance. But, as far as we know, it did not make sufficient way among the Australian aborigines to affect materially the laws of marriage and descent with which we are now concerned.

On the whole, it may be said, with regard to the Australian totemic gentes, that while in some cases they restrict matrimonial choice, and in others they may perhaps not have that effect, they are bound by the laws which bind the classes. This, at all events, is the general rule, to which there may be exceptions besides that of the Kamilaroi marriage with the half-sister.*

---

* As so many of our correspondents have questioned the assertion of marriage with the paternal half-sister among the Kamilaroi, it may be well to give the authority on which it rests.

The late Mr. T. E. Lance, an unquestionable authority, informed me that he had met with instances of marriage between Ipai and Ipatha, which the natives justified on the ground that the parties were not of the same mudji (totem). Being then in Sydney, where my friend Mr. Ridley resides, I told him what Mr. Lance had said, and urged him to follow up the clue, which evidently pointed to marriage regulations based upon totemic subdivisions of the classes He was on the eve of starting for the interior to make certain philological investigations set on foot by the New South Wales Government at the instance of Prof. Max Müller; and, on his return to Sydney, he informed me that his inquiries had resulted in the discovery of the laws of the Kamilaroi gentes He gave me a short memorandum on them, which is embodied in Tables D and E.

The Kamilaroi half-sister marriage, therefore, having been noted by an experienced observer, such as Mr. Lance, and verified by so well known an authority as Mr. Ridley, we may safely take to be an established fact as far as concerns the tribe which came under the notice of these gentlemen.

Certain curious facts connected with the totems, apart from the question of marriage and descent, have come to our knowledge in the course of these inquiries; but, as it is with this question only that we are at present concerned, those facts would be out of place here. A brief notice of them will be given further on.*

* *See* Appendix B.

CHAPTER III.

LAWS OF MARRIAGE AND DESCENT.

RULE I —*(a)* Marriage is theoretically Communal—Matrimonial Rights of a Class recognized over Wide Areas—Communication aided by Gesture Language—*(b)* Relationship is that of Group to Group—" Brother," Gentes, and Classes—Evidence of the Terms of Kinship.

Rule II —Marriage is Exogamous—This Rule binds all the Classes and Gentes—Overrides Marriage by Capture—Necessarily results from the first Class Divisions.

Rule III.—The Wife does not come into her Husband's Class or Gens.

Rule IV.—Descent is through the Mother—Shown by the Class Names and Totems—Kamilaroi Class Names no Exception—Necessary Result of the Marriage Regulations and the Constitution of the Classes.

WE have traced the inter-sexual divisions of the Australian aborigines from the two primary divisions to the four classes, and the subdivisions distinguished by totems; and we have seen that the laws of marriage and descent, founded on the first segmentation of the community, remained unaltered save in the narrowing of matrimonial selection. Those laws, already clearly shown by the various tables of marriage and descent given in the preceding chapter, now present themselves for further investigation.

They may be stated as follows :—

I.—*Marriage is theoretically communal. In other words, it is based upon the marriage of all the males in one division of a tribe to all the females of the same generation in another division.*

LAWS OF MARRIAGE AND DESCENT.

Hence, relationship is not merely that of one individual to another, but of group to group.

By this it is not meant that present usage is hereby stated, but that this is the ancient rule which underlies present usage, and to which that usage points.

II.—*All the divisions—gentes as well as classes—are strictly exogamous.* In other words, marriage is forbidden within every division of a tribe.

III.—*The wife does not come into her husband's division. She remains in her own.*

IV.—*Descent is reckoned through the mother.*

In order more clearly to illustrate these regulations, we may take one set of the class divisions as an example; and, inasmuch as the rules have been shown to be substantially invariable, we may take any one set as typical of all. Let us take the South Australian classes Kumite and Kroki, with their feminine terms Kumitegor and Krokigor.

RULE I.—*Communal Marriage and Group Relationship.*

Marriage is communal. Every Kumite is theoretically the husband of every Krokigor in the same generation with himself. Every Kroki is theoretically the husband of every Kumitegor in his own generation. It is not hereby asserted that marital rights are actually exercised to this extent at the present day; but they exist, and are acknowledged, even now-a-days, to a certain extent.

Relationship is consequently that of groups of individuals to other groups. All Kumites and Kumitegors of the same generation are looked upon as brothers and sisters. So also are all Krokis and Krokigors of the same generation.

Every Kumite is looked upon as joint father to all Krokis and Krokigors in the generation next below his own. So also with the other relationships.

(a) MARRIAGE.

The regulation given above is the ancient rule. Present usage is that every Kumite, for instance, takes as many Krokigor wives as he can get and keep; but the old rule makes itself felt still, asserting the tribal right in the women, who are now, nominally at least, the property of the individual.

Thus, among tribes which are organized like the Kamilaroi,* friendly visitors from other tribes are accommodated with temporary wives from the proper classes, and no man can refuse to furnish his quota from his own harem.

" 'Cui fœmina sit,' " we read in 'Eyre's Discoveries in Central Australia'† " eam amicis libenter prœbet Si in itinere sit, uxori in castris manenti aliquis supplet illi vires. Adversis ex longinquo accedentibus fœminas ad tempus dare hospitis esse boni judicatur . . . Senioribus mos est, si forte gentium plurium castra appropinquant, viros noctu hinc inde transeuntes, uxoribus alienis uti, et in sua castra ex utraque parte mane redire.' "

These statements are more than borne out by the plainspoken testimony of many correspondents who have been good enough to furnish information concerning the Australian blacks to Mr. Howitt and myself ‡ They, however,

* *Like the Kamilaroi* —It must be distinctly understood that these remarks are intended to apply to those tribes only which are organized like the Kamilaroi. It is their common organization which gives them the common privilege. It will be seen that there are tribes which have not that organization
† Quoted by Sir J Lubbock, "Origin, &c ," Note, p 411.
‡ [I have observed the custom referred to by Eyre frequently among the Cooper's Creek aborigines (Dieri, Yantruwunta, &c) In a communication received from the Rev. H. Vogelsang, of the Lutheran Mission, Kopperamana, during the preparation of this work for the press, he says—"The question 'Minna murdu?' is connected with eating and with hospitality. For instance, when a stranger blackfellow arrives here, the question is, ' Minna murdu?'—what are you? Kangaroo, or Rat, or Mouse, or whatever else it may be. All those of the same name go to the same camp, eat together, live together, even lend each other their women. Even alien blackfellows, from a distance of three or four hundred miles, are thus hospitably

LAWS OF MARRIAGE AND DESCENT.

are unanimous in making this important addition to Eyre's statement, that the freely-granted favours, which were naturally looked upon by him as mere promiscuous intercourse, are strictly regulated by the laws of the class divisions. Thus, Mr. T. E. Lance informed us, with regard to a tribe with which he was well acquainted, that, though most of the women are nominally the wives of the elderly men of the tribe, their husbands are obliged to lend them to the younger men on stated occasions. But the youths thus favoured must be none other than those of the proper classes And of the Clarence River Kamilaroi he wrote—

"If a Kubbi meet a stranger Ippatha—(these are intermarriageable classes, *see* Table B)—they address each other as *spouse* A Kubbi thus meeting an Ippatha, though she were of another tribe, would treat her as his wife, and his right to do so would be recognized by her tribe "

This important statement has been fully confirmed by other competent informants, in reply to a special inquiry on the subject.*

Mr. G. F. Bridgman's native servant, before mentioned, who had travelled far and wide throughout Australia, told him that he was furnished with temporary wives by the various tribes with whom he sojourned in his travels; that his right to those women was recognized as a matter of course; and that he could always ascertain whether they belonged to the division into which he could legally marry,

entertained. Our tribe, the Dieri, have different names for their Murdus from those of the neighbouring tribes, but they can always understand each other "— A W H]

* [Mr. Cyrus E Doyle, of Kunopia, Moree, N S W , wrote to me as follows, in reply to a question :—" You are quite right in supposing that any Hippi can take any Kubbatha as his wife and keep her, and that his right to her will not be questioned by her family ; and of course the same rule extends to the other names, such as Cumbo, Kubbi, &c."—A. W H]

"though the places were 1,000 miles apart, and the languages quite different." Many pages might be filled with similar testimony.

This seems to be the most extensive system of communal marriage the world has ever known. It could have held its own in no other part of the globe; for nowhere else, if we except an isolated tribe here and there, have the aborigines been so completely shut out from external impulse. Australian marriage—taking into account, for the present, those tribes only which have the Kamilaroi organization—is something more than the marriage of group to group, *within a tribe*. It is an arrangement, extending across a continent, which divides many widely-scattered tribes into intermarrying classes, and gives a man of one class marital rights over women of another class in a tribe a thousand miles away, and speaking a language other than his own. It seems to be strong evidence of the common origin of all the Australian tribes among whom it prevails; and it is a striking illustration of how custom remains fixed while language changes.

The evidence I have brought forward may perhaps be called in question. For instance, it may be doubted whether Mr Bridgman's native servant could have made himself understood among the various tribes whom he visited in the course of his travels; and it may also be objected that the inter-tribal enmity of the Australians must make his story somewhat problematical. But, in the first place, the fact in support of which his testimony is advanced, is quite independent of that testimony, being fully supported by other evidence; and, in the second place, the difficulties in the way of his journeyings may be more apparent than real.

It is quite possible for a native to make his way across the Australian continent if he passed from tribe to tribe in

LAWS OF MARRIAGE AND DESCENT. 55

accordance with certain established rules;* though, if he ventured without that passport, he might be killed—and eaten too, for many of the tribes are cannibals.

Nor would his ignorance of the dialects spoken by stranger tribes necessarily stop his way. Mr. Gason, an unimpeachable authority, tells us, in his pamphlet on the Dieri Tribe, that they have a gesture language as well as a spoken tongue; that this gesture language is common to many tribes, and that by its means natives who are "barbarians" one to another can converse with ease. Mr. Gason understands this language of signs, and has frequently employed it. I have heard of it in other parts of Australia, and have myself seen it used with great apparent readiness by two white men who had learned it from the natives.†

The importance of this subject may justify a short digression here. Gesture language, which has been advanced as an evidence of mental inferiority on the part of

---

* "*Passed on from tribe to tribe*"—This statement receives amusing confirmation from the following incident narrated by Buckley, the convict who lived among the blacks for so many years that he forgot his English :—
"They have a notion that the world is supported by props, which are in charge of a man who lives at the farthest end of the earth. They were dreadfully alarmed on one occasion, when I was with them, by news *passed from tribe to tribe*, that, unless they sent him a supply of tomahawks for cutting more props, and some rope to tie them with, the earth would go by the run, and all hands would be smothered. . . . *Passing on the word to the tribes along the coast,* some settlers at a very great distance were robbed of axes, saws, rope, and tires of dray wheels, all of which were forwarded to the old gentleman on the other side; and, as was supposed, in time to prevent the capsize, for it never happened. A tribute of this description is paid whenever possible; but who the juggling old receiving thief is I could never make out." (Morgan's "Life of Buckley," p. 58. M'Dougall : Hobart Town, Tasmania, 1852)

The Australian tribes have heralds, whose person is sacred when they are engaged in their official duties. *See* Mr Howitt's account of the Kŭrnai Leewin.

† [I have often seen this gesture language used by the Dieri and other kindred tribes By means of it the "Mŭrdŭ" of a stranger could be ascertained, and the various hospitalities connected therewith either offered or demanded.—A W H]

savages, we may yet discover to be a proof of a quite remarkable intelligence. It certainly fails to prove poverty of language. The North American Indians—some of them, at least—have it, and their languages not only suffice for all their ordinary wants, but are also copious enough to furnish materials for abundant oratory. There is no evidence* whatever that the language of savages is inadequate to express all they have in their minds; and what tongue can do more than this for the people who speak it? Gesture language is not a mere eking out of the spoken tongue. It is a most remarkable enrichment of it, and forms a valuable means of communication between tribes whose languages differ from one another far more widely than French or German differs from English. How valuable would such a means of communication be to ourselves! —a language of signs, by means of which Englishmen, speaking no tongue but their own, could make themselves understood—as far, at least, as their everyday wants are concerned—throughout a continental tour.

(b) RELATIONSHIP.

That relationship is of group to group seems to be a fair inference from what has already been shown as to communal marital rights.

* *No evidence, &c.*—Much of what has been advanced as proving the poverty of language among savage tribes seems to me to have but little weight An African traveller, for instance, observes that, when his men talk together after nightfall, they sit within the light of the camp-fire in order that their word signs may be perceptible; and he jumps at once to the conclusion that the signs are necessary in order to eke out the poverty of the spoken language. But he forgets that his men were of different tribes, some, at least, of whose dialects differ as do the Australian.

The proof required here is, firstly, that the interlocutors are men of the same tribe; and secondly, that they are *compelled* to use signs to express what their words are insufficient to express, for we know that savages often use the gesture language from choice in their conversation. It is good practice so to use it.

LAWS OF MARRIAGE AND DESCENT. 57

As to both marriage and relationship, it is the group alone that is regarded. The individual is ignored. He is not looked upon as a perfect entity. He has no existence save as a part of a group, which in its entirety is the perfect entity. It is not the individual Kumite who marries the individual Krokigor: it is the group of males called Kumite which marries the group of females called Krokigor. Hence the son of this marriage is not the individual Kroki, but the group Kroki; its daughter is not the individual Krokigor, but the group Krokigor (Table A). This son and this daughter—*i e*, group Kroki and group Krokigor—are brother and sister, and this relationship binds every member of the groups. So also with the other degrees.*

The subdivision of the two primary classes failed to alter the idea of relationship in the native mind. For matrimonial purposes, indeed, the boundaries of the group are contracted, but descent and relationship remain unaltered. The Ipai group is brother to the Kumbu; the Muri group is brother to the Kubi. So also with the gentes. The Emu group is brother to the Bandicoots and Blacksnakes; the Kangaroo group is brother to the Opossums and the Iguanas (Table D).

Further evidence is afforded by the terms of kinship in present use among the Australian aborigines. These, however, are not so conclusive in proof as are those in use among other tribes, whose terms are given in full by Mr. Morgan in his work on the "Systems of Consanguinity and Affinity of the Human Family." The systems of the Tamil speaking peoples, the North American Indians, Fijians, Tongans, and many others, follow out the strict logical

---

* [When conversing with one of the Majauka tribe, of the Darling River (whose cousin had been with me on my first expedition), as to the classes of the Cooper's Creek tribe, I said "I am Mūngalli-Lizard of the Yantruwunta." He immediately replied, "Why! I am Lizard too—Karni—and you are just the same as my brother"—A W H]

sequences of the primary relationships which result from the division of a community into exogamous intermarrying classes. When those primary degrees are known, they themselves reveal the inter-sexual laws on which the system was founded, and every possible relationship may be deduced from them by a simple process of reasoning. In every case, excepting where a few anomalous terms have been introduced, the theoretical deduction will be found to be identical with the term in actual use. For instance, when we have ascertained that a Mbau Fijian calls his father's brother *father*, his mother's sister *mother*, his father's sister *mother-in-law*, and his mother's brother *father-in-law*, we can determine with positive certainty the exact degree of relationship in which he stands to any other member of his tribe, how remote soever their relationship may be according to our own system. Nay, more, we can determine the exact relationship between any one of his descendants and any other person belonging to the tribe after the lapse of any number of generations, although, according to our system, there may be no relationship whatever between those persons.

Not so, however, with the Australian terms. In the first place, several terms are found in use which point to the older system, called by Mr. Morgan the *Malayan*—to a time prior to the first division of the community into intermarrying classes. The survival of these terms here and there need cause no surprise if we bear in mind the fact that every one of the terms logically resulting from the classificatory system of kinship is still found in everyday use among nations who advanced beyond that system—who can say how many ages ago?

And farther, an Australian aborigine, when asked to define the relationship in which he stands to other persons, frequently takes into consideration matters other than relation-

LAWS OF MARRIAGE AND DESCENT.

ship, and so gives words which are not specific terms of kinship. After years of inquiry into this matter, the humiliating confession must be made that I am hopelessly puzzled. Of one thing, however, I am perfectly sure, that there is a good reason for every one of the inexplicable terms which an Australian black gives when asked to explain a long line of descents, with several branches from the main stem; only, I have been unable to get at those reasons. In one list I have found the same degree of relationship represented by no fewer than five different words, four of which appear not to be terms of kinship at all, but to express some connection other than relationship. A difference of totem within a class may cause a difference of appellation, or it may not, apparently according to the whim of the speaker. Thus, Muri-Iguana and Muri-Kangaroo are half-brothers, for they are the sons of Ipai (Table D); but one sometimes designates the other by a word differing from the term by which he would address a Muri of his own totem, while at other times he may use the ordinary term So also with the four classes. Ipai and Kumbu are "brother" classes, but any particular Ipai, in defining his relationship to Kumbu, may use either the ordinary term for brother, or some word intelligible enough to the natives, but exasperatingly puzzling to an inquirer who is ignorant of the language. Moreover, there are certain changes of name and grade conferred at a secret ceremony called Bora, or Bura, which in some way or other, inexplicable by our informants, affects, or may affect, the words by which a man will designate his kinship, and yet does not touch their relationship It is simply impossible to ascertain the exact meaning of these words without a very full knowledge of the native dialects, added to a personal influence with the blacks powerful enough to induce them to reveal jealously-guarded secrets known to the initiated only, and a patience compared with which that of Job is furious irritability. In all probability there are not half a dozen men so qualified in the whole Australian continent; and one gentleman—who, doubtless, has the requisite knowledge—positively refused to disclose the secrets entrusted to him by the natives. He had to identify himself with a tribe before he could learn those secrets.

Nevertheless, enough can be made out from the terms of kinship in present use to show that relationship is based upon the same ideas with those which form the foundation of the system called by Mr. Morgan the Turanian. Most certainly, as will presently be shown, the terms of that system are the logical outcome of the Australian classes. The following table, though incomplete, shows that among many widely-separated tribes the same term is used for father and father's brother; the same term for mother and mother's sister; the same term for brother, father's brother's son, and mother's sister's son; and the same term for son and brother's son (a male speaking), or for son and sister's son (a female speaking).

If the reader will make out a genealogical table, or family tree, of his own brothers and sisters, or of his uncles and aunts, with their respective children, the significance of these terms, and their points of difference from our own, will be readily perceived.

In every case shown in the following table there are two terms for "brother," one signifying "elder brother," and the other "younger brother." I have given one only of those terms.

LAWS OF MARRIAGE AND DESCENT. 61

TABLE F.

M = A male speaking. F = A female speaking.

TRIBES	Paroo River, Queensland.	Dieri, Cooper's Creek.	Brabrolung, Gippsland.	Port Lincoln, South Australia.	Lake Alexandrina.	Port Mackay, Queensland.
INFORMANTS	Mr. G. O. Lyon.	Sergeant Gason. Rev. W. Homan.	Mr. A. W. Howitt.	Rev. G. Taplin.	Rev. G. Taplin.	Mr. G. F. Brídgman.
My father	Yabino.	Apiri.	Mungan.	Baápi.	Nanghai.	Tabunéra.
My father's brother	Yabino.	Apiri.*	Mungan.†	Baapi.	Nanghai.	Tabunera.
My mother	Yangardi.	Andri.	Yúkun.	Ngami.	Nainkowa.	Yunganera.
My mother's sister	Yangardi.	Andri.	Yukun.	Ngami.	Nainkowa.	Yunganera.
My brother	Takoun.	Nihini.	Tundung.	Yunga.	Tarte.	Cutanera.
My father's brother's son	—	Nihimi.	Tundung.	—	Tarte.	Cutanera.
My mother's sister's son	—	Nihmi.	Tundung.	—	Tarte.	—
My son	Tergi.	M. Athamurámi. F. Atháni.	Lit.	Kuitya.	Porlean.	Wulbura.
My brother's son — M	Tergi.	Athamurani.	Lit.	Kuitya.	Porlean.	Wulbura.
My sister's son — F	—	Athani.	Lit.	Kuitya.	Porlean.	—

* *Dieri Tribe.*—My father's brother is called " my friend father." Also, " my great father," or " my little father," as he is older or younger than my father. So also in the Fijian, Tamil, and other systems. [I think the word Athamurani is compounded of ato = I, and mūra = new, *i.e.*, a revival of myself.—A.W.H.]
† *Brabrolung Tribe.*—My father's brother is called " my other father,"

TABLE F.—Continued.

M = A male speaking.   F = A female speaking.

TRIBES	Wakeruk, East Gippsland.	Eildon, Victoria.	Fraser's Island, Queensland.	Maneroo, New South Wales.	Mota, Banks Islands.	Mbau, Fijian.†
INFORMANTS	Mr. A. W. Howitt.	Mr. A. Falconer.	Rev. E. Fuller.	Mr. A. W. Howitt.	Rev. R. H. Codrington.	L. Fison.
My father	Lung.	Manmorong.	Babūn.	Bäbang.	Tamák.	Tamanggu.
My father's brother	Lung.	Manmorong.*	Babun.	Babang.	Tamak.	Tamanggu.‡‡
My mother	Wangan.	Fatpūrung.	Navang.	Natyang.	Ravevek.	Tinanggu.
My mother's sister	—	—	Navang.	Natyang.	Ravevek.	Tinanggu.
My brother	Tidyang.	Bunganyik.	Nūn.	Tidyang.	Tasik.	Tadhinggu.
My father's brother's son	Tidyang.	—	Nun.	Tidyang.	—	Tadhinggu.
My mother's sister's son	Tidyang.	—	Nun.	Tidyang.	Tasik.	Tadhinggu.
My son	Lit.	Bubugrik.	Kūma.	Windya.	Natuk.	Luvenggu.
My brother's son—M	—	—	—	Windya.	Natuk.	Luvenggu.
My sister's son—F	—	—	—	Windya.	Natuk.	Luvenggu.

* *Eildon Tribe.*—My father's brother is called "my other father."
† *Fijian Terms.*—I have added these for comparison. The Mbau system is Turanian from beginning to end.
‡ *Fijian.*—My father's brother. See note on Dieri tribe.

The significance of the terms of kinship given in the foregoing table requires only a little attention in order that it may be clearly seen. It can be presented directly to the eye by constructing genealogical tables, or "family trees," and noting down the relationship of the persons represented therein, according to the rules shown in the table. This, however, would require considerable space, and as it will have to be done further on in a series of diagrams showing that the terms of kinship in the Turanian system logically result from the class divisions, the reader is referred to those diagrams.*

RULE II—*All the divisions—gentes as well as classes—are strictly exogamous. In other words, marriage is forbidden within every division of a tribe.*

Although matrimonial selection has so wide a range, it is strictly governed by the class regulations. A man, as already shown, has marital rights over women in a class intermarriageable with his, not in his own tribe only, but in others also far distant from his own; but under no circumstances may he take to himself a woman from a forbidden class. The Kamilaroi marriage with the half-sister by the father's side need not be taken into account here. It has been shown to be, in all probability, no more than a local infringement of a universal rule. And moreover, partial exception though it be, it proves the rule by observing its application to the gens, while it throws off its yoke as binding upon the entire class. Ipai, for instance, is allowed,

---

* The reader cannot fail to be struck with the extraordinary divergence of the Australian dialects as shown in Table F. Even among terms of kinship, where, if anywhere, we should expect similarity, we find the widest difference. In the New Hebrides again, and in other South Sea Island groups, a like confusion of tongues prevails. Here is a rich field for the philologist, if he enter upon it now. A few years hence and it will be a desert.

at least in the tribe of Mr. Lance's informants, to marry an Ipatha of a totem other than his own, but he cannot marry Ipatha of his own totem (Table E). That is to say, he cannot marry a woman of his own gens.

The rule of the two original classes—"Kumite may not marry Kumitegor: Kroki may not marry Krokigor"—prohibiting marriage within the class, binds all the subdivisions also. The tables of marriage and descent already given show that (with the local exception of the Kamilaroi marriage with the half-sister by the father's side) the subdivision of the two classes did not result in intermarriage between any two divisions formed out of one of the original classes. Thus, Yungaru was divided into Gurgela and Burbia ; but Gurgela cannot marry Burbian : he must seek his wife in one of the sub-classes into which the other original class, Wutaru, was divided (Table C). So also with the gentes (Table D). If we had found these subdivisions to be simply exogamous quà subdivisions, this would have been enough to prove that the law of exogamy still prevailed, though with contracted range. But the tables prove more than this ; they show that, not the principle only, but the range also, of the law is unaltered. And this is sufficient to prove the law, as far as the women within a tribe, or community, are concerned.

That this law of exogamy is strictly enforced, under the sternest penalties, is proved by the united and positive testimony of many competent informants. A few of them may be quoted here.

Mr. J. A. G. Little says of the Larakia tribe, Port Darwin :—

"Occasional cases of elopement between blood relations (*i e.*, persons of the same class) occur. In such cases the pair are pursued, and the man, if possible, killed; but, if he succeed in eluding capture for a certain period, the offence may be condoned"

LAWS OF MARRIAGE AND DESCENT.

Dora, a Herbert River (Queensland) native, was present when her brother inflicted summary punishment for a breach of this law, and she gave a graphic account of the incident to our valued correspondent, Mr. W. Reeve, jun. The offenders were a man of her tribe, and a woman belonging to another tribe, but of the class name corresponding to his. They were found together in the bush, cooking grubs at the same fire. After some parley, Dora's brother struck the woman fiercely with his knife, inflicting "awful wounds under the left breast and over the back." The woman recovered, and the offence was eventually condoned.

Mr. C. Giles, jun, writes concerning the Antakerinya tribe, Central Australia :—

"Marriage can take place only according to the rules given (*i e*, the class rules). Infringement of these rules is punishable by death"*

Not only is the law thus strictly enforced in all cases of ordinary marriage, but it holds good also with regard to what Mr. M'Lennan calls marriage by capture. It regulates the disposal of women who are stolen from other tribes, or captured in war.†

"It is obvious," Sir John Lubbock remarks ("Origin of Civilization," p. 80),‡ "that, even under communal marriage, a warrior who had

---

* [As to marriage by capture, and further evidence confirmatory of this statement, see Summary and General Conclusions, Part ii —A W H]

† Mr. Percival S. Friend, Stipendiary Magistrate, Rewa, Fiji, informs me that a man from Tana (New Hebrides), one of the "imported labourers," was brought before him, charged with the murder of a woman from the same island, with whom he had been cohabiting "The prisoner, after being duly cautioned, made a voluntary statement to the effect that he was *bound* to kill the woman, because she had admitted men whom the law of their land forbade to her. If she had intercourse with a dozen men of the same clan with himself, he could have no objection."
I myself witnessed the trial of a similar case in the Supreme Court of Fiji.

‡ All my references to the "Origin of Civilization" are to the Second Edition

captured a beautiful girl . . . would claim a peculiar right to her, and, when possible, would set custom at defiance . . . A war captive was in a peculiar position   The tribe had no right to her."

This seems obvious to ourselves, but the influence of the class system among the Australians makes it anything but obvious to them. They maintain the tribal right against the individual with regard to war captives as strictly as they maintain it with regard to any other women. If a warrior took to himself a captive who belonged to a forbidden class, he would be hunted down like a wild beast; and, unless he managed to keep out of the way until the hot wrath of the tribe had cooled down, he would be killed, and his captive with him. This is a strong statement, but it rests upon strong evidence.

Mr. Charles G. N. Lockhart, after giving the law of marriage between Kilpara and Mukwara, says:—

"This holds good even with regard to casual amours. It appears, further, that the neighbouring tribes have the same distinctions. I asked them how, under certain circumstances of forcible rape—no uncommon occurrence—they knew the female was not of a forbidden tribe. They said they always knew If in doubt, they asked the female "*

Mr. Reeve, already quoted, remarks further:—

"Should any children be born of such a connection (*i.e.*, between forbidden classes), they are certain to be killed, as are generally the parents also. If the offenders be spared, they are subject to the eternal gibes and jeers of the tribe.† *If a man takes in war from*

---

* "*If in doubt, they asked the female.*"—Mr. Chatfield, before mentioned, informed me that in a tribe with which he was acquainted, the raised cicatrices on the bodies of the natives are the blazon of their respective classes or totems. But several of our most trustworthy correspondents, replying to inquiries on this point, did not confirm Mr. Chatfield's statement. This, however, does not prove his statement to be incorrect, as far as concerns the tribe to which he referred.

† "*The eternal gibes and jeers of the tribe*"—So also Mr. Morgan tells us of a case among the Shyans, "where first cousins had married against their usages." The pair were "ridiculed so constantly by their associates that

LAWS OF MARRIAGE AND DESCENT.

another tribe a woman whom he cannot legally marry, and uses her as his mistress, the tribe will kill them both."

Many similar testimonies might be quoted from the letters of gentlemen who have given us information as to the tribes which have the Kamilaroi organization. Their evidence is conclusive in proof that the class law overrides marriage by capture among those tribes, and it must be borne in mind that none other are at present under consideration.

Hence it is evident that—with the one local exception already noted, which is, after all, only an exception in part—all the class divisions are exogamous, and that the law is strictly enforced. At all events, if this be not exogamy, it is not easy to imagine what exogamy can be.*

Here, then, we have exogamy, certainly not produced by marriage by capture, according to Sir John Lubbock's theory (" Origin of Civilization," p. 83), but actually compelling marriage by capture to conform to long-established exogamous rules. Nor do the Australian class regulations give more countenance to Mr. M'Lennan's theory that savages were driven into exogamy and capture-marriage by "female infanticide" resulting in a scarcity of women.†
Australian exogamy, at all events, is the plain outcome of

---

they voluntarily separated rather than face the prejudice." ("Ancient Society," p 458)

Compare Hardistry's remarks on the Tinné Indians—"A Chitsang cannot by their rules marry a Chitsang, although the rule is set at nought occasionally. But, when it does take place, the persons are ridiculed and laughed at " The words next following are strong proof of group relationship—"The man is said to have married his sister, though there be not the slightest connection of blood between them." (Smithsonian Report, quoted by Lubbock, "Origin," &c , p. 112)

* [*See* Part II , Appendix F. The Gournditch-Mara tribe This community has four classes which are not exogamous. It is, however, socially far advanced beyond the Kamilaroi organization, and the class rules are proportionately weakened The form remains, while the substance is gone *See* also the Wimmera tribe, Summary, Part II.—A W H]

† *See* the discussion of female infanticide in the Summary, Part II.

the class divisions; and similar divisions elsewhere doubtless produced similar results.

RULE III.—*The wife does not come into her husband's division. She remains in her own.*

Kumitegor marries Kroki, but her marriage does not bring her into the Kroki class. She continues to belong to the Kumite class. So also with the four classes and the gentes.

The Motu people, Mr. Codrington informs us, express this regulation by a striking figure of speech. They are divided into two intermarrying classes, called Veve, or "mothers." One veve is said to be on one "side of the house," and the other veve to be on the other side. The wife does not pass to her husband's "side of the house." She is said to be "at the door."

This is a most important fact, and, together with the following rule, it is the key to more than one difficulty concerning which there has been much speculation. There is no need for any further evidence in support of it with regard to the Australians. A glance at Tables A, B, C, D, and E will show it as a matter of fact.

RULE IV.—*Descent is reckoned through the mother.*

In every case the class names and totems shown in the foregoing tables settle this question beyond dispute. The child is of the mother's class, not of the father's: of its mother's totem, not of its father's.

Thus, Kumite's wife is Krokigor. His son is not Kumite, but Kroki. So also, if the Kamilaroi Emu marry Iguana, his son is not Emu, but Iguana (Table D).

LAWS OF MARRIAGE AND DESCENT. 69

At first sight, the descents in the four classes may seem to contradict this assertion, inasmuch as the child does not come into that particular sub-class to which its mother belongs—e g., Ipatha's son is Kumbu, not Ipai (Table B). But it has been shown that Ipai and Kumbu are mere segments of a still-existing class. Ipai is the complement of Kumbu. The two together make up a whole. The original classes are Ipai-Kumbu and Muri-Kubi; and, as far as the line of descent is concerned, the original classes only are taken into consideration. Kubi, therefore, in marrying Ipatha, marries a woman of the Ipai-Kumbu class, and his children, Kumbu and Butha, are of that class (Table B). In other words, they are of their mother's class, not of their father's.

This is still more clearly seen in the Mackay classes, simply because we know the names of the two primary classes in that tribe.

Yungaru = Gurgela-Burbia.
Wutaru = Wungo-Kuberu.

Gurgela, a Yungaru man, marries Kuberuan, a Wutaru woman. His children are Wungo and Wungoan, who are not Yungaru like their father, but Wutaru after their mother (Table C).

Why the children should be exchanged between these "brother" classes which do not intermarry—in other words, why Wungoan's children should be of the Kuberu class, and why Kuberuan's children should be of the Wungo class, is not directly apparent. Their exchange between the two primary classes is the necessary result of descent through the mother. Kumite's son must be Kroki because the mother is Krokigor. Kroki's son must be Kumite because the mother is Kumitegor. Is it possible that this exchange—which, however, as will presently appear, is more apparent than real—had become a fixed idea in the native mind when the two classes subdivided, whence it seemed to be an absolute necessity that the sub-classes also should exchange their children? This, though mere conjecture, would be thoroughly in accordance with the mode of thought among savages. To the savage ancient custom is full of sanctity, and cannot be disregarded without impiety. He reasons, not from intrinsic quality, but from the custom of his fathers; and, like that school of politicians to whom he has transmitted so many of his ideas, he cannot be happy without his precedent.

There is a curious solution of this difficulty, which seems to come within the bounds of possibility. I give it for what it is worth. It was suggested to my mind by Herodotus' "Legend of the Minyæ," who came to Sparta from Lemnos; and, apparently as a necessary consequence of their naturalization among the Spartans, *exchanged wives with them*. ("Melpomene," 145)*

A reference to Table B (p. 36) will show, if we arrange the four classes (say of the Mackay tribe) in two pairs as follows, that the marriages and the first descents are—

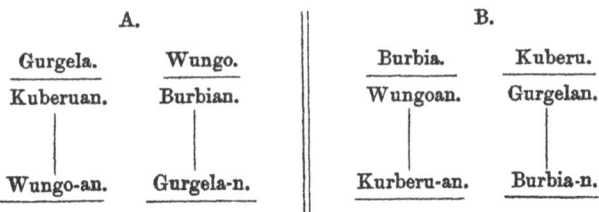

If we examine either of these pairs, we see that their *descents* are precisely those of two exogamous intermarrying

---

* The Spartans seemed to have reasoned as follows:—We admit the Minyæ *as a clan* into our community We must look upon them all—men and women alike—as Minyæ. Therefore, our clans being exogamous, their women must be married to another clan, and we must furnish their men with wives.

gentes with uterine succession, but the *marriages* are different.

Thus, if Emu and Snake be two such gentes, the identity of the descents is shown by the following diagram—males being represented:—

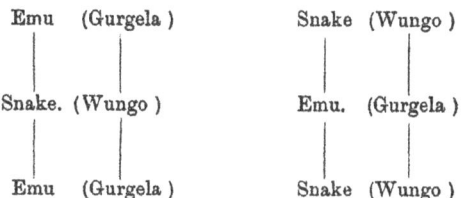

The difference in the marriages appears as follows:—
M=male; F=female.

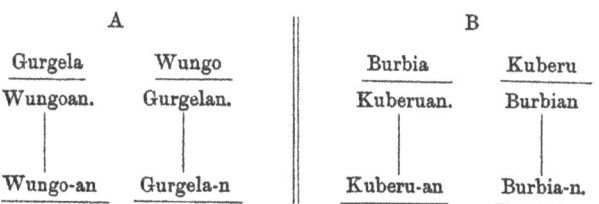

That is to say (if Emu be taken as corresponding to Gurgela, and Snake to Wungo), Emu (male) marries Snake (female), but Gurgela marries, not Wungoan, but Kuberuan, and so forth.

If the usual rule were observed, the marriages and the first descents would be as follows:—

A			B	
Gurgela	Wungo		Burbia	Kuberu
Wungoan.	Gurgelan.		Kuberuan.	Burbian
Wungo-an	Gurgela-n		Kuberu-an	Burbia-n.

Now, let us make the following suppositions:—

1. That A. and B. were at one time two distinct tribes, each consisting of two exogamous intermarrying classes— A. being made up of Gurgela and Wungo, while B. consisted of Burbia and Kuberu, as shown in the diagram.

2. That these two tribes united into one community, Gurgela amalgamating with Burbia, and Wungo with Kuberu; Gurgela-Burbia taking the Alligator (Yungaru) as its totem, and Gurgela-Burbia taking the Kangaroo (Wutaru).

3. That these amalgamating classes *exchanged wives*, as the Minyæ are said to have exchanged theirs with the Spartans, but *without altering the descents as they stood when the union took place*—in other words, that class Gurgela took Burbia's wives (Kuberuan), but retained its children, Wungo and Wungoan; that Burbia took Gurgela's wives, (Wungoan), but retained its children, Kuberu and Kuberuan, and so forth.

Then we shall have the following arrangement :—

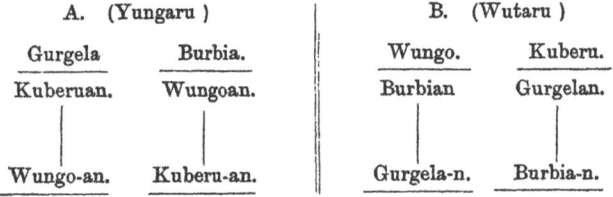

which is precisely the arrangement as it stands at the present day.

If, by any chance, this be the true solution, the four classes were formed by the amalgamation of two class-divided communities, not by the further segmentation of one such community; but the main theory set forth in this memoir will serve equally well for either supposition. And, in what way soever the four classes may have been formed, it is evident, from the fact of their wide prevalence in Australia, that their formation must be referred to a very early time, before the tribes dispersed over the continent.

It is well known that descent is still reckoned through the mother by many tribes in every quarter of the globe, and several conflicting theories have been advanced to

LAWS OF MARRIAGE AND DESCENT.

account for the fact. The Australian system shows it to be the necessary consequence of the matrimonial regulations of the class divisions. If we consider the inter-sexual arrangements at present in force among the Australian aborigines, who have what I call, for the sake of convenience, the Kamilaroi class organization, we cannot deny that the saying—cynical enough as regards civilized communities, "Maternity is a matter of fact, paternity of conjecture"—represents the plain literal truth as far as tribes such as the Australian are concerned. For, when a man has no exclusive right to his wives; when even strangers from a distant tribe, who are of a class corresponding to his, may claim a share in his marital rights; when a woman is married to a thousand miles of husbands, then paternity must be, to say the least of it, somewhat doubtful. But there can be no possibility of mistake as to maternity, and therefore it seems natural enough that children should "follow the mother," as several of our correspondents phrase it; in other words, that they should be of the mother's class and gens, not of the father's.

Moreover, this is the necessary result of the very constitution of the classes. In speaking of the "exchange of children," it was said that this exchange is more apparent than real. It appears to be a real exchange as long as our attention is fixed upon the fathers of those children. But when we turn our attention to the fact pointed out by Mr. Morgan ("Ancient Society," Part II. chap. i.), that the basis of the Australian class organization is the woman, not the man, we see that there is in reality no exchange at all. The classes are, in point of fact, not Kumite and Kroki, but Kumitegor and Krokigor. Kumite and Kroki appear to exchange their children, because each wife holds her own offspring by a law as steadfast against alteration as were those of the Medes and Persians. As far as descent is

74 KAMILAROI MARRIAGE.

concerned, the father is a mere nonentity. Descent in the male line alternates between Kumite and Kroki in alternate generations, but Kumitegor's female descendants in the direct line, through females, are Kumitegor for ever.*
From first to last, as regards descent, the father is utterly ignored, and the mother alone is taken into consideration. This is notably shown in the descents from the Kamilaroi marriage with the paternal half-sister (Table E, Diagram No. 3). Throughout the classes, and the gentes also, descent is traced through female ancestors. An Emu prides himself on being the descendant of a long line of Emus; but it was through his mother that the Emu blood flowed into his veins, not through his father. His father was no better than a Blacksnake.

Conclusion. The system which I have tried to explain in the foregoing pages is that which will, I think, be found in most of the Australian tribes; but there is so much ground yet unex-

* *Descent in the Male line and in the Female* —These descents are shown at a glance by the following diagram, which may be continued *ad infinitum* with the same results. The female line appears on the right hand, the male on the left.

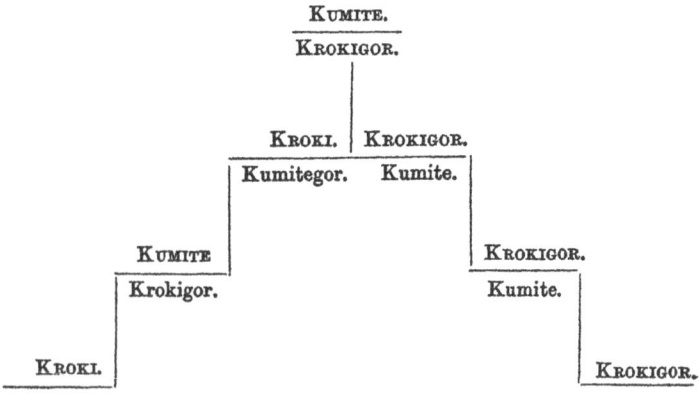

LAWS OF MARRIAGE AND DESCENT. 75

plored, that this opinion can only be held provisionally, while waiting for further evidence.

The system has been shown to prevail in Western and Central Australia, along the east coast and interior to a considerable distance inland, and in the extreme north at Port Darwin. We know that it extends beyond the places noted, but we have reason to believe that it does not cover all the area bounded by them. The usages of several tribes, which appear at first sight to be radically opposed to it, can be shown to arise directly from the enforcement of its rules under circumstances of peculiar difficulty; but we cannot affirm that the usages of all the Australian tribes which may be found to differ from those of the Kamilaroi, admit of a similar explanation. In all probability they do not. Some of the South Australian tribes, especially, point to the prevalence of a system different from that of the Kamilaroi; and a vast amount of work yet remains to be done before the question can be finally settled.

The whole subject needs thorough investigation, and it needs it now. The aborigines are dying out as if they were plague-stricken, and with them is perishing information of the highest value to anthropological science, which, if not soon obtained, must be lost to us for ever. This is a matter for the united action of the Australian Governments. A year's work by a few competent men under their auspices now would do more than could be effected by an army of savans a generation hence.

CHAPTER IV.

THE TERMS OF KINSHIP PECULIAR TO THE TURANIAN SYSTEM SHOWN TO RESULT FROM THE AUSTRALIAN CLASS ORGANIZATION.

FROM the four rules of marriage and descent shown in the various tables, and investigated in the preceding chapter, it may now be demonstrated that the terms of kinship peculiar to what Mr. Morgan calls the Turanian system, are the logical outcome of the Australian classes.

The characteristics of that system are given by Mr. Morgan in his "Ancient Society," pp. 442, *et seq.*, together with theoretical explanations which will be found to coincide in every particular with the ascertained facts. We may take those characteristics as so many propositions, and demonstrate them by means of diagrams, so as to present directly to the eye that which would otherwise require a troublesome effort to keep it clearly before the mind.

All the marriages and descents given in the diagrams may be verified by a reference to Table A. This notification is given once for all, in order to save the trouble of repeating the reference at each step of the demonstration.

Special attention is called to the terms Uncle, Aunt, Nephew, Niece, and Cousin. Strictly speaking, these relationships are not recognized by the Turanian system; and Mr. Morgan uses the terms, for the sake of convenience, to indicate relatives who are fathers-in-law and mothers-in-law rather than Uncles and Aunts, sons-in-law and daughters-in-law rather than Nephews and Nieces; while the meaning of the term Cousin varies with the sex of the speaker, and with that of the person spoken of. These points will be fully brought out in the course of the demonstration.

It must further be noted that the meaning of those terms, as applied to the Turanian system, does not coincide with that which they bear in our own. The following definitions must be borne in mind:—

I.—My Uncle is my mother's brother only; not my father's brother also, as with us.

II.—My Aunt is my father's sister only, not my mother's sister also, as with us.

III.—Ego being male, my Nephews and Nieces are my sister's children only, not my brother's children also, as with us.

IV.—Ego being female, my Nephews and Nieces are my brother's children only, not my sister's children also, as with us.

V.—My Cousins are the children of my mother's brothers, and of my father's sisters, but not those also of my mother's sisters, and of my father's brothers, as with us.

VI.—The term *collateral*, as used by Mr. Morgan in stating the Turanian characteristics, denotes relationships differing from those with which our own system has made us familiar. For instance, "my collateral brothers" are the sons of my father's brothers and of my mother's sisters. The explanation given in the introductory chapter as to the extended sense in which the terms of kinship are used, must be kept in mind. The Ego is a group, not an individual; but each individual takes all the relationships which are taken by his group.

PROPOSITION I.

"Ego being male, all the children of my several brothers, own and collateral, are my sons and daughters." ("Ancient Society," p. 442.)

Kumite.	Kumite A.
Krokigor.	Krokigor A.
Kroki B. | Krokigor B.	Kroki B. | Krokigor B.

Let Ego be Kumite, a male. All my brothers, own and collateral, are Kumite.

Let any one of them be represented by Kumite A.

Then, because my wife is Krokigor, my children are Kroki B and Krokigor B.

But the wife of Kumite A is also Krokigor.

Therefore his children also are Kroki B and Krokigor B.

But Kroki B and Krokigor B are my children.

Therefore, Ego being male, my brother's children are my sons and daughters. Q.E.D.

NOTE.—Hence is manifest the reason why my brother's children, Ego being male, cannot be called my nephews and nieces, as with us.

PROPOSITION II.

"Ego being male, all the children of all my sisters, own and collateral, are my nephews and nieces."

Kumite.	Kumitegor.
Krokigor.	Kroki.
Kroki B. | Krokigor B.	Kumite B. | Kumitegor B.

If Ego be Kumite, a male—
My sister is Kumitegor, and her children are Kumite B and Kumitegor B.
Kumite B and Kumitegor B are my nephews and nieces.
But all my sisters, own and collateral, are also Kumitegor.
And all their children are Kumite B and Kumitegor B.
But Kumite B and Kumitegor B are my nephews and nieces.

Therefore, &c. Q.E.D.

But, strictly speaking, the Turanian system does not recognize these relationships, and the proposition may be stated thus:—

"Ego being male, all the children of all my sisters, own and collateral, are my sons-in-law and daughters-in-law."

Diagram as above.

Ego being Kumite, all my sisters, own and collateral, are Kumitegor.
All their sons are Kumite B; all their daughters are Kumitegor B.
But Kumite B marries my daughter, Krokigor B, and is therefore my son-in-law.
And Kumitegor B marries my son, Kroki B, and is therefore my daughter-in-law.

Wherefore, &c. Q E.D.

PROPOSITION III.

"Ego being female, the children of my several brothers, own and collateral, are my nephews and nieces."

Kumitegor.		Kumite.	
Kroki		Krokigor.	
Kumite B	Kumitegor B.	Kroki B	Krokigor B.

If Ego be Kumitegor, a female—
My brother is Kumite, and his children are Kroki B and Krokigor B.
Kroki B and Krokigor B are my nephews and nieces.
But all my brothers, own and collateral, are Kumite.
And all their children are Kroki B and Krokigor B.
But Kroki B and Krokigor B are my nephews and nieces.
Therefore, &c. Q.E.D.

But, strictly speaking, the Turanian system does not recognize these relationships, and the proposition may be stated thus :—

" Ego being female, all the children of my several brothers, own and collateral, are my sons-in-law and daughters-in-law."

Proof as in Proposition II.

COR.—From this proposition and the foregoing it is manifest that (bearing in mind the restricted sense of the terms nephew and niece), Ego being male or female—

My nephew is my son-in-law—that is, a man who has a right to take my daughter to wife.

My niece is my daughter-in-law—that is, a woman whom my son has a right to take to wife.

PROPOSITION IV.

"Ego being female, the children of my several sisters, own and collateral, are my sons and daughters."

Kumitegor.		Kumitegor A.	
Kroki.		Kroki A.	
Kumite B.	Kumitegor B.	Kumite B.	Kumitegor B

If Ego be Kumitegor, a female—
My children are Kumite B and Kumitegor B.
But all my sisters, own and collateral, are also Kumitegor.
And all their children are Kumite B and Kumitegor B.
But Kumite B and Kumitegor B are my children.
      Therefore, &c. Q.E.D.

NOTE 1.—Hence is manifest the reason why my sister's children, Ego being female, cannot be called "my nephews and nieces," as with us.

NOTE 2.—Mr. Morgan's statement of this characteristic is as follows:—"With myself a female, the children of my several sisters, own and collateral, *and of my several female cousins*, are my sons and daughters."

The words which I have italicised are omitted from my enunciation of this proposition. They apply to the Seneca-Iroquois system, to which Mr. Morgan's statement refers, but not to the Tamil, the Fijian, and many others, which take all the terms logically resulting from the division of a tribe into exogamous intermarrying classes. Ego being female, the children of my female cousins are my nephews and nieces, or rather my sons-in-law and daughters-in-law, as shown in Proposition XIII.

PROPOSITION V.

"All the children of these sons and daughters are my grandchildren." (*See* "Ancient Society," p. 443.)

This may be more fully stated as follows:—

(*a*) Ego being male, all the children of my brother's children are my grandchildren.

(*b*) Ego being female, all the children of my sister's children are my grandchildren.

(*a*) Ego being male, all my brother's children are my sons and daughters. (Prop. I)

And the children of my sons and daughters are my grandchildren.

Therefore the children of my brother's children are my grandchildren.

(*b*) Ego being female, my sister's children are my sons and daughters. (Prop. IV.)

And the children of my sons and daughters are my grandchildren.

Therefore the children of my sister's children are my grandchildren.

Wherefore, &c. Q.E.D.

PROPOSITION VI.

"All the children of those nephews and nieces are my grandchildren."

This may be more fully stated as follows :—

(*a*) Ego being male, the children of my sister's children are my grandchildren.

(*b*) Ego being female, the children of my brother's children are my grandchildren."

(*a*) If Ego be male, my sister's children are my sons-in-law and daughters-in-law. (Prop. II.)

And the children of my sons-in-law and daughters-in-law are my grandchildren.

Therefore the children of my sister's children are my grandchildren.

(*b*) Ego being female, my brother's children are my sons-in-law and daughters-in-law. (Prop. III.)

THE TERMS OF KINSHIP.

And the children of my sons-in-law and daughters-in-law are my grandchildren.

Therefore the children of my brother's children are my grandchildren.

Wherefore, &c. Q.E.D.

COR.—From this proposition and the foregoing it is manifest that, Ego being male or female, all the children of my brother's children, and all the children of my sister's children, are my grandchildren.*

PROPOSITION VII.

"All my father's brothers, own and collateral, are my fathers."

Kroki.	Kroki A.
Kumitegor.	
Kumite B.	Kumitegor B.

---

* Sir John Lubbock observes of the Iroquois system that—"Though a man's sister's children are his nephews and nieces, his sister's grandchildren are also his grandchildren, indicating the existence of a period when his sister's children were his children." ("Origin," &c., p. 129.)

This is an evident mistake, for those relationships afford no such indication. They result from the fact that a man's sons and daughters intermarry with his sister's children. His sister's grandchildren, therefore, must necessarily be his grandchildren. They are his children's children.

Thus, Ego being male—

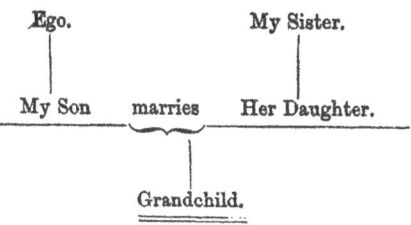

If Ego be Kumite B, or Kumitegor B—*i.e.*, male or female,
All my father's brothers, own and collateral, are Kroki.
But Kroki is my father.
Therefore all my father's brothers are my fathers.
Q.E.D.

NOTE.—Hence is manifest the reason why my father's brothers are not called my uncles, as with us.

PROPOSITION VIII.

"All my father's sisters, own and collateral, are my aunts."

Kumite.	Kumitegor.
Krokigor.	Kroki.
Kroki B. | Krokigor B.	Kumite B | Kumitegor B.

If Ego be Kroki B, or Krokigor B—(*i.e.*, male or female),
My aunt is Kumitegor.
But all my father's sisters, own and collateral, are Kumitegor.
Therefore they are my aunts.
Q.E.D.

Strictly speaking, the relationship of aunt is not recognized by the Turanian system, and the proposition may be stated thus:—

"All my father's sisters, own and collateral, are my mothers-in-law."

Diagram as above.

If Ego be Kroki B, a male, my wife is Kumitegor B,
Her mother is Kumitegor.

Therefore Kumitegor is my mother-in-law.

But all my father's sisters, own and collateral, are Kumitegor.

Therefore, they are my mothers-in-law.

In like manner, if Ego be female, it may be shown that my father's sisters are my mothers-in-law.

Wherefore, &c. Q.E.D.

NOTE.—" My mother-in-law" does not necessarily mean the actual mother of the woman whom I have as my wife. Ego being male, it means "a woman whose daughter I have a right to take to wife." Ego being female, it means "a woman whose son has a right to take me to wife."

PROPOSITION IX.

"All my mother's brothers, own and collateral, are my uncles."

Kumitegor.		Kumite.	
Kroki.		Krokigor.	
Kumite B.	Kumitegor B.	Kroki B.	Krokigor B.

If Ego be Kumite B, or Kumitegor B—*i.e.*, male or female, My uncle is Kumite.

But all my mother's brothers, own and collateral, are Kumite.

Therefore they are my uncles. Q.E.D.

Strictly speaking, the Turanian system does not recognize the relationship of uncle, and the proposition may be stated thus:—

"All my mother's brothers, own and collateral, are my fathers-in-law."

Diagram as above.

Ego being Kumite B, a male, my wife is Krokigor B.
Her father is Kumite.
Therefore Kumite is my father-in-law.
But all my mother's brothers, own and collateral, are Kumite.
Therefore they are my fathers-in-law.
In like manner, if Ego be female, it may be shown that all my mother's brothers, own and collateral, are my fathers-in-law. Q.E.D.

COR.—From this proposition and the foregoing, it is manifest that, whether Ego be male or female,

My uncle is my father-in-law, or rather the father of one with whom I have matrimonial rights.

My aunt is my mother-in-law, or rather the mother of one with whom I have matrimonial rights.

PROPOSITION X.

"All my mother's sisters, own and collateral, are my mothers."

Kumitegor.	Kumitegor A.
Kroki.	
Kumite B.	Kumitegor B.

If Ego be Kumite B, or Kumitegor B—*i.e.*, male or female, Kumitegor is my mother.

But all my mother's sisters, own and collateral, are Kumitegor.

Therefore they are my mothers. Q.E.D.

PROPOSITION XI.

"All the children of my father's brothers, and all the children of my mother's sisters, own and collateral, are my brothers and sisters."

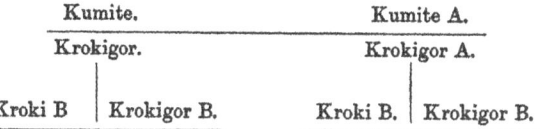

Ego being Kroki B, or Krokigor B—*i e.*, male or female, all my father's brothers are Kumite, and their children are Kroki B and Krokigor B.

Again, all my mother's sisters are Krokigor, and their children are Kroki B and Krokigor B.

But Kroki B and Krokigor B are my brothers and sisters.
Therefore, &c.   Q E D.

PROPOSITION XII.

"All the children of my several uncles, and all the children of my several aunts, are my male and female cousins."

My uncles are my mother's brothers (definition i).

My aunts are my father's sisters (definition ii).

And their children are my male and female cousins (definition v).

But since, strictly speaking, these relationships are not recognized by the Turanian system, the proposition may be stated as follows:—

(*a*) Ego being male,

1. The sons of my mother's brothers and the sons of my father's sisters are my brothers-in-law.

2. Their daughters are my wives.

(β) Ego being female,

1. The sons of my mother's brothers and the sons of my father's sisters are my husbands.
2. Their daughters are my sisters-in-law.

Kumite.	Kumitegor.
Krokigor.	Kroki.
Kroki B. | Krokigor B.	Kumite B. | Kumitegor B.

(a) If Ego be Kroki B, a male,
1. My mother's brothers are Kroki, and my father's sisters are Kumitegor.
Their sons are Kumite B.
But Kumite B marries my sister, Krokigor B, and I marry his sister, Kumitegor B.
Therefore he is my brother-in-law.
2. The daughters of my mother's brothers Kroki, and of my father's sisters Kumitegor, are all Kumitegor B.
And Kumitegor B is my wife.

(β) If Ego be Krokigor B.—*i.e.*, a female,
1. My mother's brothers are Kroki, and my father's sisters are Kumitegor.
Their sons are Kumite B.
And Kumite B is my husband.
2. The daughters of my mother's brothers Kroki, and of my father's sisters Kumitegor, are all Kumitegor B.
But Kumitegor B marries my brother Kroki B, and I marry her brother Kumite B.
Therefore she is my sister-in-law.

Wherefore, &c. Q.E.D.

Note.—This result may be formulated as follows:—

Ego being male, my male cousin is my brother-in-law—that is, he may take my sister to wife. My female cousin is my wife—*i.e.*, she is a woman whom I may take to wife.

Hence it is manifest that a man has brothers-in-law, but no sisters-in-law.

Ego being female, my male cousin* is my husband—*i.e.*, he may take me to wife. My female cousin is my sister-in-law—*i,e.*, she is a woman whom my brother may take to wife.

Hence it is manifest that a woman has sisters-in-law, but no brothers-in-law.

PROPOSITION XIII.

" Ego being male, the children of my male cousins are my nephews and nieces, and the children of my female cousins are my sons and daughters."

Ego being male, my male cousin is my brother-in-law. (Prop. XII.)

Therefore his children are my sister's children.

But the children of my sister's children are my nephews and nieces. (Prop. II.)

Therefore the children of my male cousins are my nephews and nieces.

Again, Ego being male, my female cousin is my wife. (Prop. XII.)

Therefore her children are my sons and daughters.

Wherefore, &c., Q.E.D.

In like manner it may be shown that, Ego being female, the children of my male cousins are my sons and daughters, and the children of my female cousins are my nephews and nieces.

* I am told that, in some parts of Ireland at the present day, a girl will sometimes reveal the state of her affections to the youth on whom she has set her heart, by saying, "I wish I were your cousin." And this is understood to be an offer of marriage.

PROPOSITION XIV.

"All the brothers and sisters of my grandfather, and those of my grandmother, are my grandfathers and grandmothers."

This follows as a corollary from Proposition V.

SUMMARY OF RELATIONSHIPS.

In order to understand the classificatory relationships, we must dismiss from our minds our own notions of relationship. We are accustomed to think of it as a relation between individual and individual: but we must bear in mind the well-established fact that to the savage *the group is the individual.* Where we have any one person in our mind in considering relationship, he has in his mind a number of persons, who collectively make up the group the relationship of which he has under consideration; and every one of those persons bears to all other persons in the tribe the relationship which his, or her, group bears to their respective groups. In other words, relationship, whether consanguinity or affinity, is conceived between group and group; and as is the relationship of Group A to Group B, so is the relationship of each member of Group A to all the members of Group B, and *vice versâ.*

The relationships between three generations include all the degrees with which we need concern ourselves. Above grandfathers the terms are generally second grandfather, third, fourth, and so on, or simply "ancestors."* Below grandchildren the terms are second grandchild, third, fourth, and so on, or simply "descendants." Sometimes apparently anomalous terms of great interest present themselves for

---

* Some tribes have no term for grandparents.

THE TERMS OF KINSHIP.

these degrees, but we cannot stop to notice them here. The relationships then may be classified as follows:—

I.—Relationships on the same level—*i.e.*, between groups in the same generation.

II.—Relationships between the first generation and the second.

III.—Relationships between the first generation and the third.

I.—Relationships on the same level.

1st Phratria *		2nd Phratria.	
Kumite.	KUMITEGOR.	Kroki.	KROKIGOR.
Kroki.		Kumite.	

On the same level in each phratria, as shown in the diagram, there are two groups, one male and the other female, making four groups in a generation. And the relationships are—

(α) Between the groups in the same phratria.

(β) Between each group in one phratria and those of the other.

(α) Relationships between the groups in the same phratria.

Group Kumite is brother to Group Kumitegor—

That is to say, every Kumite is brother to all the Kumitegors: he is also brother to the other Kumites.

Every Kumitegor is sister to all the Kumites, as well as to all the other Kumitegors.

So also with Groups Kroki and Krokigor.

Hence the term "my brother" does not necessarily single out the son of my actual father or of my actual mother.

---

* The same results are obtained from diagrams of a pair of intermarrying gentes—say Emu and Kangaroo. I use the terms gens and phratria here for the sake of convenience, asking permission to waive for the present any question that may arise as to their propriety.

Ego being male, it means a man of my own group.

Ego being female, it means a man of the group which is "brother" to my group.

So, also, the term "my sister" does not necessarily mean the daughter of my own father or my own mother.

Ego being male, it means a woman of the group which is "sister" to my group.

Ego being female, it means a woman of my own group.

(β) Relationships between each group of one phratria and those of the other:—

Group Kumite is the husband of Group Krokigor.

Group Kroki is the husband of Group Kumitegor.

Hence Group Kumite and Group Kroki are brothers-in-law.

Group Kumitegor and Group Krokigor are sisters-in-law. That is to say, every Kumite has (theoretically) marital rights over all Krokigors. Every Kroki has (theoretically) marital rights over all Kumitegors.

Hence the terms "husband" and "wife" do not necessarily imply actual marriage. They indicate mutual rights of cohabitation.

The term "my brother-in-law" does not necessarily single out the actual husband of my own sister. It indicates a man belonging to a group which has the right of cohabiting with the group which is "sister" to my own.

So also with the term "sister-in-law."

II.—Relationships between the first generation and the second.

Kumite.	Kumitegor.	Kroki.	Krokigor.
Kroki.		Kumite.	
Kumite-b.	Kumitegor-b.	Kroki-b.	Krokigor-b

THE TERMS OF KINSHIP. 93

Group Kroki is the father of Groups Kumite B and Kumitegor B.

Hence every Kroki calls every Kumite B "my son," and every Kumitegor B "my daughter." Every Kumite B, and every Kumitegor B, call every Kroki "my father."

Group Kumitegor is the mother of Groups Kumite B and Kumitegor B.

Hence every Kumitegor calls every Kumite B "my son," and every Kumitegor B "my daughter;" and they call every Kumitegor "my mother."

So also with the relationships between Group Kumite and Groups Kroki B and Krokigor B; also between Group Krokigor and those groups.

Again, Group Kumite is the father of Group Krokigor B, which is the wife of Group Kumite B; Group Kumite is also the father of Group Kroki B, which is the husband of Group Kumitegor B. Therefore, Group Kumite is father-in-law (or uncle) to Groups Kumite B and Kumitegor B.

So also Group Kroki is father-in-law to Groups Kroki B and Krokigor B.

For a like reason Group Kumitegor is the mother-in-law (or aunt) of Groups Kroki B and Krokigor B.

And Group Krokigor is the mother-in-law (or aunt) of Groups Kumite B and Kumitegor B.

Hence every Kumite B is the son-in-law (or nephew) of every Kumite and of every Krokigor; and every Kumitegor B is their daughter-in-law (or niece).

So also every Kroki B is the son-in-law of every Kroki and of every Kumitegor; and every Krokigor B is their daughter-in-law.

Hence the term "my father-in-law" does not necessarily single out the actual father of my actual wife. It indicates a man of a group with whose daughters my group has the right of cohabitation.

So also with the terms mother-in-law, son-in-law, and daughter-in-law.

III.—Relationships between the first generation and the third.

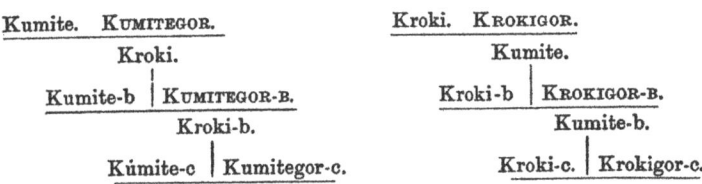

These are very simple.

Groups Kumite C and Kumitegor C are the grandchildren—

Of Group Kumite, because its son, Group Kroki B, is their father; also of Group Krokigor, for the same reason.

Of Group Kumitegor, because its daughter, Group Kumitegor B, is their mother; also of Group Kroki, for the same reason.

That is to say, all the groups of the third generation are grandchildren to all the groups of the first.

Hence the term "my grandfather" applies to all the males of my tribe in the generation next above that of my father; the term "my grandmother" applies to all the women of my tribe in that generation.*

Hence it is manifest that—

1.—On the same level the relationships are—

Within a phratria, brother and sister—consanguinity only.

Between the phratriæ, husband and wife, brother-in-law and sister-in-law—affinity only.

---

* Here, probably, we find the reason why many tribes have no terms for grandparents.

THE TERMS OF KINSHIP. 95

2.—Between the first generation and the second the relationships are—

Within a phratria, mother and child, father-in-law and son (or daughter) -in-law.

Between the phratriæ, father and child, mother-in-law and son (or daughter) -in-law.

Both within a phratria and between the phratriæ, there are relationships of consanguinity and others of affinity.

3 —Between the first generation and the third the relationships are grandparents and grandchildren.

APPENDIX A.

AT the risk of incurring a little harmless ridicule, I will endeavour to set forth the systems of group relationship more clearly by means of the following diagram. My excuse for presenting it here is that it has often helped me in my own study of this somewhat perplexing subject, showing to the eye at a glance what the mind does not readily perceive and retain without some such aid. I have used the diagram many hundreds of times in determining particular relationships among savage tribes, and it has never failed. Of course, when the relationship is more remote, it needs extension; but, how far soever it may be extended, it never changes its form. And in its simple form now given it shows all that is necessary to the understanding of the classificatory relationships.

John Smith and John Brown, two first cousins, marry one another's sisters. Each has a son John and a daughter Jane. These first cousins marry, and have issue, a son and a daughter to each marriage. The same christian names are continued.

KAMILAROI MARRIAGE.

The surnames represent the two intermarrying phratriæ, or gentes. The christian names represent the sex of the groups.

No. I.—DESCENT THROUGH MALES
(Turanian System.)

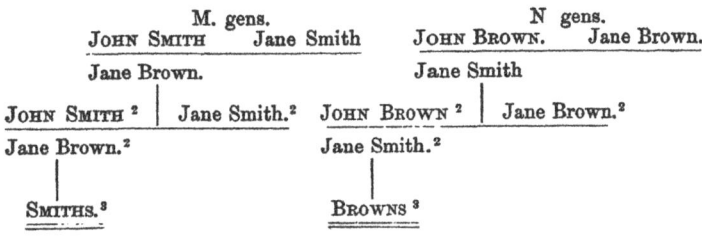

No II.—DESCENT THROUGH FEMALES
(Ganowanian System.)

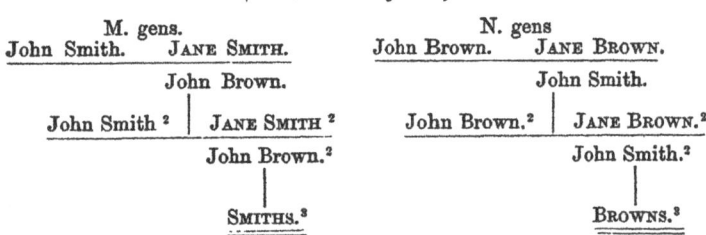

Precisely as are the relationships between the individuals in the diagram, so are the group relationships of intermarrying gentes. No. I. shows the system as it appears in tribes like the Fijians, who have descent through the father. No. II. shows the system as it is found in tribes like the Kamilaroi, who have descent through the mother. The composition of the gens, also, is shown in each case.

GROUP MARRIAGE AND RELATIONSHIP:

BY

LORIMER FISON.

CHAPTER I.

MORGAN's Theory—M'Lennan's Theory of Kinship Terms—The Group Relationships are Real Relationships—Lubbock's Theory of the Four Classes — The Ancient Gens — Kamilaroi — Half-sister Marriage— Endogamy and Exogamy—Distinction between Relationship through Females and Descent through Females—Orestes' Plea before the Areopagus—Marriage not a Contract, but a Status—The Social Unit—Inheritance of the Sister's Son.

THE characteristics of the Turanian system (as shown in Chap IV. of Kamilaroi Marriage, &c.) were drawn by Mr. Morgan from the terms of kinship found by himself and his helpers in everyday use among many tribes in every quarter of the world. The hypothesis on which he accounts for them is that they are the result of a reformatory movement prohibiting the once-prevalent intermarriage of brothers and sisters. His theory, therefore, as a whole, requires the former prevalence of what he calls the Malayan system with the consanguine family—that is to say, communal marriage of all the males within a tribe which is not divided into intermarrying classes, to all the females of the same generation, those males and those females being, consequently, at once tribal brothers and sisters and husbands and wives. *Morgan's theory.*

With that system we have little to do in this memoir, which deals with the Australian classes, whose system is the Turanian, or, rather, the Ganowanian, not the Malayan. But it may be observed, in passing, that sister-marriage is well known to have been no uncommon occurrence in the past, and that survivals of it may be found even at the present day. Ellis gives an instance which came under his notice at Hawaii:—

"Among the reigning families," he says, "brothers and sisters marry. This custom, so revolting to every idea of moral propriety, appears to have been long in use, and very recently a marriage was proposed at Maui between the young prince and princess, both children of the same parents. A council of chiefs was held on the subject, and all were favourable. . . . The individuals themselves are entirely passive in the affair." ("Polynesian Researches," vol. iv., p 435)

This is not a marriage with the half-sister, which is found elsewhere among otherwise exogamous tribes. The pair were brother and sister of full blood. Other modern instances might be given, showing that sister-marriage is still permitted, either for the preservation of a certain strain of blood, or for the transmission of property in a certain line. We have also to take into consideration the fact that the terms of kinship in present use by the Hawaiians, Samoans, Rotumans, and other South Sea Islanders, are precisely those which would logically spring from such marriages, though they do not represent present usage.

Given a community with the Malayan system in force—in other words, a state of society such as that indicated by the Dieri legend of the Murdu quoted at the beginning of the introductory chapter—and it is evident that the division of the community into two exogamous intermarrying classes, like Kumite and Kroki, would have precisely the reformatory effect which Mr. Morgan's theory requires. Kumite may not marry Kumitegor; and, since all his sisters, own and collateral, must be Kumitegor, this rule is simply a prohibition of sister-marriage, extending to tribal sisters as well as to own sisters. Mr. Morgan's theoretical divisions, induced from the terms of kinship, are identical with the two classes, found in Australia and elsewhere, of which those terms of kinship have been shown to be the logical outcome.

So far, then, his case appears to be complete; unless we can bring ourselves to agree with Mr. M'Lennan, that the terms belong to a mere system of addresses, invented by savages for the purpose of enabling them to call one another by unreal titles of kinship. But, as already stated, there are tribes whose terms of kinship are those of the Turanian system, and who, nevertheless, do not employ them in addressing one another. Moreover, the facts brought forward in the preceding chapters show clearly that the relationships expressed by those terms are as real to the Australians as are ours to ourselves. We can hardly believe that the term *wife*, for instance, if it were no more than a mere form of address, would carry with it veritable conjugal rights;* and still less can we believe that a man's taking to wife a woman who is in nowise akin to him according to our system, but whose brother he is according to the Australian, could be a capital offence unless the relationship between the parties were a real one in the eyes

M'Lennan's theory of kinship terms.

---

* "*Veritable conjugal rights*"—It is not asserted that these rights actually exist at the present day wherever the Turanian terms of kinship are found The oft-repeated caution must be borne in mind, that present usage is everywhere in advance of the system revealed by the terms of kinship. Among the Australian tribes which have the Kamilaroi organization we have seen that the term wife does actually, to a certain extent, carry with it conjugal rights wherever it applies; and even in far more advanced tribes the old range of the term is not wholly forgotten. Among the Fijian tribes, for instance, who have the patriarchal form of the family—polygamy with agnatic descent—the term "my wife" is applied to my brother's wife, and is something more than a mere form of address A man's actual assertion of the old right it expresses is looked upon with an indulgent eye, if the parties are discreet enough to keep their affairs from being noised abroad Though the practice was forbidden, it was winked at by those most nearly concerned, unless open scandal followed, in which case much virtuous indignation was displayed by the very tribe's folk who secretly allow themselves the same indulgence This shows that the prohibition of the old license had not acquired the force of a moral obligation

of the natives. Its reality is shown, not only by the infliction of the penalty, but by its motive also. The act is looked upon by the aborigines with abhorrence, and is severely punished, because it appears to them an offence against morality, such as incest is to us. It is a pollution of the entire group to which the offenders belong.

This statement may perhaps be ridiculed by those who consider savages to be "almost entirely wanting in moral feeling;" but to accuse savages of immorality because they are not moral according to our code of morality is both unreasonable and unjust. We can judge the quality of an action only by bringing it to the standard with which we are acquainted; and no more can be expected of any man than that he regulate his conduct by the law of right which is within his knowledge. As far, at least, as the inter-sexual regulations are concerned, this is done with all strictness by the Australian tribes, excepting those who have become demoralized by their contact with a civilization which, while teaching them to disregard their own moral code, neglected to teach them a better one.

The group relationships seem unreal to us only because we look at them from our own point of view; but not so do they appear to the savage. They are as real to him as our own are to us; and they bring to him the rights, the duties, and the prohibitions which ours bring to us. He has the rights of a brother, and he acknowledges the duties of a brother, towards every man of his own group; and he can no more marry a woman of a group which is "sister" to his own than we can marry our own sister.

Nor is the marriage relationship less real. We have seen that wherever a Kamilaroi native goes among tribes whose organization is that of his own, he finds the marital rights of the group to which he belongs, over the women of the group which is "wife" to his own, acknowledged by his hosts; and he is as ready to acknowledge their rights in return if they become his guests.

That the group relationships are real relationships to the native mind is further shown by the curious feeling manifested among savages between those who are connections by marriage, and especially between mother-in-law and son-in-law. It is well known that this frequently takes the form of mutual shame and avoidance, and exhibits itself in all manner of ludicrous ways. As, for instance when an Australian and his mother-in-law, compelled to address one another, stand back to back, and yell at the top of their voices, feigning to be far apart. Or as when a Kafir woman, meeting her son-in-law in the path, squats behind a bush, while he passes on hiding his face behind his shield. I once saw a man of the Wangaratta tribe (Australia) full of the utmost distress and disgust because his mother-in-law's shadow had fallen across his legs. He had been lying at the foot of an enormous gum-tree, which hid him from the old lady's view as she approached, and so the catastrophe occurred. In some tribes this feeling exhibits itself in another form—that of respectful formality between such connections. They are ceremoniously polite to one another, always using the respectful forms of address—*e g*, the pronouns in the dual or the plural instead of the singular—and in all things treating one another with a certain formal courtesy, as if they were strangers of rank, to whom such respect is due.

These customs—whether the mutual shame or the mutual respect—seem to have sprung from the same motive.* Certainly they have the same effect. Their result is *an avoidance of familiarity between the parties.*

---

* Sir John Lubbock supposes the mutual avoidance of mother-in-law and son-in-law to be the result of marriage by capture. I venture to think that his theory does not account for the facts.

And when we consider who the parties are, the customs explain themselves. It will be seen at a glance from the diagram showing the relationships between the First generation and the Second that a man's mother-in-law is a woman of the same class name with his wife. That is, she is one of a class of women who are his wives, but she herself is forbidden to him, and must therefore keep out of his way, as he on his part must keep out of hers. The slightest familiarity between them would be indecent—nay more, it would be pollution, bringing down who knows what terrible punishment from the Unseen Powers. Hence the ludicrous shifts to which these relatives resort. Among the Fijians the same mutual avoidance is seen between brother and sister, whether they be children of the same parents or not. They will not so much as look at one another. The word for the relationship between them is Ngane, and the verb formed from it means "to shun." The Fijian shuns his sister for the same reason that an Australian avoids his mother-in-law. She is a woman who is *specially* forbidden to him, and the very touch of such a woman would be pollution. These customs are powerful aids in enforcing the moral code as it exists among such tribes.

Group relationship also furnishes the reason why a person who is adopted into a gens forthwith abandons all the relationships of his own gens, and takes those of the gens into which he is adopted. Relationship being conceived, not between individual and individual, but between group and group, the relationships of the group into which he enters by adoption must necessarily bind him, as they bind all those who are members of it by birth; and, as necessarily, his former relationships must fall from him as he enters the new group. This also goes to prove that the group relationships are true relationships. We cannot suppose that the Iroquois Wolves, for instance, who, as Mr. Morgan tells us, were taken into the Hawk gens by adoption,* considered their Hawk relationships to be unreal, any more than we can suppose that a Roman who was adopted looked upon his solemn *detestatio sacrorum*, and *transitio in sacra*, as indicating nothing more than a change from one "system of addresses" to another.

Another remarkable proof that the group relationships are real to the savage mind presents itself in the well-known fact that, in many tribes who have descent through females, the son-in-law is bound to provide food for his father-in-law in times of peace, and to fight on his side in war. Thus, an Australian native cannot do as he pleases with the game he kills. He must share it out according to certain established rules; and, in Mr. Howitt's carefully-prepared list of food distribution among the Kurnai, we see that the best joints are given to the wife's father. That a man has to fight on his father-in-law's side has been noticed by several observers of savage life among tribes who have uterine succession; and it is worthy of note that this duty still devolves upon him in some tribes, who, though they have advanced to descent through males, have not yet been able to free themselves from the traditions of the older line. Thus the Rev. R. Taylor says of the Maori, who keep records carved in wood of long lines of male ancestors, and whose songs carry back those lines to the *nichts und alles*,† that the son-in-law

---

* "Ancient Society," p. 81

† "Very little," says the Rev. R. Taylor, "is thought of a chief who cannot count back some twenty or thirty generations, and the high families carry theirs even to the beginning of all things. I once obtained a pedigree of this kind, beginning with *na kore i ai*—from the Nothing the Something —which went on gradually introducing name after name, and at last terminating with that of the speaker." ("Te Ika a Maui," p 325)

This genealogy begins with The Nothing, whence came, in orderly sequence, the power of increasing, the living breath, the atmosphere, the firmament, the heavenly bodies, the dawn, the morning, the day, the earth, the god

had to go into his father-in-law's *hapu* (clan), and, "in case of war, was often obliged to fight against his own relatives."*

The reason of this custom, and the probability of its frequent prevalence among the lower savages, is seen in the fact that it is the logical result of their group relationships, when descent is through the mother. It is not that a man has to *leave his own clan*, in order to go into his father-in-law's, when he marries. He is of his father-in-law's division by birth. Thus, if Dog and Snake be the totems, or badges, of two intermarrying clans with descent through females, the daughter of Dog (male) is Snake, and the son of Snake (male) is Dog. This Dog, the son of Snake, marries Snake, the daughter of Dog. In other words, father-in-law and son-in-law are of the same division. See also the foregoing summary of relationships between the first generation and the second (*ante*, p 92), where it is shown that Kumite B is the son-in-law of Kumite

The foregoing considerations will, I think, be admitted as a sufficient answer to Mr. M'Lennan's question now to be quoted, as well as a sufficient refutation of the strong statement he makes in his own reply to the question he puts. "What duties or rights," he asks, "are affected by the

Ru, and so on, until we come to the exalted mortal at the end of the series. Pride in a long pedigree is no mere "ecstasy of the fancy," as Buckle called it. It is a "survival in culture" of an old savage notion, which was reasonable enough in its day, when he who was not the full-born descendant of full-born ancestors could not even have a place in the clan except on sufferance

* This custom, which may be said to be the rule in Australia among the tribes of Kamilaroi organization, was evidently on its way to extinction among the Maori This is manifest from the fact that there was stout rebellion against it on the part of the young men, doubtless backed up by the agnates. Some of them, within Mr. Taylor's knowledge, refused to obey the custom, and lost their wives in consequence; and whenever there is so much opposition to an ancient custom among savages, we may be sure that a new custom has gained a footing strong enough to afford a sanction to the malcontents. ("Te Ika a Maui," p. 337)

'relationships' comprised in the classificatory system? Absolutely none. They are barren of consequences, except, indeed, as comprising a code of courtesies and ceremonial addresses in social intercourse."*

Sir John Lubbock suggests that the four intermarrying classes might arise out of marriage by capture among four neighbouring tribes, who had the custom of exogamy with descent through the mother. {Lubbock's theory of the four classes.}

"After a certain time," he observes, "the result would be that each tribe would consist of four septs or clans, representing the original tribes; and hence we should find communities in which each is divided into clans, and a man must always marry a women of another clan" ("Origin," &c, p 87)

This is a possible hypothesis, but we have no need to search for hypothetical solutions of the question. The Australian divisions—which are tangible facts before our eyes at the present day—show that the four classes, and the gentes also, arose out of two primary divisions by an orderly process of evolution, such as might be expected from the forces at work. Granted the consanguine family, the prohibition of sister-marriage would give us two exogamous intermarrying classes—the Queensland Yungaru and Wutaru for instance; and we have seen how these subdivided into four, Gurgela, Burbia, Wungo, and Kuberu, and into other subdivisions distinguished by totems.

But, although the primary divisions were subdivided, they held all the subdivisions bound by their law. The four classes, for instance, are perfect in form, but they are not independent. They are like two pairs of Siamese twins, each individual being fully developed, and yet bound to his fellow by an unseverable ligament which prevents independent action. The bond here is the old law, "No

* "Studies," &c, p. 366.

marriage within either of the primary divisions." If that law did not continue to bind the subdivisions, Gurgela, for instance, could marry a woman from any one of the three remaining subdivisions, whereas he can only marry into the other primary division Wutaru, and into one only of its subdivisions (Table C). Each of the two primary divisions is, in fact, an imperfectly developed *curia* or *phratria* (phratry, as Mr. Morgan sensibly anglicizes it); and the four classes, as well as the totemic subdivisions, are gentes within a phratria.

The ancient Gens.

This use of the term "gens" may seem improper to the student, before whose mind the word calls up the Greek γένος and the Roman gens; but I venture to say, that when the social organizations of savage tribes are more fully understood, it will be seen that their exogamous intermarrying class is but the archaic form of the Roman gens, that the two are the same institution in different stages of growth, as Mr. Morgan has shown in his "Ancient Society," and that the same term may be correctly applied to both. To secure precision, it may be desirable to make a distinction between the gens which, like the Australian, has descent through the mother, and that which, like the Roman, has agnatic descent. But this is only a question of convenient nomenclature. It is not worth while to dispute about a mere "question of words and names." Our family is not the Roman familia, nor is our household the old Teutonic household; but no one disputes the propriety of the terms, whether they be applied to our institutions or to those others.

Professor Hearn, in his admirable work on the "Aryan Household," argues correctly that the gens is neither an artificial association nor an aggregation of originally independent households; but he proceeds to assert that it is the outcome of a household:—

"From the simple homogeneous household are evolved numerous distinct and related households, which, in the aggregate, form a whole, and that whole is the gens." "Aryan Household," p 168)

On the same page, however, we read:—

"There were gentes before familiæ ; and, after familiæ were known, there were gentes without familiæ The clan separated into households, but the separate households did not by any voluntary association form a clan "

I am not sure that I have grasped his meaning here. The two statements appear to be contradictory; for, if the gens were evolved from the household, how could there be "gentes before familiæ?" Setting this aside, his theory seems to be that the gens, or clan, separated into households; and that from some at least of these households— say, from each of those which were successful in the struggle for existence—a gens was evolved. These gentes, we may suppose, would again separate into households, which would again expand into gentes. So that we have an alternate series of clans dividing into households, and households growing into clans; but the original "simple homogeneous household" at the beginning of the series remains unaccounted for.*

Doubtless there were clans so formed after descent came into the male line; but there were clans of an earlier date than these. There are gentes among many tribes who have descent through females; and these could not have been evolved from a household such as that of which Professor Hearn treats in his valuable work; for there cannot be such a household without a house-father, and there cannot be a house-father until descent comes to be reckoned through males. The gens, therefore, being older than

---

* It should be noted that Professor Hearn expressly disclaims any intention of tracing the household back to the remoter past.

the household, is, à fortiori, older than the gens which was evolved from a household. It is as old as the first division of an endogamous commune into two exogamous intermarrying classes. It is needless to say that the gens of the nomad hunters—especially in so early a stage of their history as that which the Australian reveals—does not coincide with that of the civilized dwellers in cities. Like other institutions, it adapted itself to the changing conditions through which the races passed as they advanced from savagery, or barbarism, to civilization; but it never so far changed its aspect as to be beyond recognition, and I am persuaded that we shall yet be able to trace the successive stages of its development in the present usage of savage tribes, if we bestir ourselves to ascertain that usage before the tribes are "improved off the face of the earth." The great desideratum now is to trace the change of descent from the female line to the male.* From this point the gens—to use a nautical phrase—"takes a fresh departure," and the formation of the household, with its ancestral worship, becomes only a question of time.

Professor Hearn follows De Coulanges in taking ancestral worship as the basis of relationship; but in the earlier form of the gens the bond of union was certainly relationship and not community of worship. We have instances of female eponyms—the Darling River Kilpara and Mukwara are such instances—but I know of no case in which worship of female ancestors is practised among savage tribes. Mr. Morgan observes that the North American Indians,

"Though they had a polytheistic system not much unlike that from which the Greek and the Roman must have sprung, had not attained that religious development which was so strongly impressed upon the gentes of the latter tribes. It can scarcely be said that any Indian

* [In the Kŭrnai we have a community, as it were in the act of change from descent in the female to descent in the male line —A. W. H.]

gens had special religious rites; and yet their religious worship had a more or less direct connection with the gentes." ("Ancient Society," p. 81.)

I think it can be shown that they could not possibly have "attained that religious development," the reason being that, with a few exceptions, they had not reached descent through the father.

Ancestral worship seems clearly to have been an outcome of descent through males. At all events, there must have been this descent before there could be that worship. For, since the household gods were the male ancestors, the forefathers must have come into the direct line of descent before there could be household gods. And, when ancestral worship had become established, men worshipped the same gods because they were related—because they were descended from the same forefathers who had grown into gods. A common worship, therefore, was necessarily a mark of common descent; for the gods worshipped were the ancestors, and none but their descendants, either by birth or by adoption, could offer sacrifices to them. But the worship depended on the relationship, not the relationship on the worship. The worship was a mark of the relationship: the relationship was the cause of the worship. When descent comes into the male line, the eponym takes the place of the totem, and his subsequent deification is a simple growth.*

* We cannot draw a line beyond which offerings to the dead cease to be mere acts of filial piety, and become acts of worship, pre-supposing deification The savage does not think that death removes his ancestors entirely from him In some way or other, which he does not trouble himself to account for, they are still present with him, even though they have made the long journey to Hades, and they are in want of those things which they needed in this life Hence he makes offerings to them of food and other useful things, just as he furnishes his living elders with such articles, and for the same reason—because they have the claim of kinship upon him. But it can scarcely be said that the presentation of such offerings amounts to deification The ancestors *grow* into gods, and then what were mere acts of filial piety become acts of worship.

It is true that many persons were brought into the gens by adoption; and so there were men who were in nowise related according to our notions of relationship, but who nevertheless shared in the common worship. But the gens exercised the right of adoption long before it practised ancestral worship. The admission, therefore, of the adopted to the *sacra* of the gens could not have been the basis of their admission to its relationships. They were admitted to those relationships before the *sacra* were established. Among tribes who have descent through the mother at the present day, the gens has the power of assimilating members of other gentes by adoption, and these persons, when adopted, necessarily* enter forthwith into all the relationships belonging to true-born members of the gens.†

The fact that ancestral worship is consequent on the change of descent from the female line to the male explains the facts that the household god is always a male, and that the celebration of his worship is limited to males. Professor Hearn observes—

"It is remarkable that the house spirit is always masculine." ("Aryan Household," p 148)

And again—

" Admitting the worship of the house spirit, why was that spirit a male, and never a female? Why, too, was the celebration of his worship always limited to males? Until an answer can be given to these questions, our explanation of the subject, although it may be true as far as it goes, is obviously incomplete " (*Ibid* , p 163)

The answers to these questions seem to me to be very simple, and to be clearly given by the laws of marriage and

---

* *See* page 104

† [It seems to me that the formal presentation of female captives to the head man and a council of elders in the Gournditch-mara tribe before being given to their future husbands, points strongly to adoption.—*See* Part II , Appendix F.—A.W H.]

descent. Let M and N be two intermarrying gentes, three generations being represented, the males by capitals, and the females by small letters, while the successive descents are noted by figures. Descent is in the male line

M	m
M^1	m^1
M^2	m^2

N	n
N^1	n^1
N^2	n^2

When the marriages take place, m, m^1, m^2—that is, all the women of M gens—go over in marriage to N gens: n, n^1, n^2, go over to M gens, and the gentes become—

M n
M^1 n^1
M^2 n^2

N m
N^1 m^1
N^2 m^2

Each gens, therefore, consists of males who are married to women of another gens The women forfeit their own agnatic rights without acquiring similar rights in the gens of their husbands. They abandon their own line of descent without gaining a place in the other line. If any one of them do not marry, she may remain in her own gens, but she cannot transmit its blood. She cannot have a legitimate child, and therefore she cannot become an ancestor. The gens, therefore, virtually consists of males alone. Hence it is manifest that, since the ancestors are the household gods, the house spirit can be none other than a male, for all the female members are of another gens. For the same reason the celebration of his worship is necessarily limited to males. The only females who could join in that worship by right of birth forfeited their birthright by marrying into another gens; and none but males are left to make the offering "No female," says Professor Hearn, "is counted in the line of descent, because no offering is made to a female ancestor." But the fact is that no female is counted in the line of descent for the sufficient reason that no female can possibly be in that line when descent is through males. Every female ancestor was a woman of another line, and therefore no offering could be made to her.

But though this is known to have been the rule among Aryan nations, it is probable that there was a time in their history when females, and not males, were reckoned as the ancestors. It is certain that some of those nations formerly counted descent through the mother; and further investigation will, I think, show a strong probability that this was the general rule. At all events, it can be proved that tribes with whose present usage our forefathers would find themselves quite at home, advanced from that rule to the regulations now in force among them. The more advanced Fijian tribes, for instance, have descent through males, agnatic relationship, and ancestral worship They have village communities consisting of clans which are made up of households. They have the *mark*, of which each clan, and each household, knows its share. Within the *koro*, or village, they have the precinct under the dominion of the house father, often surrounded by its own fence, and the position of its house, or houses, regulated by the allowance for eavesdrip. In short, their status and regulations might be set forth in terms which would roughly serve for the Aryan tribes. And it is beyond question that they formerly had descent through females. Unmistakable marks of that line of descent are to be seen even on the most advanced tribes; others still bring the sister's son into the line of succession, while others again are divided into two exogamous intermarrying classes with descent through the mother, like the Kumite and Kroki of South Australia.

MARRIAGE WITH THE HALF-SISTER.

The Kamilaroi marriage with the paternal half-sister is specially interesting in that it affords an instance of rebellion against the class law. It is a partially-successful assertion of the independent right of a gens to choose its own wives where it will, provided always that it go beyond its own boundaries in choosing them. We should not have expected to find it among savages of so low a type as the Australian; for, as far as it goes, it is a defiance of the rule which was long obeyed by the gentes even in nations of a high culture It is marriage within a phratria.

It will be observed that this innovation of the Kamilaroi can result in marriage with the half-sister by the father's side only where descent is reckoned through the mother. For where descent is through the father, the wife comes (though only by a legal fiction) into her husband's gens, and her children are born into that gens. Consequently the half-sister must be of the same gens with her half-brother, and the Australian law forbids their marriage Ipai-Emu marries his half-sister Ipatha-Blacksnake (Table E). But if descent were in the male line, this woman could not be his paternal half-sister, for his father would be Emu, while her father would be Blacksnake. The Kamilaroi marriage with the half-sister, therefore, involves descent through the mother. And wherever we find marriage with the *paternal* half-sister, in conjunction with descent through the father, it seems probable that we may suspect it to be a survival of the older regulation.

Special attention is called to these marriages because Sir John Lubbock founds on them what seems to me to be a mistaken argument against Mr. Morgan's theory. In his " Origin of Civilization," he remarks :—

"Morgan also considers exogamy as explainable, and only explainable, as a reformatory movement to break up the marriage of blood relations, and which could only be effected by exogamy, because all the tribe were regarded as related. In fact, however, exogamy affords little protection against the marriage of relatives; and, wherever it was systematized, it permitted marriage even between half-brothers and sisters, either on the father's or the mother's side. Where an objection to the marriage of relatives existed, exogamy was unnecessary; where it did not exist, exogamy could not arise" (p. 106)

It is true that where no "objection to the marriage of relatives existed," exogamy could not rise—at least it would not be likely to arise spontaneously; but I fail to understand how it could be "unnecessary" where such an objection did exist. For how could that objection take effect without exogamy, that is, without a law compelling men to seek their wives outside the group to which they themselves belonged? And, since that group was composed of their nearest kin, how can it be said that such a law "afforded little protection against the marriage of relatives?" The only ground for the assertion is the permission of marriage with the half-sister; and even this appears to be overstated It is true that it has been permitted by some exogamous tribes, but it is a mistake to say that it has been allowed "wherever exogamy was systematized" Many exogamous tribes do not permit it

But it is not easy to make out what Sir John Lubbock means by exogamy. On page 98 of his work already quoted, he remarks :—

"Mr M'Lennan's theory seems to me to be quite inconsistent with the existence of tribes which have marriage by capture, and yet are endogamous The Bedouins, for instance, have unmistakably marriage by capture, and yet a man has a right to marry his cousin"

Sir John, therefore, looks upon marriage with the female cousin as endogamy, whereas it is strictly exogamous. For a Bedouin may not marry those cousins of his—according to our system—who are the daughters of his mother's sisters or his father's brothers. The marriageable cousin is the daughter of his mother's brother or of his father's sister, and is, therefore, neither of his gens nor of his phratria—using these terms for the sake of convenience. Under the Turanian system, which is exogamous, she is none other than his wife—*i e*, a woman whom he may take to wife. (See Kamilaroi Mar , chap iv., prop. xii)

The fact is, that Mr M'Lennan's terms, endogamy and exogamy—though very convenient, if properly used—are apt to be dangerously misleading, and require careful definition. The former is an obligation to marry within a certain group of persons ; the latter is an obligation to marry without the group But what is the group ? If we are to understand it as a constant, well and good Only, let its boundaries be defined, so that we may know what we have to deal with. *The group, however, is not a constant.* It varies ; and the range of the terms—the area to which they apply—varies with its variations. Supposing, for instance, a tribe to be an undivided commune—*i.e.*, to have communal marriage between all its men and women of the same generation—then the whole tribe would be endogamous. If it splits up into two intermarrying classes, like Kumite and Kroki, it is still endogamous *quâ* tribe; but endogamy can no longer be said to be its law of marriage, for it is composed of two strictly exogamous divisions.

A division subdivides into gentes. We may now speak of it as a phratria. As long as it holds its gentes bound by the phratriac bond, it continues to be exogamous ; for all its gentes must marry into the other phratria. But if, in the course of time, each gens establish its right to marry anywhere beyond its own bounds, then the gentes are still exogamous, while the phratria is neither endogamous nor exogamous There is no longer an obligation to marry either within it or without it. Each of its members can marry either within its limits

Endogamy and Exogamy.

or without them, as he pleases, only he must go beyond his own gens in his choice of a wife. And, still farther, when father's brothers and mother's sisters come to be looked upon as uncles and aunts, instead of fathers and mothers, the "collateral" or "tribal" brothers and sisters turn into marriageable first cousins, and the exogamy of even the gens is done away with—nay, the gens itself disappears, and exogamy is confined to the family. But this brings us down to our own marriage law; whereas it is with the Australian that we are now concerned, and with the question as to whether its exogamous law could suffice as a "reformatory movement to break up the marriage of blood relations." That it would so suffice has, I venture to think, been sufficiently proved. The law required by Mr. Morgan's theory is identical with that of the Australian classes. "Kumite must not marry Kumitegor;" and this rule most unquestionably prohibits the marriage of all kinsfolk nearer than first cousins. Nay, more, it excludes even those first cousins, according to our own system, who are the children of father's brothers or of mother's sisters. It allows no union which is prohibited by our law, and it bars marriage between many persons whom we do not reckon to be in anywise akin.

Distinction between relationship through females and descent through females.

The Australian classes show the development of the classificatory system of kinship with descent through the mother, but they take us no farther. They throw no light on the change of descent from the female line to the male. Sir John Lubbock considers this system to be a sort of intermediate stage between the two lines of descent.

"In North America," he observes, "the system of relationship through females prevails among the rude races of the north Farther south we find a curious, and so to say intermediate, system among the Iroquois and Hurons, to whom, as Mr. Morgan has shown, we may add the Tamils of India. A man's brother's children are reckoned as his children, but his sister's children are his nephews and nieces ; while a woman's brother's children are her nephews and nieces, and her sister's children are her children." ("Origin," &c , p. 127).

Farther on he remarks :—

"We cannot dismiss these peculiarities as mere accidents, but must regard them as similar, though peculiar, views on the subject of relationship."

There seems to be a confusion here between *relationship* through females and *descent* through females. Thus, on p. 127 we read—

"Relationship to the father at first excludes that to the mother; and, from being regarded as no relationship to the former, children come to be looked upon as none to the latter."

A like statement is found in Mr. M'Lennan's "Primitive Marriage," which, as Mr. Morgan points out—

"Asserts that this kinship (*i e*, kinship through females), where it prevailed, was the only kinship recognized." ("Ancient Society," p. 515)

But descent through the mother does not exclude personal relationship to the father, or to any other relative. Nor does descent through the father exclude personal relationship to the mother, or to any other relative. In fact, the line of descent does not at all affect the personal relationships. Thus, the relationships of the Seneca-Iroquois, who have descent through the mother, coincide in every important particular, save one, with those of the Fijians, who have descent through the father. The point of difference between the two lines is this. With descent through the mother, the child is not of the father's class, but of the mother's—*e g*, Kumite's son is not Kumite: he is Kroki, after his mother Krokigor (Table A). With descent through the father, he must be of the father's class. But though what may be called the *gentile* relationship is different, father and son being of the same gens when descent is in the male line, and of different gentes when it is in the female line, the personal relationship between father, and son, indicated by the terms of kinship, is the same in both cases. The "relationships of the Iroquois and Hurons," some of which appear to Sir John Lubbock to indicate kinship through males, while others point to kinship through females, have no such significance. They are (as has been proved in Kamilaroi Mar., chap. iv., props. i, ii., iii., and iv.) the necessary result of the division of a tribe into exogamous intermarrying classes, whether descent be in the male line or the female. This is what Sir John speaks of as—

"A curious system, founded on peculiar views of the subject of relationship"

Those views can hardly be said to be "peculiar," for they are of a world-wide prevalence, as he himself has shown by his carefully-gathered list of widely scattered tribes whose relationships are governed by similar views; and the system can appear "curious" only as long as we fail to perceive its fundamental principle. It is clear and simple and logical throughout.

The assertion that "relationship to the father excludes that to the mother" has been repeated by Professor Hearn :—

"Uterine succession," he observes, "that is, succession through the mother alone, ignores kinship through the father, just as agnation ignores kinship through the mother." ("Aryan Household," p. 151.)

If by kinship here we are to understand membership in the same gens—using the terms, for want of a better, to denote any exogamous tribal subdivision—the assertion is quite true. But if the assertion be that uterine succession ignores all relationships through the father, and that agnation ignores all relationships through the mother, I venture to maintain that it is incorrect. It rests on the assumption

DESCENT THROUGH FEMALES.

that there are no relationships excepting those which are within the gens, whereas we find, in the languages of many tribes which are organized in gentes, specific terms in constant use for relationships other than these.

If "kinship" be taken in its narrower—and, indeed, its strictly correct—sense, as membership in the same tribal division, then relationship is wider than kinship; for, in addition to the relationships between the members of the same gens, there are also relationships between them and the members of the gens, or gentes, with which their gens intermarries. None of all these relationships are in anywise dependent on the line of descent. They are precisely the same whether the rule be "agnation" or "uterine succession." Where descent is through the father, males only are in the direct line of succession: where descent is through the mother, females only are in that line. In other words—using the term "cognate" in a restricted sense, as contrasted with "agnate"—descent through the father brings the agnates alone into the gens *as abiding members of it*: descent through the mother brings the cognates only; but all the relationships, whether those within the gens, or those between the intermarrying gentes, are the same in both cases. In each case there is relationship between agnates and cognates, as well as between agnates and agnates and between cognates and cognates.

This may be shown directly to the eye by the diagram of the two intermarrying gentes M and N, before given. Whether descent be in the male line or the female, M marries n, and N marries m. The marriages, with the first descents, are as follows:—

Descent through Males				*Descent through Females*			
M n		N m		M n		N m	
M^1	n^1	N^1	n^1	N^1	n^1	M^1	m^1

In both cases husband and wife are of different gentes, for no marriage can take place within a gens while the gens is exogamous. In the former case father and child are of the same gens, while mother and child are of different gentes. In the latter case mother and child are of the same gens, while father and child are of different gentes. But the relationships are the same in both cases—not only those between parents and children, but all the others also. In the language of every tribe which has the Turanian system of kinship there are specific terms for the relationships which each member of one gens bears to the members of the other, as well as for those in the same line of descent.

The plea of Orestes before the Areopagus has been often quoted in proof that there is no relationship between mother and child when descent is reckoned through males. The argument is stated by Sir John Lubbock in the following words (I italicize the words on which the argument depends) :—

"—— Orestes asks the Erinnyes why they did not punish Clytemnestra for the murder of Agamemnon ; and, when they reply that marriage does not constitute *blood relationship*—' She was not the kindred of the man she slew '—he pleads that by the same rule they cannot touch him, because a man is *a relation* to his father, but not to his mother. This view, which seems to us so unnatural, was supported by Apollo and Minerva ; and, being adopted by a majority of the gods, led to the acquittal of Orestes " ("Origin," &c , p 129)

The wording of the original is as follows (Eum. 573, Camb. Texts) :—

OP. τί δ'οὐκ ἐκείνην ζῶσαν ἤλαυνες φυγῇ;
XO. οὐκ ἦν ὅμαιμος φωτὸς ὃν κατέκτανεν.
OP. ἐγὼ δὲ μητρὸς τῆς ἐμῆς ἐν αἵματι;

It appears to me that Orestes does not here deny *relationship* to his mother. He simply repudiates *mem-*

bership in the same gens with her, and thereby raises a very interesting legal point.* The charge brought against him by the Erinyes was not a charge of matricide *quâ* matricide. Had it been so, his plea of justification as the avenger of blood would have been amply sufficient. They charged him with having killed a member of his own gens, *and only on this ground could they have any hold upon him*. Their case depended upon their establishing this point, and it was on this point that their case broke down. For it was not with all cases of homicide that they had to deal. Those only in which the slayer was ὅμαιμος of the slain came within their jurisdiction. The whole gens was the body corporate, in whose veins flowed the common blood. The shedding of that blood by a member of another gens and therefore of another αἷμα, was simple homicide, with which they were not concerned. Hence their justification of themselves for not punishing Klytemnestra. But the shedding of that blood by a member of the gens was something more than man-slaying. It was impious homicide—a vital injury inflicted on the body corporate by one who was a part of that body, and therefore bound to defend it against injury, and to revenge it when injured. Even when it was accidental, it called upon the Erinyes for vengeance, which could only be averted by expiation and purification. And the reason why it called upon them

* I am gratified by observing that Mr. M'Lennan's interpretation of Orestes' case is substantially one with my own "The basis of the suit," he remarks, "is the claim of the Erinnyes to the right of punishing matricides. This was their function by special ordination, as representing a time when kinship through the mother was unquestioned" ("Studies," &c., p. 258) Mr M'Lennan, however, looks upon that function as conferred by "special ordination," whereas my theory is that it arose directly out of the constitution of the gens I may say here that this part of my own MS was written more than a year before I saw Mr M'Lennan's work, and that my references to it in the first part of these memoirs were quotations at second hand

seems to me to be as follows. When every gens had to pursue its own blood feud, there was a difficulty in the way of punishing a murderer who had killed a member of his own gens. For, with descent through males, the avenger of blood was the brother or the son of the deceased; with descent through females, he was the brother or the sister's son. In both cases, therefore, he was of the same gens with the criminal, who was consequently out of his reach. He could not kill him without bringing upon himself the guilt of shedding the blood of his own gens. Hence, man being powerless, the gods had to step in. This seems to be the reason why the offences which made a man *sacer*—obnoxious to the wrath of the gods—were all, directly or indirectly, of this kind, *i e*, offences against the body corporate by a member of that body. If this view be correct—I advance it under submission to the judgment of competent scholars—it seems to weigh strongly in favour of the reading φόνου instead of φόνῳ in v. 573. The argument of the Erinyes is that Klytemnestra being, as they maintained, ὅμαιμος of her son, was "exempt from slaughter" at his hand.

The plea of Orestes is twofold, and he certainly conducts his case with great skill. First, he pleads justification of his act on the ground that he had done no more than his bounden duty as the avenger of blood.

    ἀνδροκτονοῦσα πατέρ' ἐμὸν κατέκτανεν.

The Erinyes meet this with the rejoinder that Klytemnestra was beyond his reach as the avenger—she was ἐλευθέρα φόνου as far as he was concerned. He then pleads that the offence with which they charged him was not the impious homicide which came within their province, thus cutting away from under them the ground on which they based their argument. Having drawn from them the admission that Klytemnestra's crime did not fall within their jurisdiction, because she was not ὅμαιμος of the man she slew, he pleads that he is not ὅμαιμος of the woman he killed, and therefore they can have nothing to do with him. The Erinyes in vain repel this plea with horror. They persist in speaking of τὸ μητρὸς αἷμ' ὅμαιμον: and, when the verdict is given against them, they rave furiously twice in the same words against the innovating gods who have overridden and trampled upon the ancient laws.

And indeed, according to those ancient laws, their view was the right one. For, if we may believe the legend of Cecrops to be founded on fact, descent was formerly through the mother at Athens; and, with descent in that line, as already shown, mother and son were ὅμαιμοι, though husband and wife were not. That is to say, mother and child were of the same γένος, while husband and wife were of different γένη. But, descent having changed to the male line, those laws were no longer in force, and Orestes was acquitted. The Erinyes found, to their infinite disgust, that they had prosecuted him under an act which had been set aside by another of more recent date.

In studying this interesting case we have to set aside our own idea of "blood relationship." The αἷμα* here indicates no more than the line of descent, the ὅμαιμοι being the agnates because descent is through the father. The case turns on the question as to whether Orestes and Klytemnestra are of the same gens,† and this is not necessarily a

* The choice of the wife of Intaphernes is a case in point Darius having offered to spare one of her relatives whom she might select, she chose her brother in preference to her husband or her children With descent through males he was of her αἷμα, but these were not

† I am indebted to my friend, the Rev. J. G Fraser, M A , for calling my attention to the following passage, with regard to the Duchess of Suffolk's case, in "Tristram Shandy" (iv., c 29) :—"The judges of the consistory and prerogative courts of Canterbury and York, together with the master of the faculties, were all unanimously of opinion that the

question as to personal relationship, because there are relationships beyond the gens as well as within it.

Professor Hearn's "theory of agnation" is that it was "a consequence of the doctrine of worship in the male line," and that "this doctrine was founded on the common belief that a child proceeds from the father alone, and that the mother supplies to it nutriment and gives it birth, but nothing more." ("Aryan Household," p. 163) But, when Euripides represented Orestes as defending himself on this ground, and made him say, after going into certain particulars,

ἄνευ δὲ πατρὸς τέκνον οὐκ εἴη ποτ' ἄν—
(Orestes, 547)

he only provoked ridicule. One can imagine the shout of laughter with which the interpolated query must have been received—

ἄνευ δὲ μητρὸς πῶς κάθαρμ' Εὐριπίδη;

if, indeed, this were not an afterthought of those wicked wags who so cruelly persecuted the unhappy poet.

Father and son are none the less related as father and son because they are of different gentes, when descent is reckoned through females. Mother and child are none the less related as mother and child because they are of different gentes, when descent is reckoned through males; whence it appears that Sir John Lubbock's sequence ("Origin," &c, p. 130)—

First, a child is related to its tribe generally;

Secondly, to its mother, and not to its father;

mother was not of kin to her child. But what said the Duchess of Suffolk to it? asked my uncle Toby."

We cannot always tell without examination whether Sterne is dealing with facts, or only playing with fancies; and our lawyers would do a good deed if they would tell us whether there were anything in English laws at the time to which he refers, on which the civil doctors could base that opinion. If any such thing can be found, it will be of great interest.

MARRIAGE NOT A CONTRACT. 127

Thirdly, to its father, and not to its mother;

Lastly, and lastly only, to both father and mother—may be stated more correctly as follows:—

1. A child stands in a filial relation to the whole generation next above it, because the tribe is a commune, and is not yet divided into intermarrying gentes.

2. The child is of its mother's gens, not of its father's, because the tribe is now divided into exogamous intermarrying gentes, and descent is through the mother.

3. The child is of the father's gens, not of the mother's, because descent has changed to the male line.

4 The family has superseded the gens, and father, mother, and child are of the same family

Relationship depends, not on the line of descent, but on the law of marriage; and therefore, if we would understand the ideas of relationship which are in the mind of a savage, such as the Australian, we must clearly understand his idea of marriage. Bachofen supposes that descent through the mother arose out of a rebellion against communal marriage on the part of the women, who successfully established their rights as against those of the men; and Sir John Lubbock, while dissenting from that view, on the ground that "savage women would be peculiarly unlikely to uphold their dignity in the manner supposed," says, "It seems to me perfectly clear that the idea of marriage is founded on the rights, not of the woman, but of the man;" and he quotes "the complete subjection" of the women among the Australian blacks in support of his opinion. *Marriage is not a contract, but a status.*

Both these views appear to be based upon our own idea of marriage as a contract between the parties. But the idea of marriage under the classificatory system of kinship is founded on the rights neither of the woman nor of the man. It is founded on the rights of the tribe, or rather of the classes into which the tribe is divided. Class marriage is not a contract entered into by two parties. *It is a natural state into which both parties are born,* and they have to be content with that state whereunto they are called Kumite's consent has no more to do with his marriage to Krokigor than it had to do with the sex wherewith he found himself endowed when he came into the world Just as he was born a male, so was he born Krokigor's husband. What has he to do with the marriage contract? It is between the classes, and was made ages ago by the far-away ancestors It binds all the members of the community, and lays hold upon them as soon as they draw in their earliest breath of life

The social unit.

The Australian classes give a clear view of that tribal idea which lies at the root of land tenure, inheritance, and so many other important questions. The individual is not recognized. He has no independent rights He has, so to speak, no independent existence He is, in fact, not a perfect individual, but only an insignificant part of one. And in the tribal divisions and subdivisions we see what appears to be a steady progress towards the *individualizing of the individual* (if the phrase may be allowed), with a continued struggle against the old tribal law along all the line. First, the whole tribe, in its corporate capacity, may perhaps have been the individual holding all rights vested in itself. Whether it were so or not, we have it clearly before us, separated into two corporate bodies with partially independent rights; and we can follow the process of segmentation throughout the minor subdivisions, until at length we come to the civilized man with his personal rights and possessions, and his gospel of political economy teaching him that self-seeking on the part of the individual must result in the greatest good of the greatest number. There is something in the law of his old savage forefathers which it were well for him to take with him in his onward march. It would have saved him a great deal of trouble if he had not left it behind.

The Australian regulations explain the inheritance of the sister's son, which Sir John Lubbock calls "the curious practice that a man's heirs are not his own, but his sister's, children," and which he says "we are able to understand," because change of wife is of so frequent occurrence among the lower races that "the tie between a mother and child is much stronger than that which binds a child to its father." ("Origin," &c., p 120) *[margin: Inheritance of the sister's son.]*

This kind of inheritance arises directly from tribal subdivisions organized like the Australian, *i e*, with descent in the female line. Kumite's children cannot inherit from Kumite because they are not of the Kumite class. They are Kroki. The inheritance falls to the children of his sister Kumitegor, because they are Kumite. And this rule remains in force through all the subdivisions as long as descent continues to be in the female line. With descent through males, the children come into their father's gens and inherit from him.

And, moreover, the inheritance is inalienable. The entire estate is a public estate, and it is strictly entailed. It is held by the whole community, but no generation so holding it is the absolute owner. Each generation holds in trust for the next, and it cannot alienate the estate even by common consent of the whole generation, for its property in the estate is no more than a life interest. This is the ancient rule. Is our own an improvement upon it?

CHAPTER II.

Mr. M'Lennan's Theory of the Rise of Kinship—Of Female Infanticide—Of Exogamous Tribes and Marriage by Capture—Of Polyandry—Sir John Lubbock's Theory of Individual Marriage—Of Expiation for Marriage—The Group is the Social Unit as regards Marriage—Degradation Theory—Conclusion—Appendix C—Female Infanticide.

THE system of kinship, called by Mr. Morgan the Turanian, has been shown to be the logical outcome of the presence in a community of exogamous intermarrying divisions: these, upon examination, were found to consist of certain homogeneous groups; and, taking each group as a unit, it was shown that the relationships between group and group are precisely those which would arise and continue between individuals among ourselves if marriage were between certain first cousins, and continued from generation to generation between pairs of their descendants.

The groups represented by these cousins are found in many tribes at the present day; the terms of kinship appropriate to them are in constant use; and if, taking the groups as single units, we examine the relationship of any one group to another, we find that the term proper to that degree is used between all the members of the groups. Hence the terms of relationship, as they are heard in daily use, point out the groups; and the groups, taken as units, explain the *raison d'être* of the terms. It now remains for us to consider more fully the principal objections which have been advanced to Mr. Morgan's theory, and briefly to recapitulate the main conclusions which may be drawn from what has been advanced in these memoirs.

Mr. M'Lennan, who denies that the terms have anything whatever to do with relationship, has attempted a full explanation of them as a sequel to his review of Mr. Morgan's hypothesis, which he considers to be of an "utterly unscientific character." Having absorbed the bane of an utterly unscientific theory throughout so many pages of these memoirs, let us now apply ourselves to the examination of a scientific hypothesis by way of antidote.

Though Mr. M'Lennan opens his eighth chapter with the assertion that "the earliest human groups can have had no idea of kinship," yet in the very next paragraph he finds himself compelled to call one of those groups "a group of kindred." This seeming contradiction he explains on the supposition that the apparent bond which united the members of such a group was one of fellowship only, arising from the fact that "they and theirs had always been companions in war or the chase—joint tenants of the same grove or cave." And yet he tells us that "they were held together by a feeling of kindred." Here, then, we have a group of early savages who have "a feeling of kindred" strong enough to hold them together, but who have "no idea of kinship."

It is possible that Mr. M'Lennan makes here, in his own mind, a distinction between "a feeling of kindred" and an "idea of kinship" which is not clear to mine. His meaning may be that the early savages *felt* they were related, and yet did not perceive *how* they were related This I gather from his previous remark that "at the root of kinship is a physical fact, which could be discerned only through observation and reflection—a fact, therefore, which must for a time have been overlooked." Since this fact is the sufficiently obvious one that a child proceeds from its mother, it is not easy to understand the absolute necessity for its having been overlooked even for a time, however short. The mother, at all events, would scarcely fail to perceive it.

The process by which the early savage arrived at his system of kinship through females is given by Mr. M'Lennan as follows:—Having "perceived the fact of consanguinity in the simplest case—namely, that he had his mother's blood in his veins"—he quickly came to see that he was of the same blood with her other children. A little more reflection then enabled him to observe that he was of one blood with the brothers and sisters of his mother. On further thought he perceived that he was of the same blood with the children of his mother's sister. And in course of time, following the ties of blood through his mother and females of her blood, he arrived at a complete system of kinship through females. This is the process, stated very nearly in Mr. M'Lennan's own words. ("Studies," &c., p. 124.)

Now, though it is a great mistake to say that savages do not reason, they certainly do not reason in this way. They reason by deduction, not by induction. They do not put together a number of separate facts, and draw from them a general conclusion. Some large fact, involving a general principle, fills their minds, and they accept its logical consequences, clinging to them long after they have ceased to be able to carry them out in everyday life, with a persistence which is often ludicrous, and sometimes even pathetic. The consequences of that leading fact are, as it were, a line of rails to them. As long as it lasts they go on smoothly enough; but when it fails them—then, unless they are "shunted off" to another line, they are helpless. A striking case in point is that of the Kurnai. They are a tribe of savages off the rails.

The group relationships arising from the marriage of the exogamous divisions are precisely what the savage would perceive and adopt, while Mr. M'Lennan's process of reasoning would be altogether foreign to his mind. He did not piece together his system of kinship out of the various degrees of relationship as he perceived them one by one. Paradoxical as it may sound, it was his system of relationship which gave him his degrees of relationship.

Mr. M'Lennan's method of accounting for those relationships on the basis of polyandry* seems to be even more unsatisfactory than is the process of reasoning by which he represents the savage as arriving at their perception. Indeed, a very strong case can, I think, be made out against his entire theory of polyandry as a system of marriage. And since this is closely interwoven with his hypotheses as to female infanticide, exogamy, and marriage by capture, it will be necessary to devote some little space to the consideration of them all.

Mr. M'Lennan states his case concisely in the following words :—

"We believe this restriction on marriage (exogamy) to be connected with the practice in early times of female infanticide, which, rendering women scarce, led at once to polyandry within the tribe, and to the capturing of women from without." ("Studies," &c , p 111)

"If it can be shown, firstly, that exogamous tribes exist, or have existed ; and, secondly, that in rude times the relations of separate tribes are uniformly, or almost uniformly, hostile, we have found a set of circumstances in which men could get wives only by capturing them ; a social condition in which capture would be the necessary preliminary to marriage" ("Studies," &c , p 42)

After advancing his proofs of the foregoing conditions, he remarks—

"We now confidently submit that the conditions required for this inference are amply established." ("Studies," &c , p 109)

This gives the following sequence :—

1. Female infanticide was the general practice among savages, and resulted in a scarcity of women; so causing polyandry and marriage by capture.

---

* Origin of the Classificatory System of Relationships ("Studies," &c., pp 372-407)

2. The tribe having thus taken to capturing women, acquired the habit of so doing, and became exogamous.

3. Exogamy having thus grown into a law, and neighbouring tribes being, as a rule, hostile to one another, men could get their wives no otherwise than by capturing them. Which may be fairly summed up as follows :—

Female infanticide causes marriage by capture.

Marriage by capture causes exogamy.

Exogamy causes marriage by capture.

I cannot suppose this to have been Mr. M'Lennan's meaning, but I have failed to perceive any other.

Two things, however, are clear as forming the basis on which his theory stands—

First, that "female infanticide" was the general practice among the "primary hordes;" in other words, that they killed many more female children than male.

And, second, that exogamous tribes existed under "circumstances in which men could get wives only by capturing them;" in other words, that these tribes could not marry *anywhere within their own boundaries*, and were consequently driven to capture their wives, there being no possibility of friendly intermarriage with other tribes.

Let us now test this basis, and see whether it be secure.

Female infanticide.

It is well known that infanticide is a very common practice among savage and barbaric tribes ; and the opinion seems to prevail that "female infanticide"—the killing of female children rather than male—is the general rule. This opinion is undoubtedly correct as to many tribes, but I venture to suggest that it needs reconsideration *as far as the lower savages are concerned*, and it is with them that the theory now under consideration has to do   I think it will be found that the practice is far less common with them than it is with the more advanced tribes. And for this reason—

FEMALE INFANTICIDE.

Savages are perfectly logical people in their own way, and do not act without a motive, which, to their minds at least, is a sufficient one. So thoroughly have I been convinced of this by my sixteen years' residence among them and observation of their ways, that I do not hesitate to assert that, whenever their acts appear capricious to us, we may be quite sure there is something hidden from us in which lies what to them is a sufficient motive. Now, the savage has no hesitation in killing his infant children, whether male or female, if they be in his way, but he does not kill any one of them for the mere sake of killing; and he certainly would not kill his daughters rather than his sons without a sufficient motive. Is such a motive to be found among the lower savages?

The reasons usually given for female infanticide are thus stated by Sir John Lubbock:—

> "Female children became a source of weakness in various ways They ate and did not hunt. They weakened their mothers while young, and, when grown up, were a temptation to surrounding tribes " ("Origin," &c , p 108)

To the same effect Mr. M'Lennan observes:—

> " To tribes surrounded by enemies and, unaided by art, contending with the difficulties of subsistence, sons were a source of strength both for defence and in quest of food, daughters a source of weakness " ("Studies," &c. p 111)

The motive here advanced is that *females are an encumbrance to savages;* and for this four reasons are given:—
1. They "weaken their mothers while young."
2. They "eat and do not hunt"—*i e*, they are food consumers and not food providers.
3. They are "a source of weakness" as regards defence —*i e*, they are in the way in war time.
4. They are "a temptation to surrounding tribes."

I think it can be shown that not one of these reasons is of any force as regards the lower savages.

1. That women "weaken their mothers when young," cannot be a reason for killing female children rather than male, unless it can be shown that girls require more nutriment from their mothers than boys require.

2. The assertion that women "eat and do not hunt" cannot apply to the lower savages. On the contrary, whether among the ruder agricultural tribes or those who are dependent on supplies gathered from "the forest and the flood," the women are food providers, who supply to the full as much as they consume, and render valuable service into the bargain. In times of peace, as a general rule, they are the hardest workers and the most useful members of the community.

3. And certainly they are not "a source of weakness" as regards defence. They are perfectly capable of taking care of themselves* at all times; and, so far from being an encumbrance on the warrior, they will fight, if need be, as bravely as the men, and with even greater ferocity. Of this I could give some shocking examples which have come within my own knowledge.†

---

* They who are accustomed to the ways of civilized women only can hardly believe what savage women are capable of, even when they may well be supposed to be at their weakest. For instance, an Australian tribe on the march scarcely takes the trouble to halt for so slight a performance as a childbirth The newly-born infant is wrapped in skins, the march is resumed, and the mother trudges on with the rest Moreover, as is well known, among many tribes elsewhere, it is the father who is put to bed, while the mother goes about her work as if nothing had happened. The Rev Geo Taplin, though allowing that "aboriginal women generally suffer less during parturition than civilized women do," asserts that they "do suffer considerably in childbirth." It must be borne in mind that the natives with whom Mr Taplin was chiefly acquainted, were those who lived on the Mission Station under his charge, and therefore under abnormal circumstances. He mentions three cases of death in childbirth as the only cases within his knowledge, and these were evidently connected with congenital defect ("Aborigines of S. Australia," p. 48)

† [William Buckley, the "wild white man," who lived 32 years among

4. Finally, that they are "a temptation to surrounding tribes" does not appear to be a sufficient reason for killing them. They are far too valuable a possession to be cast away merely because the neighbours covet them. We do not find the Kafirs exterminating their cattle because they are "a temptation to surrounding tribes."

It is among the more advanced tribes that the motives for female infanticide are found, and, I believe, the practice also to a greater extent than among the lower savages.

Thus, where a costly dower has to be given with a girl in marriage, female infanticide is known to be very common. A daughter there is a special cause of impoverishment to her parents, whereas a son is a cause of enrichment. Here, then, we find a motive which seems to act with considerable power; but it does not exist among the lower savages, for with them the dower—where one is given—is provided by the bridegroom's kinsmen and presented to the parents of the girl. Here the conditions are reversed. It is the girl who is a cause of enrichment to her parents on her marriage. And this is very far from being all the advantage they derive from her. As already pointed out (Ante, p. 105), her husband has to provide her father with food in times of peace, and to fight on his side in war.

Therefore, since women are in no respect an encumbrance to the lower savages, but the reverse, it is evident that we do not find in the reasons given by Sir John Lubbock and Mr. M'Lennan a preferential motive for female infanticide.

the Port Phillip tribes says, as follows, when mentioning that those he lived with were attacked and in danger of being worsted by a numerous hostile party :—"They raised a war cry; on hearing which the women threw off their rugs and, each armed with a short club, flew to the assistance of their husbands and brothers . . Even with this augmentation our tribe fought to great disadvantage, the enemy being all men, and much more numerous. . . . Men and women were fighting furiously and indiscriminately . . and two of the latter were killed in this affair " ("Life and Adventures of William Buckley," p 43)—A W.H]

And something more than this can be shown. Another motive for killing female children rather than male is found, among agricultural tribes who have descent through the father, in the fact that a woman can transmit neither the family name nor the family estate. She passes out of the line by marriage. (See Ante, p. 113). And, with tribes who have that line of descent, and who accept its consequences as regards ancestral worship—*i.e*, who offer house sacrifice to males alone and by males alone—this is a very grave, the very gravest consideration. The dead are dependent upon their male descendants for those offerings without which their shadowy existence would be to the last degree wretched; and therefore every man is anxious to have sons, not daughters, to succeed him. If, therefore, he practice infanticide at all, he will surely kill his daughters, not his sons. But among the lower tribes this motive works the other way, for with them descent, and therefore inheritance, is through females. Hence we find in some such tribes the practice of "male infanticide"—that is to say, the practice of killing male children rather than female. Thus, the Rev. R. A. Codrington informed me, with regard to the Mota people, that infanticide was common among them, and that "male children were killed rather than female, because of the family passing by the female side."*

Exogamous tribes and marriage by capture.

We have seen that Mr. M'Lennan's postulate, as to female infanticide being the rule among the lower savages, cannot be readily granted; and we have now to examine his proposition that—

Exogamous tribes exist, or have existed, under " circumstances in which men could get wives only by capturing them."

* *See also* Appendix C.

A tribe, to satisfy these conditions, must be exogamous *quâ* tribe; that is to say, marriage must be forbidden everywhere within its limits. For if it be so constituted that its men can get their wives anywhere within its boundaries, it is not a tribe such as Mr. M'Lennan's theory requires.

His list of what he calls " exogamous tribes " is contained in the fifth chapter of his " Studies in Ancient History;" and of all those tribes there is not one which satisfies his own conditions. Without exception they are all divided into exogamous intermarrying clans; and, therefore, they can get wives without capturing them from other tribes. Each one of them is an *endogamous* tribe or community, made up of exogamous intermarrying clans; that is, it marries within its own boundaries, but it prohibits marriage within any one of its clans.

Once more we have to note a confusion arising from Mr. M'Lennan's want of precision in using the term " Tribe," and his own terms " Exogamy " and " Endogamy," all of which are equally misleading, unless the area to which they are applied be clearly defined. But, whatever be the meaning which he gives to " Tribe," the cases cited by him in his fifth chapter are of no avail. For it is evident that in these cases the word tribe must have one of two meanings, either—

(1.) The whole nation or community; or,

(2) An exogamous clan, or the exogamous clans severally into which the community is divided.

In either case the examples cited by Mr. M'Lennan are valueless, because—

(1.) If by tribe he means the nation or community, then the tribes cited are not exogamous. They marry within their own bounds.

(2.) If by tribe he means the exogamous clans, then the

tribes cited are not found "in circumstances in which men could get wives only by capturing them." The clans have peaceful intermarriage one with another.

As this statement can be verified by referring to Mr. M'Lennan's own account of the tribes which he cites as "exogamous," there is no need to trouble the reader with an examination of more than two or three of them, which seem to require special notice. Of these the first are the Kalmuks, who are "divided into four great tribes or nations," called respectively Khoskot, Dzungar, Derbet, and Torgot (or Tchoro). Their system of marriage seems to have this peculiarity, that the common people can marry within any one of these great divisions, though not within certain prohibited degrees, while the nobles must marry each without his division. The divisions, therefore, are exogamous as regards the nobles, and endogamous as regards the common people. Each division, however, is subdivided into smaller divisions, but we are not told whether these subdivisions are exogamous or not.

I know very little about the Kalmuks; and a mission station in Fiji affording no facilities for getting at books of reference, I am not in a position to ascertain more fully their system of marriage. We know, however, that the name by which they call themselves is Derben Ueirat, which means the *The Four Relatives ;* and this fact, coupled with the law of marriage among their hereditary nobles— who are likely to be strong conservatives, and given to standing in the old paths—seems to point to a time when the four great divisions were simply exogamous intermarrying clans making up one community. But, whether this were so or not, the Kalmuks will not serve Mr. M'Lennan's turn, unless we may take it for granted that there was a time in their history when they had no way of marrying save by capturing each other's women.

Let us grant this for the sake of argument, and see what comes of it. Derbet and Torgot, we will say, are two exogamous tribes living in a state of mutual hostility, and so presenting "a set of circumstances in which men can get wives only by capturing them." Now, what is the result? Say that Derbet captures a number of Torgot women, sufficient to supply its bachelors with wives, and Torgot captures Derbet women enough for its wants. We may now ask, "Are all the women on both sides disposed of?" If so, it follows that each tribe has captured all the women of the other.

But, if there be any women left uncaptured, what are they to do for husbands? Say, for instance, that a number of Derbet girls are left uncaptured by the Torgots, what is to be done with them? They cannot marry within their own tribe, for the tribe is exogamous. The Derbets must be in this perplexing strait—either they must give these women away to the Torgots (which would be a method of wife-procuring other than capture) or they must capture Torgot young men as husbands for them.

Mr. M'Lennan's theory of marriage by capture, therefore, requires, either—

(1.) That all the women of a tribe shall be captured by the men of another tribe; or,

(2) That men shall be captured for husbands as well as women for wives. Surely when a theory brings us to a conclusion such as this, it were better to lay it aside.

The Kocchs and the Hos, cited by Mr. M'Lennan in a subsequent chapter, are useless witnesses to him here, because, as Sir John Lubbock has pointed out, "they are divided into *keelis*, or clans, and may not take to wife a girl of their own keeli." ("Origin," &c., p. 117.)

Concerning the Khonds, Major M'Pherson's statement, quoted by Mr. M'Lennan, is that "intermarriage between persons *of the same tribe*" (the italics are mine), "however large or scattered, is considered incestuous, and punishable by death." This does not prove that no Khond can marry a Khond; and nothing less than this is required by Mr. M'Lennan's theory. It simply points to the fact that the Orissa Khonds are divided into exogamous clans, and that men and women of the same clan are tribal brothers and sisters. Major M'Pherson evidently uses "tribe" in the sense of "clan."

Taking the term "exogamous tribe" to mean an entire community, complete in all its parts, and forbidding marriage everywhere within its limits—the sense in which Mr. M'Lennan's theory requires it to be used with regard to the cases cited by him in his fifth chapter—I do not hesitate to say that nowhere on the face of the earth has such a tribe been found at the present day,* and that we have no trustworthy record of any such tribe having existed in bygone days. All the savage communities with which we have anything like a full acquaintance are made up of exogamous intermarrying divisions in some form or other, and, consequently, do not forbid marriage everywhere within their own limits. Such a community may properly be said to be endogamous as regards itself, if it forbids—or at least strongly discourages—marriage beyond its own boundaries, as is frequently the case; but its law of marriage cannot be said to be endogamous, because its clans are strictly exogamous. As far as I know, there is no clear instance on record of a community which is endogamous

* At first sight the Kurnai may perhaps appear to answer to this description. They "forbid marriage anywhere within their own limits;" at least, they severely punish for it But it has been shown that their community is not "complete in all its parts;" and, moreover, they are compelled to break their own rule. Mr. Howitt also shows us that, though marriage is treated as an offence, provision is made for it between the clans.

without having exogamous divisions within it. If we could find such a tribe, we should find what has been diligently sought for in vain for the last thirty years and more. It would be an undivided commune, to the former existence of which significant evidence has long seemed to point.

The case of the Ahts, quoted from Sproat's "Scenes and Studies of Savage Life" by Sir John Lubbock ("Origin," &c., p. 117), and apparently brought forward by him as an instance of such a tribe, is far from being a case in point. Sproat's account does not prove the Ahts to be endogamous, excepting in the sense that a tribe made up of exogamous clans may be said to be endogamous, because it prefers not to go beyond its own clans for its wives. If this be endogamy, then the term is of very little value, for in this sense nearly every civilized nation may be said to be endogamous, in feeling at least. Even among ourselves the "foreigner" is not looked upon as an altogether eligible husband, excepting for our princesses, and for them only for reasons of State. Derbet to Derbet for the commoners, but the Derbet princess must go to the Torgot prince. What Sproat tells us of the Ahts is that—"The idea of slavery connected with capture is so common that a freeborn Aht would hesitate to marry a woman taken in war, whatever her rank had been in her own tribe" And this feeling is a very common one elsewhere. With reference to Sir John Lubbock's notice of its manifestation among the Ahts, Mr. Walter Carew, Commissioner for Tholo, Navitilevu (Fiji), our best authority as to native customs among the hill tribes on that island, was good enough to write me the following note:—"To call a person 'a child of a captive' is a very great insult, even though the mother were of high rank." Mr. Carew goes on to remind me of a case within our common knowledge in which a chief was set aside because his mother was a war-captive, though she was a lady of high rank in one of the principal tribes in Fiji—a tribe of far greater importance than his own.

Polyandry Having examined Mr. M'Lennan's theory as to exogamy and marriage by capture, it now remains to notice his statement of polyandry.

If what we have to deal with here were no more than a statement that cases of polyandry are to be found, or even that such cases are of frequent occurrence, the controversy would be of no very great importance. But Mr. M'Lennan treats polyandry as a *system of marriage* of so extensive a prevalence, and draws with singular ability such wide inferences from it as to kinship, succession, and the change of descent from the female line to the male, that all the chief questions connected with the development of social organization are involved. His evidence ought, therefore, to be of the very strongest, and his witnesses fully competent to deal with the facts they narrate.

In forming our opinions as to the customs of savage tribes, in all cases where the significance of a custom depends upon something which underlies the visible facts, accounts given by travellers must be received with caution. They may state quite correctly each fact they observe, but they are very likely to be wrong in their interpretation of its meaning. No witness here is to be fully trusted unless he has had very full opportunities of making himself thoroughly acquainted with that which underlies the customs he describes.

This caution has a special application to evidence as to polyandry, for, as Sir John Lubbock justly observes, " when our information is incomplete, it must be far from easy to distinguish between communal marriage and true polyandry " (" Origin," &c., p. 116) Thus, the practice of the " imported labourers"* in Fiji might well be set down as true polyandry if we did not know what is beneath the outer fact. There is an exceptional scarcity of women among them, many more males than females being imported, and so a woman may be seen cohabiting with a number of men. But we have had more than one startling proof that this seeming polyandry is neither true polyandry nor mere prostitution, but only group marriage in difficulties. Women who admitted men of a forbidden class have been put to death by their countrymen (See *Ante*, p. 65, *note*), and the murderers have declared that they were under obligation to kill them. Not a few of Mr. M'Lennan's instances of so-called polyandry admit of a similar explanation; and even those cases on which he seems chiefly to depend—the Nair and the Tibetan—are anything but conclusive in his favour.

The Nair polyandry, according to the account given of it by Mr M'Lennan himself in quotations from Hamilton, Buchanan, and the Asiatic Researches ("Studies," &c, p. 149) is evidently group marriage—at least it seems so to me. A Nair woman has "a combination of husbands," but then "a Nair may be one in several combinations of husbands; that is, he may have any number of wives." Group marriage might well be described in the same words That the Nairs are divided into exogamous clans is certain from the fact that cohabitation is regulated "by certain restrictions as to tribe and caste," the plain meaning of which is that there are certain exogamous divisions on which the marriage regulations are based. And therewith the Nair polyandry resolves itself into cohabitation between permitted groups.

Mr. M'Lennan asserts that the Nair husbands are "usually

---

* Natives of other South Sea groups brought to Fiji as workmen on the plantations, &c

not brothers—usually not relatives" But in what sense does he use the words "brothers" and "relatives?" If by "brothers" he means only children of the same parents, and by "relatives" only those who are related according to our own notions of relationship, then his statement is of little weight; for a group of tribal brothers may include many persons other than these.

The Tibetan instance quoted from Turner, where "five brothers were living very happily under the same connubial compact" ("Studies," &c., p. 115), seems to be a clearer case. But even here we have no proof that it was an instance of true polyandry, and not of polyandry combined with polygynia, like the Nair custom—the custom of the Britons noticed by Cæsar*—and all the other instances given by Mr M'Lennan where tribal brothers hold their wives in common. And considering how easy it is to mistake instances of group marriage for polyandry, such proof may be reasonably demanded from one who represents polyandry as a widely prevalent system of marriage, and draws such large conclusions from it.

The law of the Levirate, which Mr. M'Lennan considers "it is impossible not to regard as . . derived from the practice of polyandry" ("Studies," &c., p 163), does not appear to me to have anything at all to do with polyandry It was a regulation to prevent the elder branch of a stock from becoming extinct Its underlying motive is found in the preferential claim to the birthright vested in the elder branch; and this preferential claim is found only in tribes who have descent through males, or at least who, having settled down to agriculture, are fairly started on their way

---

* How Mr M'Lennan could have cited the customs of the Britons in proof of polyandry as opposed to group marriage, I am at a loss to imagine What Cæsar tells us is that "groups of ten or a dozen" *(deni, duodenique)* had their wives in common ("De Bello Gallico," v. 14)

in that line. The lower savages know nothing of that motive.

Mr. M'Lennan lays stress upon the fact that the widow was the Levir's wife "without any form of marriage." But there is no proof that this is a survival of polyandry; for, in the first place, there is no need for us to look upon it as a survival of anything at all, and, in the second place, it would serve very well as a survival of group marriage. In many tribes which are organized in groups like the Australian, the widow is the Levir's wife as a matter of course. He does not always even wait until she become a widow. He is of the same group with her husband, and her group is "wife" to his.

It is not denied that cases of polyandry occur. A few instances of it have come under my own observation. But in every case the men were of a clan which intermarried with that of the woman, the circumstances were exceptional, and the custom was not the general practice—not even the frequent practice—of the tribe. In full accordance with this is the account of polyandry at Mota, sent to me by the Rev. R. H. Codrington before mentioned:—

"Polyandry exists, but is rarely practised. Never with young people, but mostly as a matter of convenience, as when two widowers live with one widow She is wife to both, and any child she may have belongs to both There are cases in which a husband connives at a connection between his wife and another man This is not counted adultery, for it is an open transaction ; and it is not polyandry, for the parties are not counted husband and wife It is not considered respectable" (*See* "Trans Royal Society of Victoria," 1879)

The existence of polyandry is not denied, but I venture to hazard the assertion that it is not *the system of marriage* in any tribe at the present day. Nay, more, it seems to me impossible that it could be the system of marriage anywhere at any time. The mere arithmetical difficulty in its way appears to me quite insurmountable.

Though such statistics as I have been able to get at in Fiji among the lately heathen tribes directly contradict the hypothesis,* still, I think we may suppose that the number of males generally exceeds that of females among the lower savages; at least, quite a number of observers declare that such is the fact. But it does not seem to have occurred to Mr. M'Lennan to consider how great his theory of polyandry as a system of marriage requires that disparity to be. Under such a system it is evident that whatever may be the average number of husbands to a wife, at least so many times more numerous must the men be than the women. If X be the number of women in a tribe, and Y their average allowance of husbands; then, since we cannot suppose that under such a system any marriageable girl would be allowed to roam in maiden meditation fancy free, the number of men must be XY, even supposing all of them to be absorbed in the " combinations of husbands."†

Nor will marriage by capture help us here; because for every woman captured there must have been Y husbands left lamenting, unless we suppose that a non-polyandrous tribe was kept in the neighbourhood of each polyandrous tribe for its convenience, and that they never retaliated upon their aggressive neighbours.

M'Lennan's theory

To sum up. It has been shown that Mr. M'Lennan's postulate of female infanticide as the rule among the lower

* *See* Appendix C

† This argument may appear to tell with equal force against the ordinary form of polygamy, under which a man may have several wives who are supposed to be his exclusively But, under this form of marriage we are not bound to suppose that every man has a wife; whereas polyandry, as a system of marriage, can leave no woman without a husband Moreover, it is a mistake to suppose that among polygamists "several women to one man" is the general rule No tribe has women enough for such a supply It is only the chiefs, or the more powerful men of the tribe, who can secure to themselves more than one wife apiece, and some of the common people are left out in the cold until a widow falls to their share, or a chief bestows upon them some cast-off member of his harem.

savages cannot be readily granted; that his exogamous tribes are not exogamous in the sense which his theory requires; and that both marriage by capture and polyandry, as systems of marriage, unless there be a fatal flaw in my reasoning, involve something which has all the appearance of an absurdity. Without claiming too much then, I think it may be said (of course with the saving clause already inserted) that the whole basis of Mr. M'Lennan's theory has been shown to be insecure. It is therefore unnecessary to examine the structure which he has built upon it. If the theory cannot account for itself, still less can it account for the classificatory system of relationships.

does not account for the classificatory relationships.

And if this be so, it is all the greater pity that Mr. M'Lennan allowed himself to treat with such contemptuous scorn the hypothesis advanced by Mr. Lewis H. Morgan, which, if correct, is subversive of his own:—

"This wild dream—not to say nightmare—of early institutions." ("Studies," &c , p 360)

"It seemed worth while to take the trouble necessary to show its utterly unscientific character." (*Ibid.*, p 371)

Before a writer permits himself to use words such as these, he should make quite sure that he has firm ground under his feet; and even then, as to whether it would not be better to leave them unsaid. "The wise may make some dram of a scruple, or indeed a scruple itself."

Sir John Lubbock's theory as to the effect of capture upon communal marriage, is stated by him in the following words:—

Sir John Lubbock's theory.

"I believe that communal marriage was gradually superseded by individual marriage founded on capture ; and that this led firstly to exogamy, and then to female infanticide " ("Origin," &c , p 81)

The manner in which this was effected is stated as follows :—

"We must remember that, under the communal system, the women of the tribe were all common property. No one could appropriate one of them to himself without infringing on the general rights of the tribe. Women taken in war were in a different position The tribe, as a tribe, had no right to them, and men would surely reserve to themselves exclusively their own prizes. The captives then would naturally become wives in our sense of the term

"Several causes would tend to increase the importance of the separate, and decrease that of communal, marriage The impulse which it would give to, and receive back from, the development of the affections, the convenience with respect to domestic arrangements, the natural wishes of the wife herself, and last, not least, the inferior energy of the children sprung from in-and-in marriages, would all tend to increase the importance of individual marriage " ("Origin," &c , p 108)

We are presented here with the following sequence:—

1. The tribe is an undivided commune. That is to say, its law of marriage—if it can be called a law of marriage—is promiscuous intercourse between all its males and all its females.

2. Members of the tribe capture women from other tribes; and each captor keeps his captive to himself, because " the tribe has no right to her."

3. By the assertion of the sole right of the captor, " the captives naturally become wives in our sense of the term"—that is to say, with the help of marriage by capture, we leap at one bound from promiscuity to individual marriage. This may take the form of monogamy if the warrior capture only one woman; but if he be very successful, he may have quite a harem of these " wives in our sense of the term."

4. "Individual marriage" being thus introduced into a " promiscuous " tribe, its reciprocal action on the affections, the domestic bliss resulting from it, " the natural wishes of the wife herself"—that is to say, the natural desire of a woman, or of several women, in a state of savagery, to be bound to one man—these, with other considerations, con-

vince the tribe of the "importance of individual marriage," and so result in exogamy and female infanticide.

Whether this be what Sir John Lubbock meant or not, it is certainly what his words mean. But, having already had frequent occasion to point out what appear to be mistakes into which he has fallen in his treatment of this subject,* we need not examine his theory at length, especially since it rests upon what can be shown by direct evidence to be a fallacy. Granting the old undivided commune, his whole theory rests upon the assumption that a warrior has a sole right, as against his tribe, to a captive taken by him in war. In support of this right Sir John advances nothing whatever beyond the assertion that it would be likely to accrue. On the contrary, it appears to me in the highest degree unlikely, because among savages the individual has no rights as distinct from the group to which he belongs; and, moreover, it is directly contradicted by evidence which can be tested at the present day †

Sir John Lubbock's theory as to expiation for marriage appears to me the true one as far as it goes; and Mr. M'Lennan's attempted *reductio ad absurdum* with regard to it is either entirely mistaken or entirely unfair.

"The general reasoning," he observes, "turns on one principle, and the evidence in its second branch on another principle The first principle is that a man might appropriate a war captive to himself because *over her the tribe had no right:* the other principle is that the appropriation must be expiated, because *it infringed the right of the tribe to the woman* The contradiction between these principles is obviously absolute, and that it exists is beyond dispute " ("Studies," &c , p 429)

The contradiction between the "principles," as Mr. M'Lennan states them, is "obviously absolute;" but then

* See ante pp 83, 107, 115, 118, 127
† See ante p 65

he does not state those principles as their author states them. Sir John's argument is, that " *as long as communal rights were in force* . . . special marriage was an infringement of these rights, for which some compensation was due," * but that these rights were *not in force* with regard to captured women. " The women *of the tribe*," he remarks, "were all common property. No one could appropriate one of them to himself without infringing on the general rights of the tribe." For *such* a "special marriage," therefore, expiation was necessary. "But," he goes on to observe, "women taken in war were in a different position. The tribe, as a tribe, had no right to them." And, therefore, no expiation was required for the appropriation of a captive, no rights having been infringed. I believe the latter clause to be entirely mistaken, but it certainly does not contradict the former.

In his argument against Sir John Lubbock's theory, Mr. M'Lennan remarks :—

"If we were to find a large number of well-vouched cases in which, on a marriage, extraordinary freedoms with the bride were permitted to men of the bridegroom's kindred, it might be plausibly maintained, in the absence of any more satisfactory explanation, that . . . there was an assertion on the one side, and a recognition on the other, of an ancient right. But the cases ought to point clearly to this The privileged persons should be men of the bridegroom's group only, and the cases should be capable of no simpler explanation than that which refers them to an ancient communal right." ("Studies," &c, p. 435)

Such cases are to be found in abundance—cases, at least, in which "men of the bridegroom's group" assert a common right to the bride, and of which, as far as I am aware, there is "no simpler explanation than that which refers them to an ancient communal right." The Kurnai practice set forth in Mr. Howitt's Latin note (p. 202,) is a clear

---

* "Origin," &c , p. 100.

EXPIATION FOR MARRIAGE. 153

case in point, as also is the fact that a fugitive wife in that tribe becomes the common property of her pursuers if they capture her, these pursuers being of her husband's kindred.* In full agreement with this is the Rev. R. Taylor's statement that, among the Maori, "formerly every woman was *noa*, or common, and could select as many companions as she liked without being thought guilty of any impropriety, until given away by her friends to some one as her future master. She then became *tapu* to him, and was liable to be put to death if found unfaithful." ("Te Ika a Maui," p. 166.) Those "companions" must be men who are of a *hapu*, or clan, which is marriageable with the woman's. To the males of that clan in the same generation with her, she is *noa* until the *tapu* of a husband is put upon her. If her husband die and his brother do not take her, she is released from the *tapu*, and becomes *noa* again. The communal right is shown also in the fact that a Maori girl is sometimes wrestled for by all the young men who have a tribal right to her.† The girl is sometimes seriously, even fatally injured in the struggle, being dragged hither and thither, regardless of her cries and sufferings. An unsuccessful suitor has been known to plunge his spear into her heart, so that no one should enjoy the prize he had failed to gain. All those youths must be "of the bridegroom's group only;" and the Maori instance is but one out of many, the custom being of wide prevalence.

* [The practice accompanying elopement among the Kŭrnai, was also occasionally followed where widows were re-married —A W. H]

† The struggle between the suitors is called *Punarua* This word is the Hawaiian Punalua, which denotes the common right of tribal brothers to certain women. A similar struggle, in a smaller way, used sometimes, in the heathen days, to take place at Vanua Levu, Fiji, between the Levir and the brother of the widow It was the duty of the latter to strangle the widow on her husband's death ; and, if the Levir wanted to keep her for himself, he had to wrestle for her with her brother, if this dragging at the woman can be called wrestling The wretched woman was sometimes almost torn in two between them

Among the Gonds and Bygars of the Sathpuras, Central Province, India, " marriage between cousins is almost compulsory, when the brother's child is a daughter, and the sister's a son." But a girl may choose any one of her cousins, either by anointing his head with turmeric and touching his feet, or by " sitting down" in his house. If, however, she thus exercise her right of choice, *any one of her male cousins has a right to carry her off if he can.* (See an extremely interesting article on " Gonds," &c, in vol. xxvi of the *Cornhill Magazine*) This case also fulfils Mr. M'Lennan's conditions, for all those " male cousins" must be of the bridegroom's group It is interesting to note that the bride's choice does not carry the *tapu* with it.

Mr. M'Lennan's objections* to some of Sir John Lubbock's instances of expiation for marriage do not seem to be upheld by what we know of savage customs For instance, Herodotus' statement that the daughters of the common people in Lydia were prostitutes before marriage, seems to point to a custom like the Maori. They were *noa* until they were made *tapu* by marriage

It is certain, also, that the forty warriors " entertained " by the " woman of the Naudowessies "† must have been of a clan with which hers could intermarry; for Carver tells us that the woman was held in great respect for what she had done, and we have conclusive proof that the admission of a man belonging to a forbidden clan would have been considered most disgraceful to both parties.

Again, Mr. M'Lennan remarks, concerning " the *jus primæ noctis*," accorded among the Nasamones, Auziles, Balearic Islanders, and others to the guests at a marriage—

" There is no indication that the guests were of the kinship of the bridegroom only, and it is not likely that they were "

---

* "Studies," &c , pp 436-443
† "Origin," &c , p. 101.

We find, among present-day savages, however, that marriage feasts are strictly "family matters." No guests attend but those who are of the parties' kin. Moreover, among many tribes it is the business of the bridegroom's clansmen to provide the marriage gift; and, according to Herodotus, it was the custom for each guest, to whom the *jus* aforesaid was accorded, to present a gift which he had brought with him for that purpose. (" Melpomene," 172)

Sir John Lubbock, however, does not clearly distinguish the group to whom the expiation for marriage was due. Granting the undivided commune with which he begins, and granting its division also into exogamous clans as the result either of capture, according to his theory,* or of a reformatory movement, according to Mr. Morgan's, the communal right is not extinguished, but *its range is narrowed from the whole tribe to the clan*. The group of men who can claim expiation for "special marriage" is no longer the whole tribe, but the group of tribal brothers who have a common right to the group of females to which the woman belongs

This common right is seen in present exercise in the cases already cited, and notably in that unmistakable preliminary to elopement among the Kurnai. We see it granted in the meeting of Kubi with the "stranger Ipatha"† and in the regulated accommodation afforded to the guest who is supplied with a temporary wife from the group corresponding to that which is "wife" to his group in his own tribe. We see its violent assertion in the fierce

---

* "Origin," &c, p 87   Sir John Lubbock's theory as to capture has this advantage over Mr M'Lennan's, that, not shutting us up to capture being the only way in which men could get wives, we are not bound to suppose either that all the women of a tribe are captured, or that young men are captured as husbands for the girls who have been left uncaught. (*See* Ante p 148)

† Ante p 53

struggle of the Maori youths for possession of the girl who is *noa*, or common to them all, and in the spear thrust into her breast by the brutal wretch in his fury of disappointment at having failed to secure her for himself. And even among tribes where there is the strong restriction of the *tapu** upon it, we see the communal right asserting itself as soon as that restriction is withdrawn, in the Maori widow who, if the Levir do not take her, becomes *noa* again to the men of his group, and in the fact of the absconding wife among the Kurnai being common to her captors. The symbol of marriage by capture, so often found among tribes of the present day, may well be a symbol of the violent breach of this communal right, just as expiation for marriage is, as it were, a compounding for it on the part of the woman.

<small>The group is the social unit as regards marriage.</small> It appears strange to me that, though the existence of the group as the social unit among savages has been so long seen and acknowledged with regard to other matters, it should still be so vehemently denied with regard to marriage and relationship.

Land tenure and inheritance are based upon it. It is seen in succession to office where there is hereditary succession; for it is not necessarily the son of the office-holder, or his sister's son, who succeeds. Qualification for office is hereditary in a certain group, but the office itself is elective among the qualified persons And these qualified persons collectively make up a group of kinsfolk. It is therefore to the group that the office descends.

Blood feud also shows the group as the social unit. A certain group is looked upon as a joint undivided body.

---

* The tapu, tabu, or tambu, can, I think, be shown in all cases to be an authoritative restriction of the communal right. The source and growth of the authority that restricts it present an interesting subject of inquiry; but there is not room for its discussion here.

THE GROUP THE SOCIAL UNIT.

If it be struck anywhere, every part of it feels the stroke, and resents it. To revenge an injury done to it is the duty of its every member; and in revenging that injury it is not absolutely necessary to strike at the injurious person himself Any one of his group will do; for not he alone is responsible for his act—the whole body to which he belongs is involved in it And the blood of that body flows in the veins of every member of it—in the veins of the helpless infant as in those of the stoutest warrior. Hence, if the offending group can be struck anywhere, it suffices * The

---

* This was put so clearly to me, many years ago, by one of the "old hands" in Fiji (one of those white men who lived as natives among the natives until they became more Fijian than the Fijians), that I may be pardoned for quoting his very words, of which I made a note at the time We weie talking about a disturbance which had arisen in the following manner A dog bit a man His brother shot the dog Its owner killed two men of their tribe in revenge; and thereupon a blood feud arose which kept cropping up for years afterwards, and was not settled without great difficulty The "old hand" maintained that the murderer was justified by Fijian custom Being then but a young resident in Fiji, and therefore naturally convinced that I knew all about the people, I disputed his assertion on the ground that the men killed had had nothing to do with the shooting of the dog Whereupon my "old hand" enlightened me as follows :—

"That makes no sort o' difference, bless you They don't care a mite s'long's its somebody belongin' to the tribe It's just like this, sir; in a manner o' speakin, say as me and Tom Farrell here has a difficulty, and gets to punchin' one another If he plugs me in the eye, I don't feel duty bound to hit him back azackly on the same spot If I can get well in on him anywhere's handy, I ain't partikler. And that's how these niggers reckons it "

One may be permitted thus once in a way to enliven the discussion of so dull a subject

See also H C Robinson's "Diary," vol i, p 453, for a striking exhibition of the same feeling on the part of a French soldier who had been cruelly treated by the Spaniards, and saved from death at their hands by the English during the Peninsular war :—

Soldier —" Ah! vous êtes Anglais : que je vous aime ! . . Mais si vous étiez Espagnol, je vous égorgerois " . .

H C R —" What! Kill me when I have done nothing to you?"

Soldier —" Si ce n'était pas vous, c'était votre frère. Si ce n'était pas votre frère, c'était votre cousin C'est la même chose On ne peut pas trouver l'individu, c'est impossible "

blood shed by the offending body is atoned for by that which flows from its wounded veins.

If, then, it be the group, not the individual, that holds land, that inherits, that succeeds to office, that strikes and is struck, what difficulty is there in the way of our accepting the fact that it is the group which marries and is given in marriage ? And if group marriage be accepted, group relationship follows as a matter of course

There will always be a difficulty in our way if we persist in measuring the group with descent through females, as it is found among the lower savages, by that with which we are familiar among the Athenians and the Romans, or even by the group as it existed among our own forefathers. As reasonably might we measure the larva by the perfect insect, and refuse to acknowledge their identity because their forms are different The later gens, or clan, or by what other name soever it may be called, is indeed, really or theoretically, a group of kinsfolk ; but it reckons descent through the father, not through the mother, and this one fact makes all the difference in the world. At least it brings into play a force which is sure, sooner or later, to make the difference. When it appears, the ties of relationship between individual and individual begin to draw closer and closer, while those between the individual and his group, and especially those between group and group, begin to loosen Separation, which was formerly difficult, becomes inevitable, and the group rapidly divides itself into smaller groups. Hereditary distinctions of rank* arise ; the right of the individual tends to assert itself more and more against that of the group ; and at length

---

* *Distinctions of rank* ---Note this one significant fact out of many With descent through the mother there can be no such thing as a base-born man The distinction between base-born and full-born men arises under descent through males, and its effects are great and lasting

property, which was formerly held in common by the many, comes to be the exclusive possession of the few. Some tie other than that of kindred becomes necessary to bind men together, and in process of time the group becomes more or less a political institution But through many a generation it builds itself still on the old lines, retains the old traditions, and uses the old terms of relationship long after they have ceased to represent the actual facts *

CONCLUSION.

IN conclusion, I repeat once more the oft-repeated caution that the terms of relationship must not be taken as showing the present usage now actually in force Thus, the fact of a group of males being called "husband" by a group of females, does not necessarily imply actual cohabitation between all the members of the groups What it implies is an ancient right of cohabitation, which, whether it were ever exercised to its full extent or not, is everywhere more or less restricted now-a-days according to the system of marriage at present in force This system, among the more advanced Fijians, for instance, is polygamy with descent through the father; among the Banks Islanders, and many other tribes, it is polygamy with descent through the mother; among the Australians it takes various forms, some of them approaching more nearly to the old license; but nowhere, as far as I know, does that license prevail to its full extent; that is to say, I am not aware of any tribe in which

---

* This is saying a great deal in a few words, and taking for granted many things which require proof But the needful proofs are, I think, to be found among tribes whose usages we may examine at the present day; and, in conjunction with my friend Mr Howitt, I hope to produce them in a future work, for which not a little of the material is already gathered

the actual practice is to its full extent what the terms of relationship imply as of former occurrence. Present usage is everywhere in advance of the system so implied, and the terms are survivals of an ancient right, not precise indications of custom as it is.

But it seems to me that no unprejudiced observer can note the significant facts presenting themselves among savage tribes without being forced to the conclusion that their system of marriage and relationship is based upon communal marriage between permitted groups, both marriage and relationship being conceived, not as between individual and individual, but as between group and group. Beyond this I do not go. Although strong evidence seems to point further still to a more ancient undivided commune, this has never yet been found; and I know of no record of which we can positively affirm that it describes such a commune, and that the writer of it was a fully qualified witness in the case. One or two passages in the former part of these memoirs, which may seem to take its existence for granted, must be read with this qualification. As far as the ascertained facts will take us is far enough for us to go, how great soever may be the possibility of a road beyond them; and the ascertained facts go no farther than to a community already divided into exogamous clans, with group marriage between them.

In attempting to support Mr. Morgan's "conjectural solution of the classificatory relationships," all I contend for is that, if the former existence of the undivided commune be taken for granted, its division into exogamous clans must have had precisely the effect which his theory requires. But, if such a community ever existed, I do not hesitate to say that Mr. Morgan's "reformatory movement" appears to me the most likely method by which it would begin its advance to a better system of marriage. And this for the very reason which would seem to make it the most improbable to many writers of our day, viz, because it would be a step in advance so difficult for men in that utter depth of savagery to take, that they would not be able to take it unless they had help from without. This might be given by contact with a more advanced tribe; but if all the tribes started from the same level, that impulse would be impossible in the first instance, and must have been derived from a higher power. And if, because of this statement, anyone take the trouble to say of me what Sir John Lubbock was pleased to say of John Williams, the martyr of Erromanga, because he believed that which Sir John Lubbock disbelieves, "a missionary so credulous and ignorant ought, one might suppose, rather to learn than to teach " (" Origin," &c, p. 174),* I shall be quite content.

And here, as I shall in all probability have occasion to write further on the evidence afforded by the customs of savage tribes as to the development of social organization, it may be well once for all to say a word on a subject to which it will not be necessary for me again to refer.

Degradation theory

It has somehow or other come to be thought incumbent upon those who hold what are called "orthodox views" to maintain that all savages were once civilized people; and eminent writers, such as Archbishop Whately and the Duke of Argyll, have advanced much ingenious argument in

---

* Compare Sir John's contemptuous words, above quoted, with the gracious declaration which ushers in his fourth chapter — "I shall endeavour to avoid, as far as possible, anything which might justly give pain to any of my readers;" also with his charitable motive for entitling that chapter the *Religion* rather than the *Superstitions* of savages—" A reluctance to condemn any honest belief, however absurd and imperfect it may be " He cannot surely suppose that Williams was not honest in his belief. Moreover, that belief is a perfectly fair conclusion from the premises which that brave missionary held; and however "absurd and imperfect " those premises may be in Sir John Lubbock's opinion, his opinion is not quite a final settlement of the questions involved

support of what is known as the degradation theory. Why that theory should be looked upon as necessary to orthodoxy I confess myself utterly at a loss to imagine.

Almost at the very beginning of history—not in the far distance behind the great nations who dwelt in walled cities, but side by side with them, men of the same time with them—we see cave-dwellers, roamers of the desert, nomad herdsmen, savages of various grades, such as the tribes whom we have before us at the present day. Why, then, need we suppose these to be descended from civilized ancestors, and not from those savages of the olden time?

And the early savages, what sort of civilization was it from which we must suppose them to have become degraded, and how was that civilization acquired? Certainly, there is nothing in Scripture to warrant the supposition that they were ever civilized at all. If we take the narrative in the beginning of Genesis to be strictly historic, we find the first human beings living in a state, not of civilization, but of innocence—" naked, and not ashamed." We see them lose that innocence, and thereupon compelled to earn their sustenance by the work of their hands, covering themselves with "aprons" of leaves, and not knowing even as much as how to make themselves "coats of skins." Surely this is no very high point of civilization from which the Bible account represents them as starting on their way. Turning our eyes upon their descendants, we see that, in the first instance at least, "sister-marriage" must of necessity have been the rule among them; and the earliest record we have of their doings tells of a cruel murder. Not until at least 500 years* have passed away do we hear of the first worker in

---

* And that, too, according to a chronology which is admitted on all sides to be uncertain in the highest degree, the Hebrew computation differing from the Samaritan, and both of them differing from that of the Septuagint.

DEGRADATION THEORY. 163

bronze and iron; and the new invention appears to have been used chiefly for warlike purposes, for the world seems to have grown worse as it grew older, until "the whole earth was filled with violence" Is it not certain that, in a state of society such as this, some tribes must have been driven away from the line of progress at its very beginning? To my mind, the only wonder is that man achieved any progress at all; and that he did so, appears to me a sufficient proof that he was not left to his own resources.

We are not now concerned with the question as to whether the narrative in the first chapters of Genesis be a historic record or not; nor is it necessary for us to enter upon that question here. What I wish to point out is, that the Bible account does not represent the first men as living in a state of civilization, and that, according to that account, their progress towards civilization must have been difficult in the extreme

The plain inference to be drawn from all history, whether sacred or profane, is, as it seems to me, that the human race started from a very low point in the social scale; that certain races have made a continuous advance, nation after nation dying as men die, but always leaving their heirs behind them; that others, after making considerable progress, came to a halt and remained stationary; while others again, who, at the very beginning, fell out, or were driven out, from the line of progress, are found in the present day at a point lower than that from which the start was made; degraded, therefore, to that extent, but certainly not degraded from a civilization to which they never attained.

And therefore, while, on the one hand, I cannot see the necessity of maintaining that savages are the degraded descendants of civilized ancestors, on the other hand it seems to me an altogether gratuitous assumption to take for granted that, because we can trace many customs of civilized races to savagism, all civilized nations must have been as utterly savage as certain tribes can be shown to be now, or to have been in the past. The theory of progress requires no assumption such as this; and—unless we give in to the hypothesis which would present us with semi-human creatures as our remoter ancestors—there is no fact in our possession which even seems to point to it. It should suffice us to know what we can ascertain and establish, and to count our acquisitions to knowledge by the facts we add to our store, and not by theories which overleap the facts.

NAVULOA, FIJI,
21st *November*, 1879.

APPENDIX B.

EVIDENCE OF AUSTRALIAN TOTEMS AS TO TOTEMISM, OR ANIMAL WORSHIP.

SIR JOHN LUBBOCK considers that the "worship of animals is susceptible of a very simple explanation, and has really originated from the practice of naming, first individuals, and then their families, after particular animals." ("Origin," &c, p. 183.)

This is surely a reversal of the true order. The Australian divisions show that the totem is, in the first place, the badge of a group, not of an individual. The individual takes it, in common with his fellows, only because he is a member of the group. And, even if it were first given to an individual, his family—*i e*, his children—could not inherit it from him. They must take their mother's totem, which is different from his, unless descent be through the father. But this is a question as to the earliest stage of totemism, and, in that stage, descent is through the mother. This, I think, we may regard as an established fact, for descent is nearly always found in that line among savages of the lowest type. It may even be stated, as a general rule (which, like other general rules, has its exceptions), that wherever a tribe of present-day savages has totemic divisions, it has also descent through the mother. And, moreover, among many tribes who reckon descent through the father, there are evident traces of its having been formerly in the other line Sir John himself has correctly pointed out the Fijian Vasu as a case in point, and many others might be advanced.

Hence, in the earliest stage of totemism, the savage could not have looked upon the animal after which he was named as indicating his paternal ancestors, because his father, and every alternate ancestor in the male line, must have borne a totem different from his own. Thus, if Snake and Emu be two intermarrying gentes, the descents are as follows (the males are indicated by capitals, their wives by small letters) :—

<pre>
         EMU.
        Snake.
          |
        SNAKE.
         Emu.
          |
         EMU
         Snake
          |
        SNAKE
</pre>

It is evident at a glance that, with exogamy and descent through the mother, father and son can never bear the same totem. The eponymous ancestors, as they are called, could not have been looked upon as forefathers in the direct line until descent came to be reckoned through the father. The supposed relationship between a man and his totem is undoubtedly fraternal. At least it is so in Australia. And this is reasonable, for the totem is a badge of fraternity. All men of the same generation who bear the same totem are tribal brothers, though they may belong to different and widely separated tribes.* Here we find an explanation of

* Note Mr. Howitt's account of how the Darling River Lizard claimed him as a brother because he had been "recognized" as a re-incarnation of a deceased Lizard belonging to the Yantruwunta of Cooper's Creek. (p 57)

EVIDENCE AS TO ANIMAL WORSHIP.

certain apparently anomalous terms of kinship. Thus, in some tribes the paternal grandfather and his grandson call one another "younger brother" and "elder brother" respectively. These persons are of the same totem. Mr. Morgan's extensive tables of terms of relationship show many other designations* which at first sight appear to be inexplicable, but which admit of a similar solution.

The Australian totems have a special value of their own. Some of them divide, not mankind only, but the whole universe, into what may almost be called gentile divisions; and they may help us to a better understanding of totemism, or animal worship.

Mr. G. F. Bridgman wrote to me of the Port Mackay tribe (Queensland)—

---

* Ego being male, my sister's child is called "my grandchild" by a Fijian mountain tribe; and by Red Indian tribes, Nos. 25, 28, 29, 30, 64, in Table II, Morgan's "Systems of Consanguinity," &c

Ego being female, my brother's son is called "my grandson" by Nos 26, 28, 29, 30, 31, 32, 36 It is worthy of note that some European nations have the same term for both nephew and grandson.

Father's sister's husband, and mother's brother, are called "grandfather" by some Fijian tribes, by the Kafirs, and by Red Indian tribes, Nos 26, 28, 29, 30, 31, &c ("Systems," &c, Table II)

The reason for these apparently anomalous terms will be seen if we take them to the following diagram :—

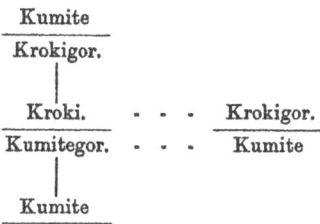

There are other terms which do not admit of this explanation For them another solution may be offered, which we cannot stay to discuss here Thus, ego being female, my brother's son is called "my younger brother" by a Fijian tribe In the Magyar, this relative is called "my little younger brother." Father's sister is called "elder sister" by the same Fijian tribe, and "grand elder sister" by the Magyar.

"Everything in nature, according to them, is divided between the classes. The wind belongs to one, and the rain to the other. The sun is Wutaroo, and the moon is Yungaroo. The stars are divided between them; and, if a star is pointed out, they will tell you to which division it belongs."

So also Mr. D. S. Stewart says of the Mount Gambier tribe (South Australia)—

"Not only mankind, but things in general, are subject to these divisions."

And he gives the following list as a specimen. Each of the totems has the prefix *bŭrt*, which means *dry*. I omit this prefix from the list. It will be observed that there are two instances of vegetable totems :—

MOUNT GAMBIER TOTEMS.

Kumite Subdivisions.	Includes—
1. Mūla = Fish-hawk	Smoke, honeysuckle trees, &c.
2. Parangal = Pelican	Dogs, blackwood trees, fire, frost (fem.)
3. Wā = Crow ..	Rain, thunder, lightning, winter, hail, clouds, &c
4. Wīla = Black cockatoo	Stars, moon, &c.
5. Karato = A harmless snake	Fish, stringybark trees, seals, eels, &c.
Kroki Subdivisions.	
1. Wĕrio = Tea-tree	Ducks, wallabies, owls, crayfish, &c.
2. Mūrna = An edible root	Bustards, quails, dolvich (a small kangaroo), &c.
3. Karáal = Black crestless cockatoo	Kangaroo, sheoak trees, summer, sun, autumn (fem), wind (fem.)

I do not know whether this arrangement is general throughout the Australian tribes; but the fact of its presenting itself in two localities so far remote from one another as Port Mackay and Mount Gambier, points to its wide prevalence. That inference, however, must be

EVIDENCE AS TO ANIMAL WORSHIP.

cautiously made; for, both in Australia and in the South Sea Islands, the closest similarities of language and custom are sometimes found in places far distant one from another.

The following are Mr. Stewart's comments, given *in extenso* :—

"All this appears very arbitrary I have tried in vain to find some reason for the arrangement. I asked, 'To what division does a bullock belong?' After a pause, came the answer, 'It eats grass : it is Boortwerio.' I then said, 'A crayfish does not eat grass : why is it Boortwerio?' Then came the standing reason for all puzzling questions : 'That is what our fathers said it was.'

"A man does not kill, or use as food, any of the animals of the same subdivision with himself, excepting when hunger compels ; and then they express sorrow for having to eat their *wingong* (friends) or *tumanang* (their flesh). When using the last word they touch their breasts, to indicate the close relationship, meaning almost a part of themselves. To illustrate :—One day one of the blacks killed a crow. Three or four days afterwards a Boortwa (crow), named Larry, died. He had been ailing for some days, but the killing of his wingong hastened his death. A Kumite may kill and eat any tuman of the Kroki, and a Kroki may likewise use any tuman of the Kumite. In the blood revenge arrangement, these subdivisions bear a prominent part Also, in cases of uncertain death, the tuman of the slayer will appear at the inquest."

Do we not find here an explanation of that curious reverence shown to certain animals and things by savage tribes? and can this reverence be said to amount to "deification?" The totem has evidently no inherent sanctity. It is reverenced only by the group which it indicates; and by them, not because it is above them as a divinity, but because it is one with them, because it is the "flesh" of the body corporate whereof they themselves are parts. It is literally "bone of their bone and flesh of their flesh." A Kumite may kill a Kroki *tuman* without shocking the feelings of the Kumites, or even of the Krokis ; but he cannot kill one of his own *tuman* without impiety. Here we see the force of Orestes' plea before the Areopagus. Klytemnestra was his mother, but she was not a part of the body corporate of which he was a part. Her *tuman* was not his *tuman*—*i e*, her flesh was not his flesh.

Much of what has been called totemism, in the sense of the deification of animals or inanimate objects, may be traced to this remarkable system. What has seemed to be an act of worship in the eyes of travellers and others, whose opportunities were not such as to enable them to look below the surface, may, in many cases, have been nothing more than acts of piety—*pietas*—demonstrations of affectionate regard towards kinsfolk. It may be objected that savages do not, as a rule, show such regard for one another; but, granting this objection (though it is quite open to dispute) it must be borne in mind that these so-called "acts of worship" are performed to the totem, not as an individual, but as the representative of the gens; and to argue that a savage can have no regard for his gens because he does not show much affection towards individuals, is to argue that we do not love our brother because we are not in the habit of manifesting special tokens of affection to each particular hair on our brother's head. To the savage, the whole gens is the individual, and he is full of regard for it. Strike the gens anywhere, and every member of it considers himself struck, and the whole body corporate rises up in arms against the striker. The South Australian savage looks upon the universe as the Great Tribe, to one of whose divisions he himself belongs; and all things, animate and inanimate, which belong to his class are parts of the body corporate whereof he himself is part. They are "almost parts of himself," as Mr. Stewart shrewdly remarks.

No wonder, then, that savages do not kill, or eat, animals of their totem, without, at least, ostensible reluctance; nor that, when driven by hunger to kill one of them, they express sorrow, make abject apologies, and sometimes tell lies to their slaughtered relative, in order to persuade him that it was not they who did the deed, or, at all events that they are not to blame for it. This is in fact their method of "purification" for an act of impiety. For to injure one of those animals is to hurt the whole body corporate to which they themselves belong. To kill one of them is murder within a gens, a crime which sets the Furies on the offender's track. To the South Australian Kumite it is bloodshedding done upon the great Kumite phratria; and so he hastens to purify himself, for he has to appease the wrath of half the universe.

APPENDIX C.

FEMALE INFANTICIDE

GENERALLY speaking, it is next to impossible to get at trustworthy statistics among savage tribes; but in Fiji we are fortunate in having had rare facilities for ascertaining them, and Sir Arthur Gordon, Governor of Fiji, has kindly placed at my disposal the lately-completed census of the native population. Let us see whether we can draw from it any information bearing upon Mr. M'Lennan's theory of female infanticide.

It is unnecessary to say that the tribes which have been for any length of time under missionary influence are useless for our purpose here, because they have been taught that infanticide is a crime; and it may be supposed that they ceased to practise it long before annexation took place, as far, at least, as regards infants who were permitted to see the light.

But in the hill country of Navitilevu, the largest island

of the group, there are certain tribes upon whom the *pax Britannica* came while they were still heathens, who appreciated missionaries only from a culinary point of view; and Government officials took the census among them within a few months of the time when they were in full practice of all the old customs, including infanticide. This was universally prevalent among them, and the Government has still much trouble to put it down. For all practical purposes, therefore, the statistics now gathered may be held to represent fairly enough what we may call their natural state. Their numbers in one of the tholo, or hill-country districts, are as follows :—

	Males.	Females.
Aged	632	678
Adults	1,675	1,717
Children	1,390	1,144

The census from which these figures are extracted was taken soon after the subjugation of the mountaineers by Sir Arthur Gordon, in the war which was forced upon him by their own misconduct, and which was ably and mercifully* conducted to a most satisfactory ending. Inasmuch, therefore, as the statistics might have been affected by the

---

* I use the word "mercifully" of set purpose, because of certain strictures which have been passed upon the conduct of the war; and, in so doing, I only repeat here what I published elsewhere at the time when the events occurred. The military executions were severe, but in their severity lay their mercy. Savages ought to be borne with as long as possible, and then just a little longer because of their ignorance; but, when it is absolutely necessary to punish them, then mercy is cruelty, and what seems to us to be cruelty is the truest mercy. They cannot understand that, when they deserve punishment, he who has the power to inflict it refrains from exercising that power from any motive other than fear of them. Be gentle with them when you ought to punish, and you encourage them to worse outrages, for which you will have to deal most severely with them. Show them once for all that you are their master, when there is need for the showing, and thenceforward you may be as merciful towards them as you please.

FEMALE INFANTICIDE. 173

war, I wrote to Mr. Horace G. Emberson, our Registrar-General, asking him to give me the numbers of a heathen tribe which had not been engaged in the war, in order that I might compare those numbers with the general statistics of the mountaineers. With his usual kindness he replied as follows:—

"Your letter is received; and, as it always has given me pleasure to please you, and always will, I set about the work at once, and hope the result, though not exactly what you wished, will yet be sufficient. I cannot find a *heathen* tribe which, in some way or other, was not engaged in the late war I have, therefore, selected two districts, of which one was for, and the other against, the Government. Their numbers are as follows:—"

	For.		Against.	
	Males	Females	Males	Females.
Aged	125	154	105	120
Adults	329	337	209	233
Children	253	183	177	140

There was no great loss on either side by actual fighting. The losing party, of course, suffered most, and the subsequent military executions fell upon their males exclusively. Nevertheless, there is not much difference between the two parties in the proportion of males to females among the adults, if we take into consideration the unusually large excess of male children over female among the Government allies.

Setting aside the "aged," with whom we are not at present concerned, the proportions of the sexes one to another among the children and the adults are as follows:—

Children
All the hill tribes—Males : females : : 125 5 : 100
Tribes for the Government : : 138 25 : 100
,, against ,, : : 126 5 : 100

Adults
All the hill tribes—Males : females : : 97 5 : 100
Tribes for the Government : : 97 6 : 100
,, against ,, : : 90 0 : 100

These statistics do not cover a population large enough to warrant the drawing of any general inference from them; but, as far as they go, they are in direct opposition to Mr. M'Lennan's theory. They show that, while the male children are in excess of the female, there are more female adults than male, which is the case among civilized nations also. We are, however, at present concerned with the adults alone; for Mr. M'Lennan's theory rests upon the supposition that the scarcity of women, caused by female infanticide, led to the capture of women for wives, and it is only among adults that the matrimonial craving would be felt The hill tribes, therefore, contradict this theory, because among them the female adults are in excess of the male. And those tribes are landowners, who reckon descent through the father, and who, therefore, have the strongest motives for female infanticide—motives which are not found among the lower savages. (See *Ante*, p. 137)

I was at first sight disposed to look upon the great excess of male children over females—an excess of 25 per cent, while that of the European nations is no more than 6—as proof positive that the hill tribes of Navitilevu must have been in the habit of killing female children rather than male. But, to my great surprise, I found the same figures—as far as regards the children—repeating themselves among the Lau or Eastern tribes, who have been under missionary influence for more than forty years, and who certainly have not been killing children after birth in the present generation. There may have been among them much of that form of infanticide which consists in killing unborn children, but this would not affect the proportion of the sexes. Their statistics show the same extraordinary excess of male children over female, and that excess is maintained nearly to its full extent among the adults also.

FEMALE INFANTICIDE.

That their males have not decreased in number between childhood and manhood, as among the mountaineers, is doubtless owing to the fact that the Lau tribes have done very little fighting since they embraced Christianity. They have been all but exempt from the slaughter of tribal wars, minor blood feuds, and private murders, which falls so heavily upon the males of heathendom, especially in those tribes who capture women for wives, and who therefore spare the females, while they kill the males.

The proportions of the sexes among the Lau tribes—in a population of 6,768 souls—are as follows, according to the Government statistics:—

Children—Males : females : : 129 45 : 100
Adults— : : 125 00 : 100

It may be noted here that infanticide, as far as I am aware, is never effected by a blow, a cut, a stab, or by violence, properly so called. Bloodshedding, or violence, would be looked upon with horror as a crime. The methods used in the South Seas which have come under my own observation are exposure, strangling, and burying alive, as in the case of the aged also, of widows, and of persons disabled by lingering illness, or otherwise disqualified by the battle of life. These methods are employed—strange as the words may sound—tenderly and lovingly. The Fijian mother will murmur "Sleep, my child," as she gently compresses the lips and nostrils of her infant till death ensues. So, also, the son will kiss and weep over his aged father as he prepares him for the grave, and will exchange loving farewells with him as he heaps the earth lightly over him.

It must also be borne in mind that in many tribes infants are not looked upon as members of the clan until they have been furnished with nutriment of some kind. I never heard of a child being killed after having been admitted to membership in the family, excepting in what was looked upon as a case of necessity. As when the townsfolk were escaping by night from a beleaguered *koro* (village), and were fearful lest the crying of their little ones should arouse the besiegers; or when a child had met with a disabling accident or sickness; or when it was deemed necessary to destroy an infant in order that its mother might suckle a child of higher rank.*

* Since this Appendix was written, the Rev J Rooney, of the Wesleyan Mission in Fiji, has been kind enough to send me the numbers of the Wainimala people, a hill tribe inhabiting fifteen villages, and numbering 1,719 souls. The census was carefully taken among them by mission agents under his direction, and the figures may be accepted as correct. Omitting the aged of both sexes, the proportions are as follows :—

Children—Males : Females : : 133·66 : 100
Adults— : : 99·07 : 100

THE KŬRNAI:

THEIR CUSTOMS IN PEACE AND WAR.

BY

A. W. HOWITT.

PREFACE TO THE KŬRNAI.

MORE than fifteen years ago I commenced, without any definite aim, to record all the information I acquired as to the Australian aborigines. Subsequently my inquiries received a particular direction through joining my friend, the Rev. Lorimer Fison, in those ethnological researches which in Australasia he has made specially his care. This present contribution to Australian ethnology is our joint production in so far as we have made a common stock of our information. It will be evident in this work, as a whole, how great a portion of it is due to my friend and fellow-labourer, who has indeed been throughout its chief architect.

I have to thank numerous correspondents in all parts of Australia for a mass of information, part of which is only made available. Where I have made use of information, I have attached the name of my informant. I desire, however, to especially express the obligations I am under, for the kindest and most unwearied responses to my many questions, to the Rev. John Bulmer, of the Lake Tyers Mission, Gippsland; the Rev. J. H. Stähle, of the Lake Condah Mission, Western Victoria; the Rev. Julius Kühn, of Boorkooyanna Mission, South Australia; the Rev. H. Vogelsang, of the Kopperamana Mission, South Australia;

180   THE KŬRNAI.

Mr. Cyrus E. Doyle, of Kunopia, New South Wales; and Mr. J. Gibson, J.P., of Stanmore, Southern Queensland.

I hope in the future to avail myself of the still unused information for which I am indebted to these and other correspondents.

A. W. HOWITT.

SALE, *March, 1880.*

INTRODUCTION.

THE aboriginal inhabitants of Gippsland, when that district was first settled by the whites in 1839, were very numerous. What the number of their population may then have been, we have now no means of accurately ascertaining. The estimates made from memory by those of the earliest settlers whom I have questioned do not agree. It is scarcely to be expected that they should do so; but, judging from all the inquiries which I have made, I think the probable number may have been between 1,000 and 1,500.

The present number can, however, be given with greater precision. An enumeration was made in 1877, at the instance of the Royal Commission concerning the aborigines, and showed that there were at that time in Gippsland 52 men, 41 women, and 66 children; of these, I believe, 6 men, 6 women, and 7 children did not belong to the Gippsland tribe, leaving 140 souls in all. There have been some deaths and some births since, of which I have no account. The diminution from 1,000 or 1,500 to 140 during a period of 32 years cannot be said to be surprising.* It

---

* For the following statement I am indebted to the Rev. F. A. Hagenauer and the Rev. J. Bulmer.

The present number of the Kurnai (January 1, 1879), classed according to their clans, is as follows:—

	Men.	Women.	Children.
Kroatŭngolŭng	26	11	12
Brabrolŭng	15	7	9
Tatŭngolŭng	17	8	22

is only in accordance with previous experience as to the fate of this aboriginal race when brought into contact with the white men throughout Australia, and it is only a further instance of a general experience of that which is going on all over the world, with greater or less rapidity, under similar contact of savage coloured races with the civilized white races.

In Australia, this extinction of the aborigines commenced with its first settlement. It may be stated broadly that the advance of settlement has, upon the frontier at least, been marked by a line of blood. The actual conflict of the two races has varied in intensity and in duration, as the various native tribes have themselves differed in mental and physical character, and as those white men with whom they have been brought in contact have differed. But the tide of settlement has advanced along an ever-widening line, breaking the native tribes with its first waves and overwhelming their wrecks with its flood. It has not ceased to flow; and from past experience I cannot conceive that it will cease until the last tribe has been broken and overwhelmed. Still, this actual conflict—bloody, and often pitilessly exterminating, as it has been, and still is—cannot account for the continuing extinction of those native tribes which, like that of Gippsland, have long submitted to the yoke of authority. The remains of such tribes have to a great extent been brought into settled homes; and their mode of life, as regards many of the younger members at

			Men.	Women.	Children.
Briakolūng	...	...	5	8	12
Bratauolūng	...	..	3	3	1
			66	37	56

I have information from Mr. Bulmer only as to the proportion of the sexes among the children. Of the 21 children at Lake Tyers, 13 are boys and 8 girls.

INTRODUCTION.

least, more or less assimilated to our own. It is clear, therefore, that some other causes must be in operation. To say, as often is said, that these causes are mysterious, is only to say that we are ignorant of their nature. Let us see whether it is possible to trace some of them. If it is possible to do so, those which we can trace may point to others which, for the moment, elude our search.

When the first settlement of white men was formed in Gippsland, the country was found to be well peopled by an aboriginal tribe. That these people were physically and mentally in accordance with the conditions surrounding them—such as climate, food, neighbouring hostile tribes—may be inferred from the fact that they existed in numerous communities in a country abounding with food. Had they not been in accord with such surrounding conditions, there would have been a want of equilibrium which could only have resulted in their becoming gradually adapted to those conditions, or extinct. Hence, we may, I think, reasonably assume that the aboriginal tribe of Gippsland was in accord with surrounding conditions. The advent of the white man, however, changed all this. Numbers were killed in conflicts with the settlers; and these aborigines were mostly, though not all, fighting men of the tribe. Other individuals collected round stations and townships. Their food was altered, and, as a whole, their society was disorganized, and their general mode of life profoundly modified. Not only were their former conditions of life, physical and mental, in complete contrast to the existing conditions of life, physical and mental, introduced by the white men, but the change which they made as regarded their old life did not extend to complete, or even to near accordance with the new life. They only adopted some of the habits of the white men; but with these they also adopted some of the vicious habits of the new comers. They fell, it may be said, not only without a struggle, but voluntarily into the fatal enticements of intoxication; their women fell, not only into intoxication, but into fatally vicious connections with the worst of the white men. This reacted again upon the tribe, for, with these newly-acquired evil habits, newly-acquired evil diseases were introduced. In addition, safeguards to health, which had become through custom part almost of their nature, were no longer regarded. A blackfellow, or a black woman, perhaps, when intoxicated, during winter weather, lay down anywhere on the wet ground, instead of sleeping in a warm hut whose site was chosen judiciously as regarded the wind and weather. I have found them, even when half-civilized and living in a house, camping on a floor sodden with moisture. It is, therefore, no wonder that colds, rheumatism, pneumonia, and phthisis have been frightfully and fatally common. Besides these diseases—produced probably in greater intensity by their own change of habits—other diseases, which the whites generally have as children in a mild form, such as measles or whooping-cough, attacked them as adults, and with fatal effects. It is difficult to point out all the directions in which change of conditions, consequent upon the settlement of Gippsland by the whites, has operated injuriously upon the native tribe.

It seems probable to me that many at present obscure or unsuspected causes have been, and are, injuriously active. From statements made to me by Dr. Forbes and Dr. Reid, of Sale, it seems that the aborigines are much infested by hydatids. It may be suspected that this frightful form of entozoic disease has been introduced to them by the domesticated animals accompanying the whites. It is, so far as I know, only of late years that the kangaroos have

INTRODUCTION.

become subject almost universally to entozoa ;* and these entozoa have infested the merino sheep in the low-lying parts of Gippsland to such a degree as to practically exterminate them. Formerly sheep were healthy, and throve well where it is now impossible to keep them. Although perhaps introduced by the whites, the actual spread of hydatids and other forms of entozoa among the aborigines may well be connected with their practice of eating only partially-cooked meat, and of drinking water from swamps and pools.

It is not necessary to continue the enumeration of instances in which altered conditions have been injurious to the aboriginal natives of Gippsland. Those I have given may suffice; and I think that, with some show of probability, I may allege that the dying out of this tribe has been the result, not of some mysterious cause, but the cumulative influence of many and various causes, all arising out of altered surrounding conditions to which either the aborigines must become adapted, or under which they must become extinct. If the aborigine could have become physically and mentally such as a white man, he would have been in equilibrium with his new surroundings. If his physical and mental nature had been able to become modified with sufficient rapidity to come into equilibrium with the changed conditions, he could have survived. But the former alternative is self-evidently an impossibility, and probably the strength of hereditary physical and mental peculiarities has made the latter alternative also an impossibility. The consequence has been that he is rapidly and inevitably becoming extinct. But it is still possible that out of all those who have been collected into missions, some

* [W. M'Gregor, Esq , M.D , the head of the medical staff in Fiji, informs me that entozoa have been found in the parrots in the hill country of Navitilevu. These were probably indigenous.—L. F.]

may leave descendants, perhaps of half-blood, who may survive; but the number will be small, and in such a case become absorbed into the general population.

The conversion to Christianity, and the settlement in the missions, of the Gippsland aborigines has tended to a great extent to break down the force of their old customs. These customs were handed down through the elders of both sexes, and collectively formed an "unwritten law" of extraordinary force. When the old people, who are the depositories of these customs, die, the knowledge even of these customs will die also. It is now almost too late to collect all the particulars of their former life. For instance, the remarkable class of "birra-arka," who professed to communicate with the dead, has been long extinct, and with its last member is gone also all possibility of ascertaining what were their mystic rites, or what claims they made to communion with the spirits, and to a knowledge of future events.

Apart from any other difficulties, the usual difficulties met with in collecting information as to the beliefs and customs of aborigines are sufficiently formidable in themselves. It is necessary that the inquirer and the source of information should have a common language. There must be complete confidence by the aborigine in his questioner, otherwise he will become perfectly obtuse. The investigator must have so much acquaintance with the habits and mode of thought of the Australian savage as to be able, as it were, to project himself into the native mind. Some of these requisites I have been so fortunate as to command. Many of the Gippsland aborigines speak English fairly, which, with the slight knowledge of their language I possess, sufficed for my purpose. I had gained their confidence through mutual acquaintance, and they regarded me almost as one of themselves, as affiliated to them, or, as they express it, a "brogan." My official position in the district gave me much influence; and, finally, among those from whom I could most easily obtain information, there was one Tūlaba who was a perfect repository of the customs and beliefs of his tribe; and that which he did not fully know was supplied by his wife. Thus I have been enabled to collect, from time to time, numerous fragments. I have now pieced them together in such order as I could achieve. That the fabric is incomplete, I fully perceive; but it may serve to show dimly what is the domestic and social life of a savage tribe, and, perhaps still more dimly, what may have been the domestic and social life of the ancestors of barbarous and of civilized races. If it is thought to do this, then my object will have been gained.*

Finally, in explanation of the title of this essay, I may mention that the name Kŭrnai is that which the aborigines of Gippsland give to themselves, signifying "man;" and it is remarkable that the word Kŭrna is similarly applied, having the same meaning, by the Dieri of Cooper's Creek.†

In writing the native words in this essay, I have followed the subjoined rules:—The consonants are sounded as in English. *G* always hard, as in *go*; *c* is not used, and *ch* as in *child*, but never where *k* would express the sound. The nasal sound of *g*, at the beginning of a word, as *ng*. The

---

* In this memoir on the Kŭrnai, I have occasionally used the present tense in speaking of their customs, when the past would have been more correct. While making this alteration, during the passage of this work through the press, in those passages which relate to their marriage customs, I have thought it well to let other minor passages stand as originally written. It is from the manuscript in its original form that Dr Morgan has quoted in his Introductory Note.

† [The name of a South Australian tribe, the Narinyeri, has the same meaning They also call all other tribes "Merkani"—wild, savage—as the Kŭrnai call other tribes Brajerak. (Informant, Rev. Geo. Taplin.) —L F]

vowels are sounded thus: *a* as in *father;* *e* as in *there;* *i* as in *fatigue;* *o* as in *old;* *u* as in *unite;* *ŭ* as in *sun;* *ū* as *oo* in *moon;* *ai* as *i* in *light;* any other diphthongs required will be illustrated in the first instance by some English word in a footnote.

THE KŬRNAI.

THE infant Kŭrnai is at first only recognized as a child— lit. The terms *boy* and *girl*—wot-woti and kuerejŭng—are not applied until the child reaches the age of eight or nine years. In infancy the young Kŭrnai is an object of love and pride to its father and mother. From observation of various tribes in far distant parts of Australia, I can assert confidently that love for their children is a marked feature in the aboriginal character. I cannot recollect having ever seen a parent beat or cruelly use a child; and a short road to the goodwill of the parents is, as amongst us, by noticing and admiring their children. No greater grief could be exhibited, by the fondest parents in the most civilized community at the death of some little child, than that which I have seen exhibited in an Australian native camp, not only by the immediate parents, but by the whole related group. In this the Kŭrnai are not singular. I have found the same feelings strongly developed among the Dieri of Cooper's Creek.

> I remember, at Lake Hope, a Dieri father proudly bringing his little boy for me to see The boy was about eight years of age ; was sharp and intelligent ; and made himself useful in fetching wood for the fire, and remained about our encampment that afternoon. The following morning, whilst we were packing up preparatory to moving off, the father returned in the greatest grief. The boy could not be found, and he supposed that I had concealed him. His countenance exhibited the extreme of grief, and tears furrowed the grime upon his cheeks He wrung his hands, and exclaimed, "My boy! my boy! Where is he? Where have you hidden him?" He could only be pacified by being allowed to feel all over the packages, to ascertain that his boy was not hidden therein.

THE KŬRNAI.

Infanticide

On the other hand, the Kŭrnai, undoubtedly, were guilty of infanticide, and the greatest risk to life through which the infant passed was probably during the first few hours of its young life. On speaking to a number of the Kŭrnai upon this subject, they gave me the following explanation. It was often difficult to carry about young children, particularly where there were several. Their wandering life rendered this very difficult. It sometimes happened that when a child was about to be born, its father would say to his wife, " We have too many children to carry about—best leave this one, when it is born, behind in the camp." On this, the new-born child was left lying in the camp, and the family moved elsewhere. The infant, of course, soon perished. The Kŭrnai drew this singular distinction, that "they never knew an instance of parents killing their children, but only of *leaving behind* new-born infants." The aboriginal mind does not seem to perceive the horrible idea of leaving an unfortunate baby to die miserably in a deserted camp, crawled over by ants and flies, and probably devoured by wild dogs. It may be that the feelings of affection arising from association and dependence have not in such a case been aroused, and the natural parental feelings seem to be overborne by what they conceive to be the exigencies of their circumstances.*

Naming the child.

When the child can walk, it is named. The name is given by the paternal grandfather or grandmother, or, in

---

* Buckley says of the Port Phillip tribes ("Life and Adventures," &c., p 143), "The women seldom have more than six children, and not often so many. So soon as they have as many as they can conveniently carry about and provide for, they kill the rest immediately after birth."

[An old Fijian chief, who counted for me on his fingers no fewer than fifteen of his children who had been killed when infants, and who were buried in one corner of his house, defended the practice of infanticide by the following curious argument:—" E senga so ni tamata na ngone sa nggai suthu vou. Sa mbera mai na yalona." Which may be rendered— " A new-born child is scarcely a human being. *Its spirit has not yet come to it.*"—L. F]

NAMING THE CHILD.

default, by the mother's parents, and may be that borne by some former member of the family.

For instance, Tūlaba, a Brabrolūng Kŭrnai, was, when a child, named Barrŭmbūlk (teal) by his maternal grandfather. This was the name of his mother's deceased brother. When, as a youth, he was initiated into manhood, a maternal uncle named him Tūlaba. This name had belonged to a grand ancestor.

The child's name became a "secret name" when the individual subsequently acquired a new one at initiation, or as an elder. To mention the secret name would be a serious breach of custom and good manners.*

Thus Long Harry in telling me his secret name of Tūrl-Būrn, did so in a whisper, when no one else was present In speaking to him of one of the Kŭrnai, I said, having mentioned his English name, "What is his Kŭrnai name?" He replied, "I cannot tell you; he might be very angry with me if I did; and our fathers have told us that we must never speak about the secret names"

The boy being now spoken of as wotti, and, as a youth, as "wot-woti," still lives with his parents, and, together with his sister, is very much under the control of his mother. The girl is called kuerejŭng, and an elder girl, approaching marriageable age, would be spoken of as tūtbŭkan.

The perforation of the septum of the nose was usually made while the boy was growing up, but some time before he was initiated. It might be that some of the men would notice him as "growing." The young men, his friends, might say to him, "You ought to have 'Ngrŭng;' † it won't hurt you." He consents. He then lies down on his back, some friend takes hold of the septum of his nose, extends it, moistens it with saliva, and then rapidly pierces it with a

Perforating the nose.

---

* I have throughout this work used the native names of the Kŭrnai even where they are reported as speaking of each other. It must be understood that I do this for the sake of clearness. The Kŭrnai never mention each other's names if it can be avoided. I have therefore often placed in speakers' mouths names of persons where they would have avoided them.

† Ngrŭng, or Ngrŭng-kong Ngrŭng = hole, Kong = nose.

sharp bone instrument. The patient must not show any sign of feeling pain. He then jumps up and extends his arms out quickly from the shoulder, and jerks each leg in succession. This proceeding being supposed to aid the "Ngrŭng-Kong" in causing him to grow big and strong.

Cicatrices not made by the Kŭrnai.

The young men were not scarred; but some few obtained these marks from the aborigines of Maneroo, their neighbours. But the young women were scarred across the back and arms, the proceeding being intended merely as an ornament. The Kŭrnai say it is to make them le-en rūkŭt, that is, nice-looking women.

Mr. J. C. Macleod, one of the first settlers of Gippsland, told me, long ago, that when he first saw the blackfellows at Buchan (Bŭkan Mŭnji) they were not scarred. He was accompanied by a Maneroo black boy, who was scarred according to the custom of his tribe. On making friends with the Kŭrnai, one of them was persuaded by my informant to be similarly ornamented. He was gashed on each arm, and others of his friends followed his example. Mr Macleod told me that he afterwards saw a number of others who had followed the new fashion.

Initiation to manhood and womanhood

When about arriving at puberty, it was considered that the young people should take their place in the community. They were no longer to be children. The old people talked it over; not only the old men, but the elders both male and female. If, after counsel, it was found that the young people were sufficiently numerous, the initiation was determined upon, and the first steps taken. Two messengers were sent from the division or the clan taking the initiative to the division or the clan nearest to it. These men were called lewin, or specially lewinda-jerra-alla, that is, the messengers of the jerraeil or initiation. Their functions were to convey the news only to the next division, or clan, which then sent out two lewin of its own people, and so on until the whole of the Kŭrnai were informed. The only exception to this custom was in the case of the

INITIATION. 193

Snowy River Kŭrnai, whose young men were not initiated.* But they are unable to assign any reason for this. The lewin may be described very sufficiently by the English term now adopted by the Kŭrnai, namely, "mailman." That is, one whose business it is to convey messages and carry news. This custom of the "mailman" is probably universal throughout Australia, and the office may also be said to partake somewhat of the sacred character of the "herald." They not only communicated between the various clans within the tribe, but also between these clans and clans of other and, perhaps, hostile tribes. I have been told by the Kŭrnai that lewin have been sent by them to the Brajerak or Maneroo tribe, with whom, otherwise, no communication was kept up excepting of a hostile character.

I have met with similar "mailmen" in Central Australia The extraordinary rapidity with which messages were sent often surprised me On the first day on which I reached Cooper's Creek, when searching for the lost explorers, Burke and Wills, my arrival was *telegraphed* by two "mailmen" to the Yantrūwŭnta, a clan of the Dieri-speaking tribe, with whom the survivor of Burke's party was then living. Similarly, news of the whereabouts of the explorer, M'Kinley, was conveyed by the Dieri natives, and from them to me by successive "mailmen," who commenced to travel not far south of the tropics and among tribes beyond the Dieri boundary In one case I halted for the night close to an encampment of the Dieri, and only separated from them by a narrow sheet of water. Two "mailmen" had arrived that evening from the south, and retailed their messages and news to their hosts The assembly was kept up until late in the night, the speeches of the "mailmen" being accompanied by the *tap tap* of the stones with which the women were pounding seeds for cakes

News of the intended initiation having been thus conveyed from clan to clan through the length and breadth of the Kŭrnai country, the proceedings commenced in the clan with which they had originated. The time was fixed

---

* The Gouinditch-mara tribe, of Western Victoria, according to the Rev. J. H Stähle, had no ceremonies of initiation.

on the return of the *lewinda-jerra-alla*. The particulars which I now give as to the ceremonies have been collected from those who participated in the last ceremony ever held, now many years ago. The settlement of the country by the whites, the establishment of mission stations—where the native customs are viewed with the utmost disfavour—and the rapid extinction of the Kŭrnai, all these causes together have broken down the custom, and it has become a thing of the past for ever. In order to ascertain as clearly as possible what the ceremonies were, I prevailed upon some of the Brabrolūng and Tatūngolūng men to give me a representation. I regretted it was not a dress rehearsal; nevertheless, the actors were in their parts *con amore*. The past seemed to revive in them. They were no longer the wretched remnant of a native tribe dressed in the cast-off garments of the white men, but *Kŭrnai*—

Ceremony of initiation.
the descendants of Yeerŭng*—performing a ceremony handed down to them through their ancestors from the mystic pair, Yeerŭng and Djeetgun.† The ceremony commences by the women beating their rolled-up rugs in slow time—not all at the same place or at the same moment, but scattered round the camp, and, as it were, answering each other. The youths and girls are seated in a long line on the ground. The youths in the front row, with legs crossed under them and their arms folded. They look straight forward. Behind each youth sits a girl called krau-un.‡ She is his companion, and each pair has been allotted after careful consultation by the elders § But the krau-ŭn is only a comrade, and no more—the Kŭrnai

---

* The Yeerŭng is a small bird, the Emu-wren (*Stipiturus Malachurus*).
† The Djeetgŭn is the Superb warbler, *Malurus Cyaneus*.
‡ *Au* as *ow* in "how."
§ The Krau-ŭn was, for instance, a female cousin, and the Bŭllerwang a male cousin.

carefully pointed out that they were but like sisters, and not like wives. Each girl sits behind her comrade in the same attitude as his, but with her eyes cast down. Behind the pair stands the boy's mother, holding her "yamstick"* erect, resting on the ground. The young people are dressed and ornamented to the height of Kŭrnai elegance. They are painted with pipeclay and red ochre (mŭrlū and naial). The boys have feathers about them, and the girls have, in addition, the ears of the native bear† tied above their own, and the tails of the native dingo‡ hanging down the back. From each side of the head depends one of the skin aprons worn by the men (bridda bridda), made from the skin of a kangaroo-rat. Each girl wears the woman's kaiŭn,§ and the whole of her person from the waist down is concealed by an opossum rug. All is attention. At a signal, given by the remainder of the women beating their rugs in slow time, the mothers stamp their yamsticks, and each youth and girl reclines the head sharply towards one shoulder; at the next beat of the rugs and stamp of the yamsticks the heads sharply recline over the other shoulder. But the body remains unmoved, the arms are still crossed, and the boys still keep their eyes to the front, while the girls keep theirs cast down. Then is heard the sound of slow chaunting in the forest. The sounds come nearer, and all the men appear in line. They keep step and time with their

* A long pointed staff used for digging roots, and also for defence. When a girl is growing up, her mother gives her a "yamstick," which, among other purposes, is used to keep off importunate admirers.

† *Phascolarctos Kouala.*

‡ The wild dog has a handsome bushy tail.

§ The kaiŭn was a kind of apron formed of strings of twisted opossum fur. It extended from the waist nearly to the knee, and concealed the thighs. It was worn by every young girl until she was married. A Kŭrnai, in speaking of this, said to me lately, "By-and-bye the bra (husband) breaks the string which holds it, and throws it away." The kaiŭn was only worn by the girls.

chaunt. They are thickly smeared with charcoal. Their heads are ornamented with feathers, and painted with naial. Down to the waist they are all wound round with frayed stringybark in thick folds. From the waist downwards they are naked. Each man has a thick bushy tuft of grass passed through the perforated septum of his nose. In one hand each bears a long flat strip of thick bark As they wind rapidly forward, each one beats his strip of bark on the ground with a hollow sound. They chaunt—"Yeh! yeh!* Wah! wah! wah! Yeh! yeh! Yeerŭng! yeerŭng!" When they reach the space in front of the seated line of youths and girls, the men run round in a ring, beating their strips of bark on the ground and chaunting as before. Then they form before the line, a man before each pair, and again the chaunt commences. The ground is beaten, the boys and girls move their head from side to side, the mothers stamp the ground with their sticks. It is faster, but the time is perfectly kept

The man facing the boy is his "büllerwang," who has to look after him during the ceremony, and he is painted about the eyes to resemble the "black duck," after which he is named. The next part of the ceremonies is that the boy rises to his feet, and, at a given signal, each büllerwang raises his boy up into the air, the boy aiding by giving a spring. He is now no longer a wot-wotti, but a tūtnŭrrŭng.

Boughs are now spread on the ground, and on them the boys are laid side by side on their backs. They neither move nor speak, but when they are in want of anything, they call the büllerwang by imitating the chirping note of the yeerŭng. The boys lie there all night, there is no sleep in the camp, the chaunting continues, the women beating

---

* This is sounded like the termination of our Hurray! and is said by the Kŭrnai to be an exclamation of triumph

time on their rugs. Next morning, about ten o'clock, there is a respite, and they get breakfast. About noon the ceremonies recommence. So it continues for two or three days. At length, early in the morning, about daybreak, the old women are heard chaunting "Yeh! yeh! Wah! wah! wah! Yeh! yeh! Djeetgŭn! djeetgŭn!" A line is formed—the mothers stand in front of their sons; behind them stand the bŭllerwangs—each one holds a branch in his hand—their arms and legs move and quiver rapidly—the branches rustle —the sibilant note of the djeetgŭn is heard, and at this the boys rush forward past their mothers; the bŭllerwangs catch them, and hasten away with them into the forest. There the boys remain several months, as the Kŭrnai express it, "frightened at the sorrow of their mothers." But the initiation is not yet completed. During their absence they live together, and are visited by the bŭllerwangs alone. They eat opossum, native bear, kangaroo, but not porcupine; and of these animals they are only permitted to eat the males— the females are forbidden to them.*

About a week after the boys have run away from their mothers into the bush, the old men go out and make certain wooden instruments called tŭrndūn. The women are not permitted to know anything about this. Three or four of the very old men who cannot hunt remain with the lads to look after them. In the evening after supper time, when it is beginning to be dusk, the other old men come up, each bringing with him a tŭrndūn. Each lad has his head covered up in a 'possum rug, so that he cannot see anything but the ground. An old man puts a throwing stick under the rug, and says, "Look at the mŭrrawŭn—look where it is going to!" Then he lifts the mŭrrawŭn, pointing upwards, the boy's eyes fixed upon it. Then he points to the old

---

* Porcupine *(Echidna Hystrix)* is reserved as food for the elders.

men round, who, in the twilight, are sounding the tŭrndūns, and says, "See the tŭrndūn!" This has been done to all the boys at the same time. They stare at the strange sight—a wonderful thing, such as they have never seen before. Each boy is held by an old man by the back of the neck with the left hand, while in the right he points a spear to the boy's eye, and says, "If you tell this to any woman you will die—you will see the ground broken up and like the sea; if you tell this to any woman, or to any child, you will be killed."*

When the time has arrived at which the youth may return, his face is painted with pipeclay and red ochre; feathers are placed in his hair. The mothers are placed in a line—before each one is a bark vessel full of water—before each one stands her son. She stoops to drink—he splashes a little water in her face—she rises up with a mouthful of water, which she squirts over his head; and she repeats this till he is well wetted. The ceremonies are now ended. He is no longer under his mother's control. He is a man. He is no longer wot-wotti, or tūtnŭrrŭng, but jerra-eil. From this time the young men (brewit) are no longer part of the paternal and maternal group, but live in a camp of their own.

All the jerra-eil who have been initiated at the same time are brothers, and in the future address each other's wives as "wife," and each other's child as "child."

It was from Tūlabā that I first obtained particulars of this custom, and who afterwards arranged the rehearsal of the ceremony I said jokingly to him, "I am jerra-eil now." He replied, "Yes, now you are my brogan" Being his brogan, it followed, as I have said, that a peculiar relation was established, and in accordance with the custom, his wife often addressed me as "brā bittel" (my husband), whilst I spoke to her as "rūkut bittel" (my wife).

* *See* Appendix E.

THE YOUNG MAN.

The ceremony which I have described may seem to us but trivial, but to the Kŭrnai it has been an ancient custom of great moment. It formed a bond of peculiar strength, binding together all the contemporaries of the various clans of the Kŭrnai.* It was a brotherhood including all the descendants of the eponymous male and female ancestors, Yeerŭng and Djeetgŭn.

The young man, or brewit, after his initiation may be said to have commenced a life independent, to some extent, of his parents. He lived with the other young men, and with those who were initiated with him and are his "brotheis." On the other hand, the girl still lived with her parents. After a while the young man thinks it time to be married. For him a wife might not be within the prohibited degrees of brother and sister, which include all those whom we call cousins. She might not be of his division of the clan—nor, as I shall show later on, at least in some cases, of the division to which his mother belonged. She might even be a "Biajeiak,"† could he find one to accept him, or could he acquire such a woman by conquest. But properly she should be a Djeetgŭn as he is a Yeerŭng.

<small>The young man, or brewit.</small>

Brūthen Mŭnji, whom I shall often mention, together with his nephew Tūlaba, were both Brūthen Brabrolūng—the former got his wife from the Kroatŭngolūng, of Lake Tyers, the latter from the Brt-britta, at the Lakes entrance They both ran away with them. Subsequently Tūlaba had a second wife after the death of the first, who was a Brabrolūng of Wy-Yŭng He did not run off with her, as she was a widow

The Kŭrnai have told me that they were frightened to go to Maneroo for wives, but that the Brajerak, who were a strong tribe, used to

---

* The Kroatŭn Kŭrnai were not initiated. They cannot assign any reason for this

† This word is used to designate any other aboriginal native than one of the Kŭrnai tribe As Kŭrnai means *man*, so Brajerak means *wild man* from Bra—man, and yeerak or jeerak—angry or savage.

come down thence for wives to Gippsland. I am told that sometimes they stole them, but that occasionally a strong party would come down and suddenly appear at a camp of the Kŭrnai at break of day, and by threats compel them to give up women to them for wives

Marriage customs

The young Kŭrnai could, as a rule, acquire a wife in one way only. He must run away with her. Native marriage might be brought about in various ways. If the young man was so fortunate as to have an unmarried sister, and to have a friend who also had an unmarried sister, they might arrange with the girls to run off together; or he might make his arrangements with some eligible girl whom he fancied, and who fancied him; or a girl, if she fancied a young man, might send him a secret message, asking, "Will you find me some food?" And this was understood to be a proposal. But in every such case it was essential for success that the parents of the bride should be utterly ignorant of what was about to take place. It was no use his asking for a wife excepting under most exceptional circumstances, for he could only acquire one in the usual manner, and that was by running off with her.*

* As my friend and correspondent, the Rev. J. Bulmer, of Lake Tyers mission, expressed doubts to me as to the accuracy of my informants' statements on this point, I not only re-examined them, but, in order to obtain a check, I went to the Ramahyŭck mission, and there questioned four women who were most likely to be able to speak positively. They were of the Briakolŭng and Bratauolŭng clans. I questioned them as to the marriage customs of the Kŭrnai *before the white man came*. Of these women, one was young, one middle aged, and two old; and all were, or had been, married. One woman, "Nanny," is the oldest living Gippsland aborigine, having been a widow, with grey hair, when Angus M'Millan discovered the country. She stated positively that the rule was that all young women ran off with their husbands; and she could only recollect three cases where girls had been given away. Her own was one of these, and she explained it by saying that she had no parents, but only brothers, who gave her to a friend; and that in such a case there would be no necessity for running away, or for the husband having to fight his wife's relatives. This instance proves the rule and explains the exception, at any rate among the Briakolŭng Kŭrnai. There are, however, indications that this rule, as also the rules regulating intermarriage between certain divisions, were relaxed among the Brabrolŭng and the Kroatŭngolŭng.

MARRIAGE CUSTOMS.

A Tatūngolūng man gave me the following illustration: "Perhaps a Kroatŭn would want a wife. Perhaps he might be a nice-looking young man. He would go down into the Tatūngolūng country. He would sneak about till he saw a nice young girl. They would look at each other and smile; but not too near, or the father and mother would see. Then, at the corroboree in the evening, the young man would say, 'I like you; we will run away, only not yet.' Then they wait for the next corroboree and run off. The father and brothers are very angry, and look out for him to fight him"

Sometimes, however, it might happen that the young men were backward. Perhaps there might be several young girls who ought to be married, and the women had then to take the matter in hand when some eligible young men were at the camp. They consulted, and some went out in the forest, and with sticks killed some of the little birds, the yeerŭng. These they brought back to the camp, and casually showed them to some of the men; then there was an uproar. The men were very angry. The yeerungs, their brothers, had been killed! The young men got sticks; the girls took sticks also, and they attacked each other. Heavy blows were struck, heads were broken, and blood flowed, but no one stopped them. But the Kŭrnai tell me that those young men only fought who might get married, not those newly-made jerrali, who were supposed to stand back, not liking to see the women's blood.

Perhaps this fight might last a quarter of an hour, then they separated. Some even might be left on the ground insensible. Even the men and women who were married joined in this free fight. The next day the young men, the brewit, went and in their turn killed some of the women's "sisters," the birds djeetgŭn, and the consequence was that on the following day there was a worse fight than before. It was perhaps a week or two before the wounds and bruises were healed. By-and-bye, some day one of the eligible young men met one of the marriageable young women; he looked at her, and said, "Djeetgŭn!" She said, "Yeerŭng! What does the yeerŭng eat?" The reply was, "He eats so and so," mentioning kangaroo, opossum, or emu, or some other game. Then they laughed, and she ran off with him without telling any one.*

In all cases, therefore, excepting those rare instances where a girl had no parents,† and her brothers gave, or exchanged, her away, or in the case of widows, the bride had to run off with her chosen husband. The bride's family were furious. The male relatives searched for her—sometimes with success, sometimes without success. If the couple could remain away till the girl was with child, it is said that she would be forgiven. If, on the contrary, she was found and brought back, or if she herself returned, she was severely punished. Her father, perhaps, speared her—through the leg or both feet—and her mother and brothers might severely beat her. As for her husband, whenever he returned, he had to fight her male relatives, and he was unable ever to look at, speak to, or live in the same camp with his wife's mother. It might become necessary for them to elope two, or even three, times before they were forgiven. At length the family becoming tired of objecting—the mother might say, "Oh! it's all right, better let him have her." It is not more than three years since a young girl, who was being educated at one of the missions, ran off thus with a young Maneroo black boy.

It is said to have often occurred that, where a man's wife

---

* Hujusmodi institutum apud aborigines constabat, juvenem prius sodalibus suis consilium suum per socium (Brogan appellatum) indicere consuêsse, quàm a castris adolescentulam abduceret. Postridie in loco quodam idoneo, a castris remoto, juvenes delecti e gente ejus abductam seriatim strupraverunt; inde domum reverterunt. Postea autem abductoris primi femina omnino habebatur.

† I have been told that in rare instances the father has been prevailed upon by his son to *give* his daughter away in the first instance.

had an unmarried sister, the father would, when the first elopement had been condoned, give the second sister to his daughter's husband—the alleged reason being that the parents would then have a double supply of food;* and there is no doubt that the husband had a right to his deceased wife's unmarried sister, which would be admitted by the father in some clans, or, among others, could only have effect if the widower could carry off his wife's sister from the camp before her relatives could prevent him.

The curious custom, in accordance with which the man was prohibited from speaking to, or having any communication or dealings with, his wife's mother, is one of extraordinary strength, and seems to be rooted deep down in their very nature. So far as I know it is of wide-spread occurrence throughout Australia.† The relation between son-in-law and mother-in-law.

A Brabrolŭng, who is a member of the Church of England, was one day talking to me. His wife's mother was passing at some little distance, and I called to her. Suffering at the time from cold, I could not make her hear, and said to the Brabrolŭng "Call Mary, I want to speak to her" He took no notice whatever, but looked vacantly on the ground. I spoke to him again sharply, but still without his responding. I then said, "What do you mean by taking no notice of me?" He thereupon called out to his wife's brother, who was at a little distance, "Tell Mary Mr. Howitt wants her," and, turning to me, continued reproachfully, "You know very well I *could not* do that— you know I cannot speak to that old woman"

The young Kŭrnai, having at last succeeded in obtaining a wife, and in being recognized by his wife's family, may be said to be free of two divisions. He commenced a partly The Kurnai family.

* As to the obligation to supply food to the wife's parents, *see* Appendix.
† [This is confirmed by many of my informants. Among the Kamilaroi, if a man be compelled to speak with his mother-in-law, the pair will turn their backs upon one another and shout as if they were far apart. A Queensland correspondent writes—"If a man be accidentally brought in contact with his mother-in-law, their mingled fear and shame are a sight to see."—L F]
The same custom is found in some of the South Sea Islands also

independent family existence of his own. He wandered over the country in which his fathers and fathers' fathers were born. It was his inheritance; but he also might wander in the country of his wife's ancestors.

There was no restriction as to a man having one wife, or any number of wives. On the death of the husband, his wife went by right to his brother; and, if he had two or more wives, they then went to his brothers, if he had any, in order of seniority. It is given as a reason, that the brother is the proper person to support his brother's widow and his brother's children. The widow might, however, exercise a choice. She might refuse to go to her husband's brother, and choose some one else. In this case the brother-in-law had no remedy except, as I am told, by endeavouring to kill her by būlk, that is, by witchcraft.

Customs at childbirth. When the time arrives at which the birth of a child is expected, the father is sent away. The women at the camp attend the mother, and it is only after a lapse of two weeks that the father is permitted to see his wife or the infant. During that time he has made his fire apart, and waits. When the time has come at which he is permitted to see his wife and his child, the paternal grandmother carries it to some brebba mūngan, that is, "other father," or, in other words, the father's brother. The mother goes and sits by the father's fire, and, after a time, the paternal grandmother carries the infant to them.*

* Among the Kūrnai it was not customary to tie the umbilical cord before severing it. My informants tell me that it was cut by means of a piece of quartz (groggin), a mussel shell (nandūun), or a strip of reed (gowūt). The Rev. Mr. Bulmer, of Lake Tyers, confirms this. The Rev. A. F. Hagenauer, of the Ramahyuk mission, states that the cord was not separated from the placenta for some four hours. It was then generally cut (not broken) with a shell or a reed. The string, after being cut, was never tied up, but was turned a little upwards, and covered with some fur-skin, or pelt. Nothing else was done. The Gournditch-mara tribe of Western Victoria first tied the cord with a piece of kangaroo sinew, and then cut it

The husband expected strict fidelity to himself from his wife, but he did not admit any reciprocal obligation on his part towards her. They say, in explanation, "Oh, a man căn do as he likes" The expected fidelity towards the husband was enforced under severe penalties. In the event of a woman eloping with some other man, all the neighbouring men might turn out and seek for her, and, in the event of her being discovered, she became common property to them until released by her husband or her male relatives.* The husband, on his part, probably speared her. Her life was in his hand. In some respects the Kŭrnai differed as regards their women from some, if not from many other tribes. Each man not only expected his wife to be faithful to himself, but he, on his part, never lent her to a friend or to a guest.†

<small>Obligations of the marriage</small>

<small>This is, for instance, the case among the Dieri tribes of Cooper's Creek, where it is a hospitable custom to provide a guest with a temporary wife. Not only is this the custom, but, in their gesture language, there is a particular sign—a folding of the hands—which signifies this custom, and may either mean a request or an offer, according as it is used by the guest or by the host</small>

<small>either with a sharp piece of flint or with a reed—(The Rev J H Stähle, Lake Condah Mission). Among the Kamilaroi of the Gwydir River, N S W, the cord was knotted in itself, and then severed by the nails of the gin attending the mother—(Mr Cyrus E Doyle, Werrina, Moree, N S W) The Chepara tribe of South Queensland tied the cord with kangaroo sinew, and then cut it—(Mr. J. Gibson, J P , Stanmore, Queensland).

My attention was drawn to this by Mr Fison, who also, at the request of Dr M'Gregor, chief medical officer of Fiji, made inquiry into this matter, and found that the cord is never tied by any of the tribes in that group The Rev George Brown, F R G S , informs us that the same practice prevails in the Navigator Islands

* A similar punishment was inflicted by the Fijians. There is a special term for it in their language. The punishment was inflicted openly in the $ra_i a$, a public square of the town —L F]

† The custom referred to in footnote, p 202, seems to contradict this, but, I am convinced, is but a survival of a once common right.

[Taylor, in his " Te Ika a Maui" (p 166, 2nd Ed) remarks that, among</small>

THE KŪRNAI.

Although a man might kill his wife under certain circumstances, and his act would be then approved by custom and by public opinion, yet, under other circumstances, he might not do so without incurring blood feud. For instance, I am told that a Brabrolŭng Kŭrnai once killed his wife near the Lakes. Her male relatives collected and fought with him. He was nearly killed, but ran off and escaped. After this they forgave him. The fact of this being regarded as an exceptional instance, may be said to prove the general assertion.

We might expect from the fact that, among these savages, the pairing family is strictly established—at least on one side—that the domestic life, the arrangements of the family circle, and the division of labour should conform, more or less perfectly, to that condition. Let us see what evidence of this there is.

The family duties shared by the man and woman. The man has to provide for his family with the assistance of his wife. His share is to hunt for their support, and to fight for their protection. As a Kŭrnai once said to me, "A man hunts, spears fish, fights, and sits about." The woman formerly built the home of bent sticks thatched with grass tussocks, but since the aborigines have obtained iron tomahawks, the home is made of sheets of bark

the Maories "every woman was *noa*, or common, and could select as many companions as she liked without being thought guilty of any impropriety, until she was given away by her friends to some one as her future master. She then became *tapu* to him, and was liable to be put to death if found unfaithful."

If her husband put her away, his *tapu* no longer guarded her against the communal right, and she became *noa* again.

It was a common occurrence for all the young men who had a common right to a girl to have a struggle for her, each one endeavouring to drag her away from the rest. The girl was often seriously, or even fatally, injured by her fierce suitors dragging her hither and thither; and sometimes a baffled pursuer, seeing that he had no chance of securing her to himself, would plunge his spear into her breast, so that no one else might enjoy the prize he had missed.—L. F]

stripped from the trees by the man. The woman caught fish and cooked it She gathered the vegetables, fruit, or seeds, which formed part of the food supply, and she wove rush bags or made nets.

When the man went out to hunt, we may, for the sake of illustration, assume that he had other men with him. In the event of game being killed, these were entitled to a share, more or less, according as they had either actually assisted in killing the game, or had only been present. For example, in the case when a kangaroo was killed by one man, and two others were present and assisted, the following division would be made:—The tail and one hind leg to one assistant; the other hind leg and the haunch to the other assistant; the remainder to the chief hunter. Such game as a kangaroo would be probably cooked in the bush before being carried home. Lesser game might be cooked, or might be carried home raw. In every case, however, whether large game or small, the cooked food was divided by the procurer into certain portions, which were allotted by custom to various members of his family group. *[margin: Common right in the catch in hunting.]*

In the above instance, of the remainder kept by the hunter, the head, neck, and back piece down to the termination of the ribs would be "neborak," and belonged to his wife's father, who, in his turn, divided his portion with his family. The rest would be mŭk-je-ak, and would be given to the man's father, who divided it with his family.* *[margin: Common right to food in the family.]*

Similar customs, regulating the food supply, appear to have obtained among the tribes of Maneroo, N S W., but they vary somewhat in detail, and particulars of which will be found given in the Appendix.

---

* Of neborak no translation can be given. It means the meat given by the man to his wife's parents. Mŭk-je-ak is derived from muk = large or great—a term of comparison, as muk-le-en = very nice, or very good—and from the word jeak = flesh.

No provision of food laid by.

It would scarcely be expected of a race of savages roaming over a certain tract of country, and depending upon their success in hunting, or in gathering plants, roots, fruits, and seeds for their daily support of food, that they should make provision for the morrow unless forced to exercise prudence and foresight by the dire necessity of want. Under conditions such as those of Gippsland, this necessity would rarely arise. The grassy forests and plains were stocked with kangaroo and other varieties of herbivorous marsupials; the forest trees harboured opossums, the native bear, and the iguana; the rivers and lakes swarmed with varieties of fish and eels; various plants, bushes, and trees afforded edible substances in roots, berries, or seeds; and, both on land and water, birds were of great number and variety. Food was, therefore, widely spread throughout the country, and included almost everything, from the larvæ of insects to the great kangaroo. In a country lying as does Gippsland between the Pacific Ocean and the great snowy ranges of the Australian Alps, droughts such as periodically desolated a greater part of the continent were not likely to occur. Here, then, perhaps less than in any other part of Australia, were the aboriginal natives likely to be driven by dire experience to develop habits of forethought. I am not aware that in any case the Kŭrnai stored up food, or even hesitated to consume or waste an over supply through thought for the morrow.

The only instance in which I found any provision made for the future was in the country inhabited by a tribe allied to the Dieri, immediately south of Sturt's Stony Desert. I there found, carefully concealed in a bush, a basket, or small hamper, made of twisted grass, and having a lid The outside was plastered with clay. It contained about a bushel of the seed of the *Portulaca oleracea* (Purslane), which those natives use for food, and which is only procurable after rains

Customs regulating the camp

Not only did custom regulate the distribution of uncooked or cooked food among the members of the group to

CUSTOMS REGULATING THE CAMP. 209

whom it was common, but it also strictly defined the position which might be occupied by the various members in the camp.

In order to learn something of these rules, I once asked some Kŭrnai to point out on a piece of ground where various members of a family group, whom I named, would camp From their statements I formed a diagram, and from it I extract the following particulars :— The starting point is supposed to be the camp of a man and his wife. The directions are given approximately by compass bearings, and the distances by paces. The nature of the ground required that the camps should extend in a particular direction

    Son and son's wife, 5 paces north
    Father and mother, 20 paces N 30° E
    Brother and brother's wife, 20 paces N 60° E
    Wife's father and mother, 100 paces or more E
    Wife's brother and wife, near the last.
    Father's sister and husband, 10 paces S 30° E
    Mother's sister and husband, 10 paces S 60° E.
    Mother's brother's son and wife, 20 paces S

In this example the relative places and distances are not, of course, intended to convey that those directions and those number of paces would in all cases be followed, but as indicating a case which might occur and which is an example of the general rule. It is necessary to point out that the term translated as father's sister's husband would also include mother's brother's wife—the relative positions of those persons would therefore be the same.

In the home, also, custom regulates the position of the individual. Taking, as an instance, the central group in the above, namely, the husband and wife, I may state that the former would sleep on the left hand side of the fire, the latter behind it; and, close behind her, the children; nearest to her, the little boy, if any; next to him, the little girl. In the event of the man's father and mother being with them for a night, the grandfather would occupy the right-hand side, the grandmother behind him further back in the hut, and the son's wife and children would move to a corresponding position near their own " housefather."

It would be a rule that the wife's sister, although called " wife " by her brother-in-law, and calling him husband, would not sleep in his hut, but somewhere near at hand. Other rules would apply to other members; and a " brogan," although calling the man's wife " wife," and she calling him " husband," would have to camp with the young men, if any were there, or else by himself. Rules such as these appear also to have obtained among the Maneroo aborigines *

<small>The Kŭrnai as an old man.</small> When the Kŭrnai arrived at mature age, and when he may be supposed to have taken his place among the elders of his clan, and was designated " boldain," he acquired a new name. The designation which he received as a child became his " secret name " when he received a new one at initiation, and this again often gave way to some name bestowed by his contemporaries from some personal peculiarity. This last name was usually compounded of two words, one of which, " Būnjil," is a constant, and may be freely rendered " elder," the other describing some quality or peculiarity. This name was probably his last, and he retained it to his death.†

---

* According to the Rev Julius Kühn similar rules obtained in the Tŭrra tribe, South Australia He says, " A man's parents fix their camp to the right-hand side of their son's camp His brothers to the left side, sister-in law to the right side or near his father's ; and from whatever cardinal point they arrive, they accordingly fix their camps at some distance from the former In the camp the husband sleeps at the right-hand side of the fire, his wife behind him, and her young children behind her

† It is worthy of note that Būnjil or Pūnjil was, among the Yarra or Westernport tribes, a supernatural being, apparently equivalent to the baukan of the Kŭrnai A Westernport blackfellow once told me that Pūngil was an old man who lived in the mountains at the sources of the Yarra river, where he possessed great numbers of cattle We have here an aboriginal belief modified by contact with the whites It is further worthy of note that among those aborigines, so far as I know, Būnjil = Eaglehawk.

[Such "modified legends " are not uncommon among savages. A Tongan

THE KŪRNAI AS AN OLD MAN. 211

Among the Kŭrnai the names given to two of the elder men whom I knew were as follows :—Būnjil Balejan (platypus), in consequence of his skill in spearing that animal. Būnjil Tambūn (Gippsland perch —*Lates Colonorum*), for his skill in catching that fish A leading man in the Briakolūng clan was Būnjil Kraura (west wind) It was supposed that he could cause the great west wind to blow so violently that the Kŭrnai could not climb the swaying trees for opossums or native bears He could be propitiated by presents of food His name designates one of the divisions of that clan.

Another of the Briakolūng was Būnjil Dauangŭn He was renowned for making canoes much turned up in front (Dauangŭn = to turn up) His brother Būnjil Ban received his name from a supposed extraordinary power in that form of sorcery

As an illustration of the way in which such names are acquired, I note the following :—The Mitchell River flows for some thirty miles through a gorge-like and inaccessible valley. In order to examine this, I caused two Kŭrnai to make canoes at the upper end, and therein we floated down together The gorge was unknown to them, and the navigation was regarded as a great feat in consequence of the numerous rapids For some time it was spoken of among the Brabrolŭng, and the name of Būnjil Gŭyŭrgŭn (rapids) was given me

Similarly, among the Dieri clans of Cooper's Creek, the word Pinnarū (pinna = great) is the analogue of Būnjil. Among those natives I was known, and am now, after nearly twenty years, remembered as Worrawotti Pinnarū (worrawotti = emu-camel), from having had a number of camels with my expedition My friend M'Kinley, the explorer, was known as Whilpra Pinnarū, from having with him a spring-cart The term whilpra being a corruption of wheelbarrow, which the Lake Torrens natives have acquired from the whites as the name for a cart or waggon.

Among the Kŭrnai age meets with great reverence. A man's authority increases with his age. If without age he possessed naturally intelligence, cunning, bravery, beyond his fellows, he might become a man of note, weighty in council, and a leader in war; but this is exceptional, and it may be stated as a general rule that authority attaches to age. It follows from this that there is no

Authority of the elders.

once told me a legend which set forth that Napoleon I. was a Tongan who went to France to deliver that unhappy country from the tyranny of Wellington —L F]

212   THE KŬRNAI

hereditary authority and no hereditary chieftain. The authority which is inherent to age attaches not alone to the man, but also to the woman. In affairs of moment the women have a voice, and it is not without weight. They consulted with the men about the ceremonies of initiation. They kept alive the stringent marriage laws. They are also, with the men, repositories of the ancient customs, and strongly influence public opinion. It may be said that the head men of the clans were, first of all, those who were oldest; secondly, perhaps, those who, to some age, added exceptional qualifications. This principle, regulating authority, I believe to be not peculiar to the Kŭrnai, but to be general to the whole Australian race.

Brūthen Mŭnji, whom I have before mentioned, is admitted by the Brabrolūng to have been one of their men of most note He was not only old, but is described as having been very strong and courageous; sagacious in council and cunning in strategy This man had a brother named Bembinkel, who was also noted for bravery and intelligence; but in these he was eclipsed by his brother To such an extent did Brūthen Mŭnji outshine Bembinkel, that Tūlaba, the son of the latter, always speaks of the former as his father; and it was only after years that I found out that Brūthen Mŭnji was his "other father" (=father's brother).

At the southern verge of Sturt's Stony Desert I encamped for a day near a small number of friendly natives speaking the Dieri language. In the afternoon a number of old men came to me, and requested that I would go and see a very old man at their camp. They spoke of him as "pinna pinnarū." I went, and found him seated in a small hut. He was the oldest aborigine I had ever seen up to this time His age I can only conjecture. Had he been of white race, I should have said he must have been a hundred years old. Being an Australian aborigine, he might be eighty or ninety. That which I have now to point out as remarkable is the extraordinary respect and reverence shown to him, not only by the women and children and men, but also in as great a degree by the elders, who had formed a deputation to ask me to visit him.

Leadership in war.   I have pointed out that there were no hereditary chiefs, but that men who were eminent, either by age or by mental

LEADERSHIP IN WAR. 213

or physical qualities, took the lead.* This latter, indeed, is no more than we observe daily in all walks of life with us; and it is a well-known observation that great occasions produce great men. This is only stating in other words that in momentous times those men who are intellectually or physically superior to their fellows come to the front. As illustrating this, and as affording a glimpse into the past life of the Kŭrnai, I may give the following, taken down almost verbatim from the words of my informant:—

A number of Kŭrnai were encamped high up on the Tambo River, near the Brajerak country Some of the men came upon fresh tracks of Brajerak Brūthen Mŭnji was there. He was a very strong man, and was very skilful He returned to the camp, and said to the others — "Someone must go and see where they are" He told Tankowillŭn to go, because he was very cunning and of very sharp sight † Such a man is called Benning Benning (spy) By-and-bye he returned, saying, "I found them; lots of women and children" Brūthen Mŭnji said, "Yŭkka tūn" (well said) Then they got their spears ready Some men went to hunt for food to leave with the women, for they might be two or three days away. Other men fixed sharp pieces of quartz in their spears with gum. Brūthen Mŭnji said to the women, "Go away down the river to Jillŭn (about 25 miles). If we do not catch them where they were, we shall not be back to-morrow; then all of you go on to Brūthen." This was why the men had caught so many 'possums for the women Brūthen Mŭnji sent spies off again. The Kŭrnai had to wait a good while before two of them returned at nightfall. "Where are they?" "Down there at the same place where they were this morning." "Yŭkka tūn," said Brūthen Mŭnji The Kŭrnai then said, "Well, what shall we do?" The two spies replied, "The two others are waiting there till night." About sleeping time these returned, and gave a signal whistle (the sound here made by the narrator was produced by pulling out the lower lip between the thumb and forefinger and sharply drawing the breath through the fold) All the

---

* *See* Appendix F, as to the Gournditch-mara tribe of Western Victoria.
† This Tankowillŭn was the father of another Tankowillŭn now living, whom I shall have to mention later on, as also performing the part of a spy. His name is untranslatable to ears polite.

Kŭrnai then had a corroboree;* they danced nearly all the night. But they did not sing They were quite silent, and only made gestures and stamped their feet In the middle of the night they all marched off well armed. They walked until they were about two miles from the Brajerak, then they had another silent dance Then they marched again, and, when near morning—there was no moon— they got close to them, not more than half a mile away Two spies went first Two other spies who had gone on now met them "Where are they?" They reply, "Just here" The dawn was coming Then all rapidly painted themselves with pipeclay—red ochre is no use, it cannot frighten an enemy—and divided, so as to surround the camp The spies whistled like birds, to tell when all was ready Then all ran in; they speared away, they speared away! They only speared the men, and perhaps some children Whoever caught a woman kept her himself Then they eat the skin of the Brajeraks †

Adoption of captive children.

My informant, in further speaking about this night attack, said that, in such cases, children might be saved and adopted. If a boy, he would take the place of a son in the family of the man adopting him. The boy, on growing up, might be called the "Brajerak boy," but he would not harbour any revenge, as he would have the "Kŭrnai tongue" A girl, under such circumstances, would be the same as any other girl of the clan.

Cannibalism.

Long before the white men came into Gippsland, a large number of the Brabrolŭng Kroatŭngolūng and Tatŭngolūng went towards Maneroo on the war path At Gellingall, about twenty miles up from Buchan, on the river of that name, they left their women, and proceeded to a place now known as Fanwick, where their spies

* This is not a Kŭrnai word, but has been introduced by the whites I do not know from what tribe it was originally derived—probably of New South Wales
† The skin of the slain Brajerak was flayed from the thighs and from the side This was roasted and eaten by the men Women were not permitted to witness the proceeding, nor to taste the spoils of the slain.
[In Fiji, also, at least among some of the tribes, cannibalism was forbidden to the women. It is said, however, that some of them indulged on the sly. The prohibition does not seem to have extended to the mountaineers of Navitilevu. In a fight, within my own knowledge, a woman rushed upon a fallen warrior, tore his body open with her teeth, and drank his blood —L. F]

surprised two Brajerak—an old man and his son. The former was killed, but the latter escaped The skin of the slain man was eaten, and his legs cut off, and carried to the camp, where the old men roasted them and shared the flesh among the boys, in order " that, when the old men were dead, the boys might know what to do."

The last narrative was told me by two men who were then boys, and shared in the feast One was Tankowillŭn (the younger), whom I have mentioned; the other was Blair, whom I shall have to mention as an actor in the last known blood feud. They told me that the flesh was "very good; much sweeter than beef."

From the preceding statements it will, I think, be evident The clan that the direction of those affairs which generally concerned that indefinite number of families which, in their aggregate, constitute the division, was in the hands of the elders. Those elders, individually, were the heads of families. While an aggregate of families, all being intimately related by common descent through the father, form the division, two or more divisions form the clan, to which alone a distinctive name is given.

As all men are Yeerŭng, and all women Djeetgŭn, it follows that, whereas the women, when married, were drafted off to other divisions and to other clans, the men remained; and, in accordance with partial descent through the male, it is through them that the divisions and the clans have perpetual succession. The sons follow the father's class, Yeerŭng; and the daughters follow the mother's class, Djeetgŭn.

The clan may be seen to have resulted from the natural spread of families over a tract of country, all which families were bound together by a common recognized descent. Those families which were most nearly related through known ancestors, and whose "country" adjoined along the rivers, were naturally most closely bound together, and

216   THE KŭRNAI.

dependent upon each other for mutual aid and protection. The nearness of their descent forbade intermarriage, and they constituted that aggregate which, in default of a better term, I have called the division. An aggregate of divisions formed the clan.

The blood feud.
As the members of a division may be regarded as in fact members of an expanded family, and dependent upon each other for aid and protection, and, as regarded many of the members, for food, we can see readily that they might well be expected, individually or collectively, to prosecute the feud or the blood feud of a member, or mutually protect each other from the effects of a blood feud. I mention the blood feud at this place because the instances which I shall give refer, perhaps, rather to its aspect as regards the clan than the individual. I now proceed to give several instances of the prosecution of the blood feud, and shall then be in a better position to point out certain interesting conclusions to which they lead.

Many years ago, a brother of Tūlaba, named Barney, woke from sleep in his camp, and found a Talūngolūng Kŭrnai named Bŭnbra (also known as Jetbolan = liar) standing over him, who said he had come for some fire. The next day Barney fell sick, and told his friends that Bŭnbra had bewitched him during the night. By and bye Barney died The male relatives sent to Bŭnbra to desire him to come and fight. At the time and place appointed, Bŭnbra arrived, with many Talūngolūng and Kroatŭngolūng men and women On the other side, the male relatives of the dead man arrived, backed by Brabrolūng, and, I believe, Briakolūng men and women. The two parties faced each other at a little distance. Bŭnbra had two shields for his defence, one for use, and the other in reserve. The relatives of the dead man had great numbers of missiles, as boomerangs, kŭllŭks,* and kŭnnin (a straight stick, pointed at each end). The boomerang was the fighting boomerang, which does not return to the thrower.

The proceedings commenced by Bŭnbra saying, "I want to tell you I never hurt that poor fellow." The reply was, "You must fight."

* Kŭllŭk = gallak = wood.

THE BLOOD FEUD. 217

Boomerangs were thrown, as my informant said, like a flock of parrots. Bŭnbra successfully dodged and warded them off. At last a kŭnnin was thrown, which passed through his thigh. The women then rushed in and stopped the fight The feud was at an end.

A well-marked instance, and the last known to have occurred in Gippsland, happened about fifteen years ago, and is characteristic. In the extreme of East Gippsland, in the Bidwelli country, lies a small tract of grazing ground, surrounded by vast extents of dense and almost impenetrable jungles A track leads to it alone from the territory of New South Wales beyond the eastern boundary of Victoria At the time when the following events occurred, the common boundary of the two colonies was not ascertained, and the place I speak of was, in point of fact, "No man's land" It was occupied by some white men as a cattle station, and they had as stockman a Brajerak. The Kroatŭngolŭng Kŭrnai were in the habit of occasionally following the coast to Twofold Bay, to assist as harpooners in whale fishing The Brajerak stockman invited a party thus travelling to visit him They did so; and he took occasion, under protection of the armed white men, to shoot one Kŭrnai, Bŭbŭk, and carry off his daughter from the midst of her friends and relatives. The Kŭrnai escaped to their own country, and the Brajerak kept the girl as his wife The relatives of the murdered man prepared, however, for revenge So far as I am aware, both the agnates and the cognates—using the latter term as implying only uterine descent—took part, and, the party being ready, set out under guidance of the brother of the murdered man. The result was that they tracked the Brajerak to another station, and found him there living with the girl he had carried off. They then killed him, and recovered her The man who first speared him was the sister's son of the deceased *

The last blood feud in Gippsland

The following narrative concerning the last great battle of the Gippsland clans, which occurred at Bushy Park, near Stratford, about the years 1856-7, was related to me by Bŭnda-wal,† otherwise Bobby Brown, a Gnarrawŭt Tatŭngolŭng, who, it will be seen, bore a prominent part in the events narrated. I give it in full, as illustrating many points of great interest respecting these savages. I have as much as possible preserved the letter as well as the spirit of

The last battle of the clans.

---

* [This is a marked trace of former descent through the mother.—L. F]
† Bŭnda = bite, wal = spear.

his tale. As a preface to this narrative, the following statement from Gliŭn-kong, of whom more anon:—

In consequence of the Omeo and Gippsland men having become acquainted through the white men and made friends by them, one of the Omeo men, Billy Blew, obtained a Briaka woman to wife He ill-used her, and her father, Kaiŭng, fought with and speared him, of which he shortly died. Billy Blew's kin in return killed Kaiŭng, together with another Briaka, and were assisted in so doing by Johnny, the brother of Bŭnda-wal. In revenge for this a Dargo man, Jimmy, the nephew of Kaiŭng, killed Johnny Flanner, the brother of Gliŭnkong, and other relations of Johnny, finding his skin hidden in a tree at Aitkin's Straits, followed Dargo Jimmy, and killed him at Erin Vale, at Merriman's Creek

This preface is connected with Bŭnda-wal's narrative, as the events form one whole, and are thus necessary to each other. I now give his narrative in his own words:—

I had two wives, both from Brt-britta One of these had been married to the Dargo man who killed my brother Johnny at Aitkin's Straits. I then collected all the men from Brŭthen, Wy-yung, and from Binnajerra, for all my own men had died or been killed, so that only boys were left But those others were also like my own people We all sneaked round south of the Lakes, and to Merriman's Creek, where we found the Dargo man Flanner, whose brother he had also killed, speared him We let him lie there, and we did not eat his skin, for he was a Kŭrnai, one of ourselves As he was a friend of the Briakolŭng, we went up to the Heart, near Sale, to look for them We found a number of Dargo, Briaka, and Brataua there, and we fought; but we were beaten, because they had guns as well as spears, and were helped by two black police and a white police trooper We ran away, and left everything behind us, our blankets and clothes, and only took our spears We ran back to where we had left our women, near to Meetung; near to that place where the wild dog turned the Kŭrnai into stone * Our enemies and the police followed us up as far

---

* They have a belief that the wild dog sometimes speaks, and that to hear this is fatal, the listener being turned into stone The narrator refers to a belief that at Meetung a camp of Kŭrnai were literally petrified by hearing one of their dogs (Ban) say, "You are eating fish, and have given me none." A Kŭrnai told me that, when a boy, he once heard a dog commence to howl something; he only caught one word "bring" (bone), when he ran off as hard as he could, and so saved his life.

THE LAST BATTLE OF THE CLANS

as Lake Tyers, but they could not cross, and we escaped. For a long time we were quiet, but at last we went up to Maneroo to get the Brajerak to come down and help us. By this time the white men had brought so many Brajerak down from Maneroo and Omeo that we had become friends. So we got the Maneroo men to help us, and with them went round the mountains to Omeo. There we got Nūkong, their head man, to help us, and we left our women there. Nūkong also sent lewin (messengers) to the men of the Ovens River and Mount Buffalo to send help; and it was arranged that we should meet them at Kŭtbŭntaura (Bushy Park). Then we all went off by way of Dargo, but we found no one there. At Bushy Park the men from the Ovens River and Mount Buffalo met us. We went to that place to get some food, and also to see some Brabrolŭng men of Wŭk-Wŭk, who were living there, pretending to be friends of the Briakolŭng and Dargo men. There could not have been less than two hundred of us—at least the white men counted and told us so. From that place we went round the country looking for our enemies. We sent out four spies in the daytime, while the main body lay concealed in the scrub, and only travelled at night. Sometimes I was one of the spies, sometimes Tankowillŭn was one of them with me. We went all over the country, even down to the Tarra, but could not meet our enemies. At length we pretended to be friends, and returned to the Mitchell. We waited a while, and then sent to the Snowy River men, who came to us. But the blackfellows from Maneroo and from the Ovens returned home, and only a few from Omeo remained to help us. While this was going on, the Dargo and Briaka sent messengers (lewin) to me, saying that we would fight and then be friends. It was decided by the Dargo old men that the fight should take place near to Deighton, at a place called Yowŭndeet. We met there and fought, but no one was killed. They were too strong for us, and ran us back to the Mitchell River. We now again waited for some time, till Charley Buchanan* brought us a message from the head man at Dargo that we should be friends. It was their custom to do this by sending a spear jagged with quartz as a token † This one had much glass on it. We

---

* A Brabrolŭng native from the west side of the Mitchell—I believe of the Wŭk Wŭk division.

† Sometimes one of the skin aprons worn by the men was sent round thus as a token, suspended to the point of the spear. I may here note that this apron (bridda bridda) was made from the skin of the kangaroo rat; the legs and tail were cut off, and also, I think, the front part of the head; half of it was cut longitudinally into strands. Two bridda bridda were worn, one in front and one behind, suspended from a waist belt made of about fifteen

said among ourselves, "We will pretend to make friends, and wait till by and bye." The spear was passed on by way of Brŭthen, and sent up to Omeo, and so round back to Dargo. Then we all gathered, only the Kroatŭn (Snowy River men) would not come, for they were frightened—two of their men had been speared. Brŭthen Mŭnji told us, "We must send a message to the Dargo men where to meet us—but we must be very quick and get up to Bushy Park." We had with us some Omeo men, with their head man, Nŭkong. Our head man was Brŭthen Mŭnji. On the morning we were to fight we were all ready—we were painted with pipeclay. This was because we were very angry at our two men being killed, and to frighten our enemies, who were painted with red ochre because they had killed our men. We were seated in a long row—our spears on the ground ready. Our women were in front, beating their 'possum rugs. Nŭkong was at one end, just behind our row; Brŭthen Mŭnji was at the other end of the row, standing behind close to me. It was about noon. He looked up at the sun and said, "We will eat first." The enemy were not in sight, but were not far off. Then a Brabrolŭng man came to us—he was a messenger—he was sent to us, but we knew him—he was our friend, and the husband of old "Nanny." He said, "There are not many of you!" Brŭthen Mŭnji replied, "Never mind how many—we will see." Then he ordered the women to go back out of danger. He made us a great speech. He told us that we would beat them. There was "no gammon about him." Then we fought, and when Billy the Bull's father speared a Kŭtbŭntaura man the others ran away. There was a running fight; they ran off and left all their things behind them. By and bye I shot one man, and others were speared. Several of the women were caught. Some of the Brabrolŭng young men from Swan Reach ran down a Brt-britta woman. They could not, however, keep her, because they were too near to her—like cousins—and as she wanted to have me, and had no father, her brebba mŭngan (father's brother, or mother's sister's husband) gave her to me. He could do this because she had been caught in a fight and was not a young girl. This was how I got my first wife from Brt-britta.

From the preceding instances we may, perhaps, draw two conclusions. First, that in the case of a member of the

feet of cord of twisted opossum fur, wound round the waist. As I have stated elsewhere, the women wore a large fringe of opossum fur string suspended from the waist until they were married; afterwards nothing.

same tribe, a blood feud is not necessarily to the death, but may be expiated by his undergoing a certain ordeal * Second, that in the case of members of an alien tribe the blood feud is fatal, and cannot be satisfied but by the death of the offender ; and, further, that the feud attaches not only to the individual, but also to the whole group of which he is a member

We may also gather that the blood feud would be prosecuted not only by the immediate relatives of the dead person, but also by the whole division, or even by the whole clan. It would be the duty of the agnates of the person aggrieved, as nearest to him, and it would also be the duties of his cognates, as is evident from the fact that, in the case of Būbŭk, it was the sister's son who avenged him. The duty would lie, therefore, not only upon the division to which the father belonged, but also upon the division from which the mother had been taken. In regard to blood feud as against an alien, as every Yeerŭng was the brother of every other Yeerŭng, the obligation to revenge blood would attach, if necessary, to every Kŭrnai from the sea to the Snowy Mountains, and from the jungles in the east to the jungles in the west.

The alliance of some clans with the alien Brajerak was an innovation brought about by intercourse with the whites.

I have felt some doubt whether the Kŭrnai would or

[* It seems to me that the quarrels between the clans scarcely amount to blood feuds In the case of a man suspected of witchcraft, my informants tell me that the "fighting" is all on one side, the person accused acting on the defensive only. This appears to be a sort of expiation for a supposed offence against the body corporate by a member of it —L F]

After the Kŭnnin had pierced Bŭnbra, he drew it out and threw it at his assailants. The women then rushed in and put a stop to the ordeal. Blood had been shed in return for the supposed murder of Barney, and the feud was quenched In this instance, at any rate, I think the term "blood feud" justified. There are, however, other cases where the term "feud" alone would certainly be more accurate.— A.H.

THE KŪRNAI.

Hospitality protected an alien friend

would not recognize any obligation of hospitality to protect a member of an alien tribe, as, for instance, a Brajerak, who, being known to the Kŭrnai, might seek refuge from the avenger of blood. The opinion seems to be, after consultation among a number of the Kŭrnai, that no protection would be given.

That some protection is, however, afforded by the rights of hospitality to a member of an alien tribe appears from an occurrence which took place, perhaps, about twenty years ago

Two Brajerak families came into Gippsland in company with some Brabrolŭng from the Dargo River The Kŭrnai (Briakolŭng), among whom these visitors were encamped, did not molest them because "they were brought in by the Dargo men who were Brabrolŭng and our brothers" It was only when the Brajerak families quarrelled with their hosts, and separated, that the Biaka men attacked and killed them

Punishment of alien friend by the clan for an offence against rights of hospitality

If, therefore, protection might be given to an alien friend, it should follow that an alien friend might be punished for some offence, in accordance with which feud, or blood feud, would ensue. Such might, for instance, be the introduction of white men into the country of his hosts. Being aware of such an instance in the Dieri tribe at Lake Hope, in Central Australia, which I will mention, I consulted the Kŭrnai, who said that if the offender were Brajerak he would be killed wherever found; but, if one of their own people, the old men might probably endeavour to get rid of him by "būlk" (magic).

When exploring Central Australia, I obtained the services of a blackfellow from a South Australian tribe at Lake Torrens, and who, being on the border, spoke both his own language and that of the Dieri He was with me some time, and I am informed that, after his return, the elders of the Dieri tribe considered that he had been very culpable in leading white men through their country, and decided that he must be killed He was accordingly speared when sitting in the camp of a clan of the Dieri living at Tinga Tingana (Strzelecki's Creek) *

In considering the combats which are known to have so frequently occurred between the various clans of Gippsland, and of which I have given instances, it must be pointed out that there is an evident and marked distinction to be drawn between combats of Kŭrnai against Kŭrnai, and those of Kŭrnai against Brajerak In the battles between the clans, those who might be slain were not eaten; but when alien enemies were killed, portions of them were eaten † Such a fight as that described between Bŭnbra and the kin of Barney might, under certain circumstances, have extended from a "duel" to a general combat, and it may serve for an illustration of my first statement The slaughter of the Brajerak by the Briakolūng, and the slaughter of the Brajerak by the Brabrolūng under Brūthen Mŭnji, was, in both cases, followed by the skin of the thighs and that from the sides of the victims being flayed off, roasted, and eaten by the victors. These are illustrations of my second statement. It seems to me probable that this distinction is of general application ‡

Mr. Bulmer tells me, as to the Maneroo natives (Brajerak), that they did not eat the slain in battle, who were left lying to be buried by their friends, but they eat parts of the

---

* [I am inclined to think, from what I know of other savage tribes, that this poor fellow's offence may, perhaps, have lain in his not having respected the common usage as to the introduction of strangers In Fiji, for instance, a stranger must be forwarded in company with either a recognized *mata* = lewin, or a man appointed specially by a chief who is friendly with the tribe whose country has to be entered upon —L F]

† [Some of the Queensland tribes carefully flay the slain, and preserve the skin, with the hairy scalp and even the finger nails attached They look upon it as a powerful "medicine," and cover their patients with it as with a blanket —L. F]

‡ [Its general application is confirmed by all our correspondents — L F]

victims whom they murdered. The parts eaten were the hands and the feet, and this was accompanied by expressions of contempt for the person murdered. These persons whom they murdered were their real enemies; the persons with whom they engaged in open warfare were their friends with whom they had a quarrel.

Mr. Bulmer further tells me that the Murray River natives always had a great horror of those enemies who prowled about; they called them Thinanmalkin (one who spreads a net for the feet), and Koorinya-nat-ola (one who seizes by the throat). These were their real enemies, and when they caught them they blotted them out by eating part of them.

A frequent cause of quarrel was the stealing of wives by the men of one clan from the men of another clan; and this appears to have been especially the case in respect to those clans, or divisions of clans, from whom, in the ordinary course, they would have procured wives Such an instance was that when some of the Tatūngolūng stole all the women from a camp of Briakolūng on the Upper Avon River, the result being that a great battle was fought. We have here the Tatūngolūng clan, regarded in the aggregate as having stolen the women, undergoing that expiation by battle which the individual similarly underwent when he obtained a wife by running off with her from the custody of her father and brothers.

The tribe an aggregate of the clans. As a number of families inhabiting a certain locality formed that aggregate which I have termed the division, so did a certain number of divisions inhabiting a larger area form that aggregate which I have termed the clan. The distinction between these aggregates is one which was well recognized by the Kŭrnai, but which I have found it difficult to define in a satisfactory way. It may, perhaps, be said that the division consisted of a number of related

THE TRIBE AN AGGREGATE OF CLANS.

families, the individual members of which were forbidden by custom to intermarry with each other. The divisions were also named, in all clans but one, after the principal locality round which their components were clustered; and, in that exception, all the divisions but one were named after some man of note.

The clan, on the contrary, although in its divisions subject to the rules as to marriage, may be defined as including all those individuals acknowledging a common descent, inhabiting a certain area including several divisions, and claiming certain distinctive qualities. Thus, the last division of the last clan in the annexed table is named from the place Binnajerra, and a member of it would be a Binnajerra Kŭrnai, or "man of Binnajerra." But this last clan is named Tatūngolūng, or, freely translated, "South men," from its position as regarded the whole Kŭrnai tribe. Again, the second clan in the list is known as Brabrolūng, a name which may be freely translated as "*the* men." The aggregate of the clans formed a whole, each male individual of which called himself Kŭrnai, or *man*.

In the following table (A) I have given all information as to the divisions, clans, and the tribe of the Gippsland Kŭrnai which I have been able to collect. This information is unfortunately very imperfect, but the difficulties standing in the way are, in some respects, insuperable. It is all that can be now rescued from oblivion, and must suffice.

As illustrative of the exceptions met with to the general rules in accordance with which I have compiled the table, the following may serve :—Raymond Island (Baul = island)* although separated from the Brabrolūng country by a narrow strait, and from the Tatūngolūng country by several miles of lake, is claimed by the latter. Its inhabitants

---

* *Au,* as *ow,* in " how "

stated themselves to be "partly Tatūngolūng and partly Brabrolūng, but most Tatūngolūng" All the males of the family bore in succession the surname, "Gliŭn-kong" (Gli=a small bird, probably the curlew sandpiper *(Ancylochilus Subarquatus)*—kong=nose=beak). Each received it from the then owner at his initiation, and held it until the initiation of the next male of the family. The oldest male had authority, and the men were collectively called Būnjil Baul. Wives were obtained from e, f, h, l, n, p, q, but not from the Tatūngolūng, because these lived on the same lake; nor from such as i or o, as being too distant; nor from the adjoining Brabrolūng, with whom they were not friendly. The present Gliŭn-kong tells me he could not marry a woman of c for his mother was of that division; and, having been born at Lake Tyers, it is his country by birth, as Raymond Island is by inheritance from his father.

The women of Baul went to almost all the divisions, so far as I can learn.

The swans' eggs laid upon this island were the property of the Būnjil Baul, and any stranger taking them without leave would have to fight. There was no other restriction as to game against friendly Kŭrnai who might visit the island.

TABLE A.

THE ABORIGINES OF GIPPSLAND (see Map).

Tribe.	Clans.	Divisions.	Wives from.	Wives to.	Remarks.
Kŭra = men, claimed the whole of Gippsland from near Cape Everard to near Cape Liptrap, but a strip of debatable land lay on the borders; for instance, the Gippsland and Maneroo aborigines both claimed the Snowy River above Buchan, and the Gippsland and Omeo aborgines both claimed the valley of the Upper Tambo River.	1. *Kroatŭngolŭng* (Kroat = East, lung = father),* claimed all the sea-coast from near Cape Everard to the Snowy River; all that river, with its tributaries, up to about Willis; the sea-coast from the Snowy River to Jimmy's Point, near the entrance to the Gippsland Lakes, with all the streams flowing into Ewing's Marsh and Lake Tyers.	(a) Ben—Sydenham Inlet. (b) Dŭra—Orbost Station, near the Snowy River mouth. (c) Würnungatti—Lake Tyers. (d) Brt-britta—Jimmy's Point = a hollow in the ground.	b, c, d c, a, t e, f, k e, t	Twofold Bay, Mallagoota Inlet. c, a, t e, f, k, t b, t	All the divisions are named after places near which was the head quarters of the division, excepting l, m, n, which were named after some contemporaneous man of note. In this table the division and the clan may be taken to represent very nearly the "gens" and "phratry," of Mr. L. H. Morgan respectively.
	2. *Brabrolŭng* (Bra = man) claimed all the country watered by the Tambo, Nicholson, and Mitchell rivers, with their tributaries, to their extreme sources, and west of the Mitchell River to Providence Ponds, with a frontage to the Gippsland Lakes.	(e) Brithen — on the Tambo River. (f) Waiung—Bairnsdale = Widgeon (this word, as Wy-Yung, gives a name to a parish near Bairnsdale. (g) Wŭk-wŭk = Lindenow Flat = ? wŭrk wŭrk = ground, soil. (h) Mŭnji—North shore of Lake Victoria = there ! (i) Daŭrgo—Dargo River.	b, c, d, k c, e, g, t f	b, c, f, g c, e, g f	

* See note, p. 229.

TABLE A.—THE ABORIGINES OF GIPPSLAND—*Continued.*

Tribe.	Clans.	Divisions.	Wives from.	Wives to.	Remarks.
Kŭrnai. (*Continued.*)	3. *Briakolŭng* (Briak derived from Bra = man and yak = west) claimed all the country west of Providence Ponds, watered by the Avon, Macalister, Thompson, and Latrobe rivers, down to the junction of the two latter, thence following the eastern side of the Latrobe to Lake Wellington, thence eastward by the lakes to somewhere near Roseneath, thence northward to the Providence Ponds.	(*k*) Kŭtbŭntaura—Bushy Park. Kutbun = to carry or have, taura = fire—the name of a hill.	*d, i, e, h, l*	*d, i, l*	
		(*l*) Bŭnjil Nŭlŭng—the country between the Avon and the eastern boundary of the clan, south of Stratford; nŭlŭng = mud, the name of a man.	*k*	*k*	
		(*m*) Bŭnjil · Dan — the country between the Avon and Macalister and Thompson rivers, the name of a man, Dan = Snow.	*e, o*	*e, o*	
		(*n*) Bŭnjil Kraura — all the country of the clan west of (*m*); Kraura = west wind, the name of a man.	*i, o, q*	*i, o, q*	
	4. *Bratauolŭng* claimed all the country from the Latrobe River to near Cape Liptrap, and from the southern watershed of the Latrobe River to the sea.	(*o*) Kŭt · wŭt — Agnes River.	*m*	*m*	
		(*p*) Yau-ŭng — Warrigal Creek.	*n*	*n, q*	
		(*q*) Drelin — Merriman's Creek.	*p, i, t*	*p*	

TABLE A.—THE ABORIGINES OF GIPPSLAND.—*Continued.*

Tribe.	Clans.	Divisions.	Wives from.	Wives to.	Remarks.
Kŭrnai. *(Continued.)*	5. *Tatŭngolŭng* (Ta = South) claimed all the country west of the Kroatun (1) and east of the Brataua (4), and lying between the Gippsland Lakes and the sea, together with all the islands in the Lakes, excepting Flanagan Island, which belonged to the Brĭ-britǎ division of the Kroatungolŭng clan.	(*r*) Yunthŭr — adjoining and east of (*q*). (*s*) Ngarrawĭt — south side of Lake Victoria. (*t*) Binnajerra—Baul-baul.	*m* *e, m, q, t* *d, e, f, g*	*m* *e, m, t* *d, g*	

NOTE.—"Lŭng."—This word, which is found as a terminal in all the clan names, appears to be disused among the Kŭrnai generally, in what was probably its original sense. The Kroatŭngolŭng understand it as "father," in which sense it occurs in the language of their neighbours, the Bidwelli. Similarly the word Tŭtbŭkan, which I have translated elsewhere as "girl," is used by that tribe as signifying "daughter."

The table A shows us that marriage was forbidden in the division, but was occasionally permitted in the clan, as, for instance, between the Brabrolūng divisions *e*, *f*, *g*, or in a more limited manner between the Tatūngolūng divisions *s*, *t*, and the Bratauolūng divisions *p* and *q*. It was a general rule, also, that the inhabitants of the same river were considered too nearly related to intermarry, but we find an exception in the divisions *f* and *g*, which adjoin An inspection of the fourth and fifth columns will raise a strong presumption that the rule was that divisions mutually obtained wives from each other where right to intermarry existed But there are also apparent exceptions, which might be capable of explanation had I more knowledge. For instance, Gliŭnkong states that the men of his island did not like to travel far from the lakes in search of wives, while the women of his family ran off with men who came from distant places.

The divisions are only approximate.* There aie others

* In a communication lately received from the Rev F. A Hagenauer, he tells me of four "tribes" whose localities indicate them as belonging to the Bratauolūng (3) and Briakolūng (1) *Tarrawarracka*, living at Port Albert, Tarraville, and Alberton ; *Bellum-Bellum*, at Woodside, Prospect, and along the sea-coast by Reeves Lake ; *Woollum-Woollum*, at the Hill Top and along the Latrobe River as far as Rosedale. Lastly, *Mooma* and *Ngat-ban*, from Stratford to Lake Victoria I have, at present, no means of comparing these "tribes" with the divisions which I have recorded in the same localities, excepting the last, which are the equivalents of that group which, on the authority of "old Nanny," I have noted as "Bŭnjil Nŭllŭng" *Tarrawai racka—i e*, "the Tarra country" ("men" being understood)— and *Bellum-Bellum* may be synonyms or neighbours of Kŭt-wŭt and Drelin Woollum-Woollum fills a space in the boundary between the Bratauolūng and Briakolūng My informants as to the former were men of the Tatūngolūng and Briakolūng, whose knowledge of the divisions of that clan was principally gained by their remembrance of the matrimonial regulations subsisting. It would have been possible, ten years ago, to have obtained complete information—now it is impossible But what I have desired to show is the general distribution of the Kŭrnai tribe and the matrimonial arrangements of the various exogamous groups—*i.e.*, the divisions, not the complete enumeration of all the lesser groups.

THE TRIBE AN AGGREGATE OF CLANS. 231

which I have noted, but which have not been sufficiently confirmed on further inquiry. I have, therefore, only recorded those divisions upon which the evidence of the Kŭrnai agreed. Others may have been subdivisions—incipient divisions which, in time, might have attained an independent existence. For instance, the Kroatŭn inhabiting the western part of their territory, whose division I have, upon preponderance of evidence, named from Brt-britta (Jimmy's Point), are also called Ngrŭngit (entrance to the lakes). The two places are about three miles apart, and the inhabitants might be named from either Again, the members of the Būnjil Nŭllŭng division (*l*) are also claimed as belonging to Kūtbŭntaura (*k*). The evidence showed me that this was a subdivision of *k*, but of such dimensions as to require a separate notice.

It is remarkable that while the designations of the divisions of clans 1, 2, 4, 5 are all territorial, those of 3 are, with one exception, derived from men of note who were still living when the country was settled by the whites * For instance, Būnjil Kraura, who is said to have had control over the winds It was believed that he could call up the great west wind (gwera-ale, kraura) if he was not well supplied with food. He would make it so to rock the trees that the blackfellows could not climb in search of game. When duly propitiated, he would charm the storm to rest by tying a band of twisted stringy bark round his head and chanting this spell—" Kŭtbun-a-wang, kŭtbŭn-a-wang, kraura, &c , &c "

(Kūtbŭn=carry or wear ; wang=a band or string)

* As illustrating how the men of division *l* are spoken of as "Būnjil Nŭllŭng's mob," I may note the following :—King Charley, a leading man among the Kroatŭngolŭng, lately described himself to me as "Tūna wanjanata Brabrolūng, Kroatŭn Kŭrnai ngiu," or "I say that I take with me the Brabrolūng and Kroatŭn men " Tūna=to say or declare ; wanjana=to carry or hold ; Kŭrnai=men ; ngiu=I

Each of these divisions, therefore, received its designation from an *eponym*, who, however, changed with each generation.*

It is now possible to take a general view of the tribe. It mattered not that differences of dialect distinguished the clans most distant from each other. It mattered not that feuds arose between their members either through direct violence or through the belief in secret magic, nor that the hunting grounds of certain families were carefully defined, and, if necessary, protected as to certain food (*e g*, swans' eggs) and trespassers warned off;† these differences mattered little when placed face to face with the fact that they were all Kŭrnai. They spoke essentially the same language; they were connected by widely-ramifying relationships; the same corroboree-songs and dances which enlivened their social gatherings were brought by the mysterious Birraarks from cloudland—the bright home of their dead ancestors; and, finally, they were bound together by the great ceremonial of jerraeil, which embraced all Kŭrnai except the "men of the east," the Kroatŭngolūng. This great ceremony, which introduced the young of both sexes, as we may say, to membership in the community, is a commemoration—even a species of rude worship—by the tribe of the eponymous ancestors, Yeerŭng and Djeetgŭn.

---

* The position of authority of such a man as Bŭnjil Kraura (*see* Table A) might easily, under favourable conditions, become permanent and hereditary, as the Rev. J H Stähle says was the case with that of the head man of the Gournditch-mara tribe. (*See* Appendix F)

† For instance, in the case of Raymond Island, which I have already noted, and also Lake Kurlip, at the Snowy River, and other similar breeding places of the black swan, whose eggs were claimed by the Kŭrnai who claimed the several localities In the case of Lake Kurlip, the eggs are still claimed by a man and his nephew—the brother and son of Bŭbŭk, by right of inheritance. This is interesting, as showing the growth of the idea of personal possession of property and its transmission by inheritance, under the exceptionally favourable circumstances of the Kŭrnai.

It may be said to form the great central idea of Kŭrnai society, and that central idea is community of descent. Every descendant of Yeerŭng is a brother, every descendant of Djeetgŭn is a sister; all else are Brajerak, savage men, aliens to their blood, having no part in their descent, their ceremonies, or in the land, their birthright.

Looking at all this, we can perceive the extraordinary isolation of this tribe. Other tribes of Australia—spread over a vast extent of continent in New South Wales, and in Queensland, following the long course of the Murray and the Darling into South Australia—were bound together by the great class divisions of Eaglehawk and Crow. It mattered not from how distant localities two men might be, their speech might be unintelligible to each other, their status of family and their customs might have marked variance, yet the common bond of class and "totem" was a brotherhood which they would not fail to acknowledge.

But as regarded the Kŭrnai, this bond with any other tribe was, so far as we can learn, even from themselves, wanting. The Eaglehawk and Crow class divisions of their neighbours, the dreaded Brajerak of the Maneroo tableland, or of even their still nearer neighbours, the jungle Bidwelli, were, so far as I can learn, utterly unknown to them; and any former connection with the Eaglehawk class can only be suspected from the admiration with which they regard this bird,* and the part which his plumage plays in their magic ceremonies.

They were completely isolated, and it may be affirmed, with great probability of truth, that thus protected against external influences, many of the marked features of their domestic and social conditions had an original development. Change is inherent to human affairs; history and our own

* *Aquila audax.*

experience teach us that the social condition of no community remains for any time absolutely the same. We know well that in those portions of a country where there is the greatest facility of communication with surrounding districts, the greatest local changes occur. On the contrary, in those portions of a country where access to and from other localities is difficult, we know well that the social conditions change more slowly, and we call such places "old-fashioned."

Thus, in a district like Gippsland, cut off by the physical features of the country from facile intercourse with the remainder of Australia, we should naturally expect to find the social conditions of the people "old-fashioned" A continuance of this isolation throughout long periods of time would tend to differentiate their customs from those of their co-descendants of a common stock; and this would take place in two directions. There would be the social conditions of the Kŭrnai resulting from the slow evolution of new conditions within their own society; and there would be a similar, but probably more rapid, evolution of the social conditions of their co-descendants elsewhere in less isolation These lines of change would be divergent. It is impossible to conceive that the forces acting upon each social organization could be so similar that at any given period of time the progress of each society should be parallel to that of the other

Such would, I think, be the *à priori* conclusions, but they are not borne out by a consideration of the facts before us. The family of the Kŭrnai is a far advance upon that of other Australian tribes; for example, the Kamilaroi. In it has been established a strongly-marked form of the Syndyasmian, or pairing family; there is the power of selection by the woman of her husband, and there is descent through the father, although as yet incompletely recognized.

THE TRIBE AN AGGREGATE OF CLANS

In face of such facts, which are only an example of others which I might instance, we cannot call the Kŭrnai "old-fashioned," but must regard them rather as "new-fashioned." Where we find such a surprising social advance in a tribe which has existed in such isolation, we must, I think, believe that the forces which produced this advance acted from within and not from without.

It may be held, probably with truth, that Gippsland was colonized in the first instance by a family, or by several families, forming a community, who, coming from the east, the north, or the west, forced the natural barriers of the country. The terms of kinship and affinity of the Kŭrnai imply that at one time they were in that family condition in which a group of brothers had their wives in common, or a group of sisters their husbands in common This group being, therefore, exogamous, would consist of two classes or "totems," and we may well suspect that their class—or totem—names were those of the birds Yeerŭng and Djeetgŭn That we have not yet met with these as existing classes or totems in other tribes amounts to very little It could only amount to something if all the class and totem names of all the tribes were known, and their absence in that case from those of any tribe might be satisfactorily explained, by showing that in some tribes certain totems appear to have become extinct *

If we may assume that Yeerŭng and Djeetgŭn were the class or totem names of the male and female members of the original Kŭrnai stocking Gippsland, the remaining

---

* [Even if all the totems of all the tribes were known to us, and we did not find Yeerŭng and Djeetgŭn among them, I do not think the absence of those totems would be of any great moment As far as I know, most of the totems are animals whose habitat is the locality occupied by the tribe using them If a tribe migrate to a country in which their totem is not found, they will, in all probability, take as their totem some other animal which is a native of the place —L F]

steps might be pointed out with more or less probability of truth.

A study of the classified terms which have been collected by Mr. Fison and myself, denoting the inter-sexual relations of the various Australian tribes, and of the class names governing marriage and descent, has shown what might have been à priori expected—namely, that there are no two systems which are precisely alike. Taking one in which the Turanian system is most strongly marked, the remainder can be placed in a series, of which some will come before, and some after, that taken as a reference. That of the Kŭrnai would be found to stand early in the series.*

I now give, in Table B, the terms used by the Kurnai to define the degrees of kinship and affinity.

TABLE B

Kŭrnai Terms.	English Equivalents
Wehntwin	- Father's father, father's father's brother.
Wehntjŭn	- Father's sister.
Nallŭng	- Father's mother, f m's brother, f m. sister

---

* I make use of the terms employed by Dr. Morgan ("Ancient Society," p 27), as they precisely define that which I desire to illustrate, and have been, in fact, framed to meet analogous conditions met with elsewhere. I extract the following definitions :—

1. *The Consanguine Family*, founded upon the intermarriage of brothers and sisters in groups It created the Malayan system of consanguinity.

2 *The Punaluan Family*, founded upon the intermarriage of several brothers to each other's wives in a group (or *vice versa*) It created the Turanian system of consanguinity.

3. *The Syndyasmian Family*, founded upon the pairing of a male and female, but without exclusive cohabitation.

It was Dr. Morgan who first clearly systematized the evidence upon which the above terms have been based In the subsequent part of this work I have found it convenient to use the terms, "Undivided commune," as representing the Consanguine Family; "Segmented exogamous commune," as representing the Punaluan Family ; and I used the terms "Individual Family" and "Pairing Family" as synonyms.

TERMS OF KINSHIP AND AFFINITY

Kŭrnai Terms.	English Equivalents.
Nakŭn	Mother's father, m f brother, m f sister
Kŭkŭn	Mother's mother, m m brother, m. m sister

All the above terms also imply the reciprocals, as *son's son*, &c

Mŭngan	Father, f brother, mother's sister's husband.
Yŭkan	Mother, m sister, father's brother's wife
Mŭmmŭng	Father's sister, mother's brother's wife
Babŭk	Mother's brother, father's sister's husband
Tŭndŭng	Elder brother, father's brother's son, father's sister's son, mother's brother's son, mother's sister's son, wife's sister's husband, husband's sister's husband
Bramŭng	Younger brother, father's brother's son, father's sister's son, mother's brother's son, mother's sister's son, wife's sister's husband, husband's sister's husband
Baŭ-ŭng	Elder sister, father's brother's daughter, father's sister's daughter, mother's brother's daughter, mother's sister's daughter, wife's brother's wife, husband's brother's wife
Lŭndŭk	Younger sister, father's brother's daughter, father's sister's daughter, mother's brother's daughter, mother's sister's daughter, wife's brother's wife, husband's brother's wife
Maian	Wife, wife's sister, husband's sister
Jambi	Wife's brother (Bennung = Jambi)
Bra	Husband, husband's brother
Lĭt	Child, brother's child (male speaking), sister's child
Bengŭn	Brother's child (female speaking)
Bendŭk	Son's wife, husband's father, husband's mother
Ngaribil	Daughter's husband (male speaking), wife's father
Que-a-bŭn	Daughter's husband (female speaking)

Note —The fraternal terms are always used according to the respective ages of the persons concerned.

In order to show what is the theoretical form of family amongst these savages, I shall discuss those terms which, it seems to me, most fully disclose it.

The theoretical form of the Kurnai family

Kŭrnai Term.	Indicates English Equivalents.]
1. Wehntwin	Paternal grandfather, grandfather's brother
2 Nallŭng	Paternal grandmother, grandmother's sister and brother
3 Wehntjŭn	Paternal grandfather's sister
4. Nakŭn	Maternal grandfather, grandfather's brother and sister
5 Kŭkŭn	Maternal grandmother, grandmother's brother and sister.

These terms are reciprocal between grand ancestors and grandchildren. We may consider this group under two aspects. First, that in which, according to the Kamilaroi system, marriage would take place between the children of brother and sister; second, that in which no intermarriage would necessarily take place between them. Each case would, I conceive, be equally Turanian. In the first case, there would be no distinction drawn between the grand relations of the Turanian and of the Malayan system. In the second case there would be a distinction; for, while the husband, husband's brother, mother, and mother's sister form one complete group, having their children in common— the father's sister on the one side, and the mother's brother on the other side—would be units of two analogous families; they would not stand in the parental relation to the children of the first group; and these distinctions would be carried out into the grand relations. Applying these considerations to the Kŭrnai grand ancestral relations, I perceive that they partially conform to the second case. A distinction is evident between the relations of the grandfather's sister and the grandchildren, but there is no corresponding distinction between the relations of the grandmother's brother and the grandchildren. On the female side of the paternal grand ancestors, the terms are such as would conform to the second system I have pointed out. On the female side of the paternal grand ancestors, the terms conform to the requirements of the Kamilaroi system, while, on the male side, they conform to the requirements of the other system, which I have pointed out as possible. The Kamilaroi system does not, I think, explain the difference. The maternal grand relations of the above group are such as would be common to the Turanian (Kamilaroi) and Malayan systems. We may, perhaps, have, in the terms applying to the paternal grand aunt and the grandchildren, a survival of previous relations under the Malayan system.

THEORETICAL FORM OF KŪRNAI FAMILY.

Kŭrnai Term.		Indicates English Equivalents.
6 Mŭngan	-	Father, father's brother.
7. Yŭkan	-	Mother, mother's sister.
8 Mŭmmŭng		Father's sister
9 Babŭk	-	Mother's brother
10 Lĭt -	-	Child, brother's child (male speaking), sister's child.
11 Bengŭn	-	Brother's child (female speaking)

We have, in these terms, the equivalent group to that of the grand ancestors in their relations to their children. We have here again the group, consisting of two brothers, theoretically the husbands of each other's wives, and the parents of each other's children, and a father's sister and a mother's brother who are units of two analogous but distinct families. In the relations of the first and second generations the same peculiarity appears that I have pointed out in respect to the grand ancestors, but it is found here in an expanded form. The parental relation does not exist between the children and their father's sister, nor between the children and their mother's brother, as regards the children; he is their babŭk, not their mŭngan, but they are still his lĭt. This suggests to me that the parental relations ceased sooner in the father's sister than in the mother's brother. It may be well to consider whether any reason can be assigned for this, which would, indeed, indicate a passage from the Malayan to the Turanian system—from the Consanguine to the Punaluan families of Dr. Morgan It is, I think, probable that changes which have taken place in the constitution of the family have affected a limitation as regarded the woman rather than the man. This tendency is evident in the present status of the Kŭrnai, in which the woman is bound to fidelity under penalties, but the man is not The change in language would slowly follow the change in custom; and, if the limitation was against the woman rather than against her husband, the change would be complete in respect to her and her relatives before it would affect fully the man and his relatives.

Thus, of the brother and sister, the latter would soonest cease to be, in language as in fact, the *mother* of her brother's children; she would be their *aunt*. The reciprocal terms would follow.

Kŭrnai Term.		*Indicates English Equivalents.*
12 Tŭndŭng	- Elder brother	⎫ Paternal and maternal cousins, hus-
13 Bramŭng	- Younger brother	⎪ band's brother's wife, husband's
14 Bau-ŭng	- Elder sister	⎬ sister's husband, wife's brother's
15. Lŭndŭk	- Younger sister	⎭ wife, wife's sister's husband.

The inter-relations of this group are, I think, strictly Malayan in theory, for they are all regarded as brothers and sisters to each other. This is further carried out in their relations towards each other's children, except when they stand in the relation of Mŭmmūng (8), and Babŭk (9). It is highly significant that in these instances, as in others which may be perceived on examining the Table B, the secondary relations, if I may so term them, are such as should be indicated logically by the primary terms themselves. It lends much strength to the belief that they have arisen at first through adaptation of language to existing relationships, and not as mere terms of personal address.

For comparison I give in Table C the principal Kŭrnai terms, together with analogous ones used by two far-distant tribes. The comparative simplicity of the former will be apparent.

THEORETICAL FORM OF KŪRNAI FAMILY

TABLE C.

Terms in English	Kurnai Tribe, Gippsland, Victoria	Turra Tribe, Yorke's Peninsula, S A	Kamilaroi, Kunopia, N S W
Father	mŭngan	ishalee	binan
Father's brother	mŭngan	ishana	wŭrŭmai
Mother	yŭkan	ishee	ŭmbathi
Mother's sister	yŭkan	angira	ŭmbathi
Wife	maian	gertŭ	goleed
Wife's sister	maian	ishibŭ	ŭngeena
Husband	bra	uba	goleed
Husband's brother	bra	dŭnna	goleed
Brother (elder)	tŭndŭng	yŭnga	tiathi
Sister (elder)	bau-ŭng	yakana	bŭrrian
Wife's sister's husband	tŭndŭng	yŭnga	diarthy
Wife's brother's wife	bau-ŭng	arna	boarthy
Husband's sister's husband	tŭndŭng	arna	diarthy
Husband's brother's wife	bau ŭng	ishibŭ	boarthy
Father's brother's son	tŭndŭng	—	tichandi
Father's brother's daughter	bau-ŭng	—	bŭchandi
Mother's sister's son	tŭndŭng	mangŭnie	tichandi
Mother's sister's daughter	bau-ŭng	mangŭnie	bŭchandi
Child	lĭt	yŭngana	kye
Brother's child (male speaking)	lĭt	wongara	wŭrŭmingi (boy) gnamŭa (girl)
Sister's child (female speaking)	lĭt	wongara	gŭnŭngarthy (boy) cŭrrŭgandi (girl)

Note —I have in the above only used the elder fraternal terms In the list compiled for me by the Rev Julius Kühn (Turra tribe), the following equivalents occur:—Ishana = anilbie ; dŭnna = yŭnga dŭnna ; yŭnga = bangyarie, arna ; ishibŭ = yakana ; mangŭnie = bangya ; wongara = yŭngana, mangana. Bangya = younger brother or younger sister For the terms of the Kunopia tribe I am indebted to Mr C E Doyle, of Werrina, N S W

The Tŭrra tribe is divided into two primary classes —Wiltŭ (eaglehawk) and Mŭltŭ (seal) There are numerous sub-classes (totems). These classes are exogamous, and the children follow the father's class There is individual marriage Consent of the woman's parents is necessary before marriage ; if this is refused, the pair occasionally elope Wives were also obtained by gift, exchange, or capture A female captive belonged to the captor, subject to recovery by her relatives in an arranged fight If unsuccessful, they attempted to capture some other woman in her place. The Kŭnopia tribe is one of those speaking the Kamilaroi language. Mr C. E Doyle tells me that it has the class divisions and totems fully developed. Group marriage is the rule on an extended scale. For instance, "a Hippi can take any Kubbath as his wife and keep her, and his right to her will not be questioned by her family. The same rule, of course, applies to all other names, such as Kumbo, Kubbi, &c." The three systems tabulated belong to three representative tribes—Kŭnopia, having group marriage; Kŭrnai, having individual marriage (the pairing family); and the Tŭrra tribe, standing between the two.

The terms which I have discussed suggest a family in which a group of brothers had their wives in common, or in which a group of sisters had their husbands in common, but in which it did not perhaps necessarily follow that the brother's children were the husbands and wives of the sister's children. They also, I think, strongly suggest a more archaic form of family, in which marriage was consanguine. We may perceive that language has slowly adapted itself to social changes.

This, then, may be said to be the theoretical family of the Kŭrnai. What the real family is I now propose to show by shortly recapitulating my previous statements

<small>The actual form of the Kurnai family.</small> The family of the Kŭrnai is strongly Syndyasmian, or pairing, but it is not completely so The man is not limited to one wife, although that number is, as a fact, the rule. But he jealously keeps his wife or wives to himself. The marriage is by consent of the woman, and the children follow descent—if boys, through the father's, if girls, through the mother's class. Marriage is forbidden in the division. It seems to me probable that the passage through the various stages of family indicated by the survival of terms designating inter-sexual relations, which no longer fit the actual relations, has been more rapid than analogous changes which we may suppose to have taken place in other tribes as to which we have data; and I cannot but suspect that the Kŭrnai probably branched off from the parent stock when that stock was in an early stage of the Punaluan family.

The Kŭrnai having, then, become completely isolated, had a peculiar development of social system, while the other Australian tribes mutually reacted more or less upon each other In many tribes, as among the Kamilaroi, the Punaluan family obtained an extraordinary development which is stereotyped in their language, while it may be supposed that among the Kŭrnai the passage through that state was more rapid into the Pairing family.

When an individual of the Kŭrnai tribe died, the relatives rolled the corpse up in an opossum rug, enclosed it in a sheet of bark, and corded it tightly. A hut was built over it, and in this the bereaved and mourning relatives and friends collected The corpse lay in the centre, and as many of the mourners as could manage to find room lay on the ground with their heads upon the ghastly pillow. There they lay lamenting their loss. They would cry, "Why did you go? Why did you leave us?" Now and then the grief would be intensified by the wife uttering an ear-piercing wail—"Penning i tŭrn!" (my spouse is dead); or the mother—"Lit i tŭrn!" (my child is dead) All the others would join in, using the proper term of relationship; and they would cut and gash themselves with sharp instruments, until their heads and bodies streamed with blood. This bitter wailing and weeping would continue all night; the less closely related persons and the friends alone rousing themselves to eat, until the following day. This would go on for two or three days, when the corpse would be unrolled for the survivors to look at and renew their grief. If by this time the hair had become loose, it would be carefully plucked off the whole body and preserved by the father, mother, or sisters in small bags of opossum skin. They then again rolled up the body, and it was not opened until it was so far decomposed that the survivors

Death and funeral ceremonies.

could anoint themselves with "oil" which had exuded from it* The only explanation which the Kŭrnai can give me of this horrible custom is, as they say, "to make them remember their relative or friend" Sometimes the body would be opened, the intestines removed and buried, in order that the corpse might dry more rapidly The ghastly relique, in its bark cerements, was carried with the family in its migrations, and was the special charge of the father and mother, of the wife, or of other near relatives or connections. Finally, the body having, after years, become merely a bag of bones, would be buried, or put into some hollow tree. Sometimes the father or mother carried the lower jaw of the deceased as a memento

<small>Belief in the protective power of the dead hand</small>

The most remarkable custom in connection with the dead was that of the "Brett" or hand Soon after death the hand, or both the hands, were cut off, wrapped in grass, and dried. A string of twisted opossum hair was attached so that it could be hung round the neck and worn in contact with the bare skin under the left arm. It was carried by the parent or child, brother or sister The belief of the Kŭrnai was, and even, I think, still in many cases is that such a hand on the approach of an enemy would pinch, or push the wearer. The signal being given, the hand would be taken from the neck and suspended in front of the face; the string being held between the finger and thumb The person would then say, "Which way are they coming?"† If the hand remained at rest, the question would be again put, but now facing another point of the horizon, and so on. The response was by the hand

---

* This horrible anointing is practised at Drummond Island, also in the Kingsmill group

† In one case "Mūnjū! Mūnjū! Wŭnman? Mūnjū! tūnamŭn nganjū—brappŭrna ma banja!" Mūnjū=there, wŭnman=where, tūnamŭn =speak to, nganjū=me, brappŭrna = to throw, ma=to, ban=wild dog; or "Speak! Where are they? Or I throw you to the wild dogs"

vibrating in some direction, and it was thence that the danger was supposed to be approaching. My informants tell me that the vibrations were often so violent that the hand would almost "come over on to the holder."

From what I have said as to the community in food, the community in the right to hunt (with a narrow limitation), and from the community in personal property, which is evidenced by the rapidity with which clothes and other articles pass from member to member of the group, we should expect to find that the personal property of the deceased might become the property of his kin. It is difficult to collect evidence on this head In the first place, the personality is very limited in extent, and in reality can only include weapons, implements, and garments. But the garments, and very often the weapons and implements of the deceased, were rolled up with his corpse or buried, from a reluctance on the part of his relatives to have constantly before them, after the funeral ceremonies, anything which might recall his loss and their grief.* In questioning several of the Kŭrnai as to what might be done in case a valuable tomahawk were left, it was said that the following order of succession might be observed, in the event of its not being buried with him:—It would go to the father, elder brother, younger brother, paternal grandfather, in the order stated, supposing all of the above series to be living; the father inheriting before the elder brother, and so on Whether such a case has happened is not within my knowledge, but the statement shows that, in the opinion of the Kŭrnai, inheritance would be in the male line; and this is in accordance with the fact that descent follows the father's class so far as boys are concerned.

Inheritance.

---

* It seems difficult to reconcile this feeling with the practice of carrying the deceased about with them.

Ancestral spirits supposed to visit the Kŭrnai in dreams

The deceased was supposed by the Kŭrnai to pass to the clouds, as a spirit. But he did not necessarily remain there, for male and female spirits are also believed to wander about in the country which they inhabited in the flesh, and may be properly spoken of as ghosts.

They are believed to be able still to communicate with the living, through persons whom they have initiated into the secrets of spirit land; of these people, called birraark, I shall speak more fully later on. They are also believed to occasionally communicate with their descendants in dreams.* These "ghosts" may be said to be the ancestors of those with whom they communicate and, to be, therefore, well disposed to them; but there are other "ghosts" which are believed to be evil disposed, which are thought to prowl about and to endeavour to capture the Kŭrnai, and we may well regard those as representing the deceased enemies who in the flesh also prowled about intent on evil.

A Tatŭngolŭng man related to me that when, as a child, sleeping in the camp with his parents, he was woke by the outcries of his father, and, starting up, found him partly out of the camp on his back kicking, while his wife clutched him by the shoulders. His father said that, while lying by the fire, a "Mrart" came up with a bag, and tried to pull him out of the camp by the foot. That he then cried out, and his wife held him fast by the shoulders, and the "Mrart" vanished.

Tūlaba states that his "other father," Brŭthen Mŭnji, occasionally visits him when asleep, and communicates to him charms (songs) against sickness and other evils. He states, further, that if he could remember all his father teaches him in sleep, he should be a mŭlla mŭllŭng (doctor). One charm which he has thus learned, and which I have heard him use to cure pain in the chest, by singing monotonously over the sick person, runs thus:—"Tūndŭnga Brewinda nŭndū ŭnga ūgarinda mri mŭrriwŭnda;" or, freely translated—"Oh

---

* Since this essay was written, the Rev. H. Stähle, of the Lake Condah Mission, Victoria, informed me, in answer to a query as to the tribe Maia, that "they believe the spirit of the deceased father, or grandfather, occasionally visited his descendants in dreams, and imparted to them charms (songs) against disease or witchcraft."

ANCESTRAL SPIRITS. 247

tŭndŭng! I believe Brewin has hooked me with the eye of his throwing-stick "*

A Kŭrnai told me that, when gathering wild cattle for a settler near the Mitchell River, he dreamed one night that two "Mrarts" were standing by his fire They were about to speak to him, or he to them (I now forget which), when he woke They had vanished, but on looking at the spot where they had stood he perceived a "Būlk," which he kept and valued much †

Quite lately, when Tankowillŭn and Tūrl-bŭrn were walking, after nightfall, past a fenced-in garden, they were much alarmed by observing what seemed to them to be a fiery eye intently watching them between two of the palings Believing that a "Mrart" was there hidden on the watch, they became afraid, and ran away to their camp

Mr C J Du Vè, a gentleman of much experience with the aborigines, tells me that, in the year 1860, a Maneroo blackfellow died when living with him The day before he died, having been ill some time, he said that, in the night, his father, his father's friend, and a female spirit he could not recognize, had come to him and said that he would die next day, and that they would wait for him Mr Du Vè adds that, although previously the Christian belief had been explained to this man, it had at that time entirely faded, and that he had gone back to the belief of his childhood ‡

In the first instances which I have given there can be no doubt that the *nightmare* under which the Tatūngolūng man suffered, and the dreams which Tūlaba and the other Kŭrnai had, were regarded as realities. I give the last example as showing a similar belief in a Brajerak, but I do not rely upon the evidence, as he might have unconsciously been influenced by ideas imbibed from Christian teaching.

Such being the belief held by the Kŭrnai as to the

---

* Tūndŭng, supposed to be a substance like frayed stringybark, which the doctor sometimes professes to extract and exhibits as the cause of the disease; Brewin = an evil spirit; nŭndŭ ŭnga = to believe or think; ugarinda = to hook or catch; mri = eye; mŭrrawŭn = throwing-stick. The throwing-stick is supposed to have magical properties

† For Būlk, *see* p 251.

‡ [I could give many similar instances which have come within my own knowledge among the Fijians; and, strange to say, the dying man, in all these cases, kept his appointment with the ghosts to the very day —L F]

248   THE KŬRNAI.

White men thought to be ghosts

existence after death, it is not surprising that, when they first saw white men wandering in the bush, they regarded them as "ghosts" This belief follows naturally upon the other, and is universal all over Australia.

A Brabrolūng told me that when, as a little boy, near the Tambo River, he saw a white man for the first time, he felt sure that it was a "Mrart," and he ran away. He said he was sure it was a "Mrart," partly from its strange appearance, and partly because it was "so very pale"

In Central Australia I have, when exploring, frequently been greeted with cries of "Kūchi!" when coming suddenly upon the natives It was occasionally varied to "Pirri-Wirri Kūchi" The former was explained, by my own blackboy, as meaning "Debbil-debbil," and the latter, "Walk-about debbil-debbil"—in other words, "ghost," or "wandering ghost"

Belief in the ngurrung mri.

Before the white men entered Gippsland, vague rumours of their existence had passed from tribe to tribe. "Lewin" had described them with the exaggeration natural to rumour. The strange sight of ships sailing by the shore had been a wonder to the Kŭrnai; and the "Lo-an," when he arrived, was recognized as a "Mrart"—a "Yamboginni" —a ghost—an apparition of the dead. When Tūlaba described to me how, when the Kŭrnai first beheld white men, and exclaimed, "Lo-an! Lo-an!" I always observed that he looked down, and moved his head uneasily from side to side, as one would do who expected a sudden blow. On inquiry I have learned that the belief was general that the white man possessed supernatural powers in his eye. He was supposed by a glance to be able to suddenly draw together the two banks of a river, and cause them to meet, or instantly to flash death to the beholder. This was called "Ngŭrrung-mri,"† meaning "Sinew-eye;" and I have, I think, also heard it called "Mlang-mri," or "lightning-

† Ngŭrrŭng = sinew, mlang = lightning.

eye." Hence it was that, when white men were seen near, the Kŭrnai would make off, crying to each other, "Don't look! don't look! or he will kill you!" I think we may see, in this curious belief, a distorted account of the bridging of rivers, and a more direct account of the act of taking aim and discharging a firearm.

Independently of the reluctance to name the dead,—which we may connect with the belief that they might be wandering near unseen, there is also a strong feeling against naming the dead, or seeing anything belonging to them, lest the sorrow should be again revived. This may seem strange, but I am convinced that it is a true reason. Shallow as are the feelings of the aborigines, they are intense while they last; and they may be easily roused again in all their former strength.

Reluctance to name the dead

Bŭnbra (otherwise Jet-bolan = liar), a Tatŭngolŭng man, lost a daughter some years back Not long ago he suddenly thought of her, tears coursed down his face in streams, and he became quite frantic with grief Those who saw him quite believed that he had only just learned the news, until another blackfellow said, "Oh! that fellow dead boy long ago!"

When cruising about on the Gippsland lakes some years ago with a crew of Kŭrnai, searching for the bodies of two murdered aborigines, I heard two of my men discussing where we could camp; and one, on mentioning a place, said, speaking his own language, that there was "le-en nobler"* I said, "There is no nobler there" He then said in English, "Oh! I meant water" On inquiry, I learned that a man named Yan (water) had died shortly before, and that, not liking to use that word, they had to invent a new one †

Quite lately, I told some Kŭrnai that I had "Lewin" (news) from "a friend, from Windigerwŭt" for them One said, "Oh! you must

---

* Le-en = good; nobler = spirituous liquor.

† [This is a common occurrence in many South Sea Island tribes. At some of the islands, if a very great chief have for his name a word of common use, or even if such a word be only part of his name, the word may be utterly blotted out of the language on his death —L F]

not call him that " I said, " Why not ? it is his name " He replied, "But his Babŭk (mother's brother) of that name is dead, and it would make his friends very sad to hear his name spoken "

Beliefs as to disease

It is not difficult to see how, among savages, who have no knowledge of the real causes of diseases which are the common lot of humanity, the very suspicion even of such a thing as death from disease should be unknown Death by accident they can imagine; death by violence they can imagine; but I question if they can, in their savage condition, imagine death by mere disease. Rheumatism is believed to be produced by the machinations of some enemy

Seeing a Tatŭngolŭng very lame, I asked him what was the matter ? He said, "Some fellow has put *bottle* in my foot" I asked him to let me see it I found he was probably suffering from acute rheumatism. He explained that some enemy must have found his foot track, and have buried in it a piece of broken bottle The magic influence, he believed, caused it to enter his foot

When following down Cooper's Creek in search of Burke's party, we were followed one day by a large number of blackfellows, who were much interested in looking at and measuring the footprints of the horses and camels My blackboy, from the Darling River, rode up to me, with the utmost alarm exhibited in his face, and exclaimed, "Look at those wild blackfellows !" I said, "Well, they are all right " He replied, "I am sure those fellows are putting poison in my footsteps !"

Phthisis, pneumonia, bowel complaints, and insanity are supposed to be produced by an evil spirit—Brewin—"who is like the wind," and who, entering his victims, can only be expelled by suitable incantations. I have mentioned how Tūlaba is possessed of a chaunt to cure chest disease. Another Kŭrnai, who is said to be a great mŭlla mŭllŭng, professes to cure, among other diseases, such ones as colic.

Some years ago, his old father was ill of colic The mŭlla mŭllŭng laid him on his face and chaunted his charm over him. When tired of this, he varied his performance by bawling out every injurious epithet he "could lay his tongue to" against Brewin In order that Brewin might be sure to hear this, he shouted in that direction in which Brewin was supposed to have entered After a time the old man was better. Brewin had been expelled.

Thus the belief arises that death occurs only from accident, open violence, or secret magic; and, naturally, that the latter can only be met by counter-charms. At p. 216 I have given an instance in the case of the "Kin of Barney v. Bŭnbra," where death was believed to have been occasioned by magic. Every individual, although doubtful of his own magic powers, has no doubt about the possible powers of any other person. If the individual himself fails, he supposes that he is "not strong enough." There is scarcely a Kŭrnai of those who are not Christianized who does not carry about with him a būlk—a rounded, generally black, pebble * It is supposed to be of general magic power. For instance, if buried together with the excreta of any person, that person receives the magic "būlk" in his intestines and dies. The touch of it is supposed to be highly injurious to any one but the owner. I have seen girls or women greatly terrified when I have offered to place one of these būlk in their hands.

The small leg bone of the kangaroo is also held to possess great power. When pointed at a sleeping person, it is supposed to cause sickness and death.

Similarly it is supposed that if the hair of a person is tied on the end of the throwing-stick, together with the feathers of the eaglehawk, and roasted before the fire with some kangaroo fat, the person to whom it belonged will pine away and die.

_{Various forms of magic.}

* It is believed that a būlk has the power of motion For instance, during the writing of this essay, Tankowillŭn told me that he and Tŭl-bŭrn had, the evening before, seen a būlk, in the shape of a bright spark of fire, cross the roof of a house and disappear on the other side. Also that they ran round to catch it, but it had vanished

From all this we may infer the belief to be that some secret influence passes from the magic substance to the victim. But the belief extends beyond this; the magic influence may, they suppose, be communicated from the magic substance to some other substance, for instance, a throwing-stick, a spear, a club, or any other weapon.

Charley Rivers, a Tatūngolūng, once explained to me how he got a wound on his head which would not heal, and how he was cured of it. Some Melbourne blackfellow (Brajerak) had put some substance like būlk in a bag containing a club of Charley Rivers'. Being drunk, the latter wanted to chastise his wife, but, in flourishing his club, hit his own head and cut it open. The magic from the Brajerak būlk had gone into the club, and thence went into anything it hit His wound therefore became so bad that the English doctors could not cure it. One of the Kŭrnai, however, who was a very strong mŭlla mŭllŭng, cured it by singing over and by sucking it He extracted the būlk from the wound in the shape of something which looked exactly like a glass marble

Barn.

Not only, therefore, is death in some cases attributed to the acts of a sorcerer, who may be any man they meet, but death is also believed to occur by a combination of sorcery and violence. Such a proceeding is that known as Barn.*

Some three or four years ago, some Brabrolūng Kŭrnai had a grudge against Būnda-wal, a Tatūngolūng They determined to try barn They chose a tall He-oak, lopped it to a point, drew the outline of a man (Yamboginni = apparition) on the ground, so that the tree grew out of his chest; cleared the ground of all rubbish for some distance round—a sort of magic circle—and were then ready. They stripped, smeared themselves with charcoal and grease, and chaunted incessantly a magic charm. This went on for several days, as I am informed, but without effect They, at last, decided that they "were not strong enough" The effect which they expected was that the victim, wherever he might be, should rise and walk to them in a trance—"like it

---

* Named from the barn—the casuarina. Two varieties occur—one, *C. suberosa*, having an erect, and the other, *C. quadrivalvis*, a pendent habit. The former is locally known as He-oak, the latter as She-oak. The He-oak is barn

sleep " On entering the magic circle, the Bŭnjil barn are supposed to throw pieces of the He-oak wood at him. He is believed then to fall, and the magicians are supposed to cut out his tongue and send him home to die

Brūthen Mŭnji, the "other father" of Tūlaba, is said to have been the last victim recorded of this form of magic Tūlaba has repeated to me his counter-charm, but I cannot remember if he obtained it in a dream It runs :—" Nūmba jellŭng barnda," or, freely translated, "Never the sharp barn (shall catch me) " This is incessantly repeated in a monotonous chaunt

There can, I think, be little doubt that, given the belief in the magic powers of the individual and in his survival as a "ghost," another belief would follow—namely, that those of the deceased, who in life were possessed of highly magical powers, might as ghosts exert their evil influence upon their enemies. But I have no direct evidence to give in support of this suggestion.

I have mentioned men called Birraark,* who professed to have communion with ghosts Unfortunately, the last Birraark died long before I knew the Kŭrnai. He was killed in the early contests with the whites.

The Kŭrnai tell me that a Birraark was supposed to be initiated by the "Mrarts" when they met him wandering in the bush. In order that they should have power over him, he must, at the time, have a certain bone ornament called gūmbert, thin, and pointed at each end, passed through the perforated septum of his nose. By this they were supposed to hold and convey him to the clouds—some

---

* It is most interesting to note how widespread has been this belief. Among the Gournditch-mara of Western Victoria, according to the Rev. J H Stähle, there were the precise analogues of the Birraarks The Rev. Julius Kühn, of Boorkooyanna, S A , tells me of the Tŭrra tribe, "There were 'Gūrildris,' men who professed to learn corroboree songs and dances from departed spirits They also professed to learn songs for the dead, which were sung to make happy the departed who were gone to another country to live for ever, but to return no more "

254   THE KŪRNAI.

say up a rope—and there initiate him. On returning to earth he was a Birraark.

It was believed that he learned from the ghosts the songs and dances which he taught the Kŭrnai; and it was from the ghosts that he obtained replies to questions concerning events passing at a distance, or yet to happen, which might be of interest or of moment to his tribe One of the Tatūngolūng told me that he had been present at an invocation of the ghosts, which bears a strange resemblance to a modern spirit *séance*:—

> On a certain evening, at dusk, the Birraark commenced his invocation The audience were collected, and silence was kept. The fires were let go down The Birraark uttered the cry "Coo-ee" at intervals At length a distant reply was heard, and shortly afterwards the sound as of persons jumping on the ground in succession This was supposed to be the spirit "Baukan," followed by the ghosts A voice was then heard in the gloom, asking, in a strange intonation, "What is wanted?" Questions were put by the Birraark, and replies given At the termination of the *séance*, the spirit voice said, "We are going" Finally, the Birraark was found in the top of an almost inaccessible tree, apparently asleep It was alleged that the ghosts had transported him there at their departure At this *séance* the questions put related to individuals of the group who were absent, and to the suspected movements of the hostile Brajerak

The spirits Brewin, Bullum-dut, Baukan

I have already mentioned Brewin, who may be said to be an evil spirit. The Kŭrnai speak of two other spirits—Būllūm-dūt and Baukan. Of the Mrarts (ghosts) the Kŭrnai speak with some precision; of Brewin they speak with somewhat less certainty; but of Būllūmdūt and Baukan little can be learned I can only say that their qualities, so far as I can ascertain, are negative. They are not so bad as Brewin. They are not very powerful, and are, consequently, not much feared. The teachings of the missionaries have, to a certain extent I suspect, connected the idea of the Deity with Būllūmdūt and Baukan. But in the minds of the Kŭrnai, these three spirits—Brewin,

Būllūmdūt, and Baukan—are, at the most, but dim and indistinct figures.*

Being desirous of learning what Brewin, Būllūmdūt, and Baukan were supposed by the Kŭrnai to be, I questioned two of the most intelligent men Both were Tatūngolūng—one, a member of the Church of England, the other, an intelligent savage and a scamp I said, "What is Brewin?" They consulted, and after a few minutes one of them said, "We think that he is Jesus Christ" I said, "Well, I think you had better consult again; I do not think your Catechism teaches you that" They then consulted somewhat longer, when he said, "We have talked about it, and we think it must be the devil"†

The usual charges which are made against the Australian aborigines generally, also lie against the Kŭrnai The counts of the indictment may be said to be—Superstition, untruthfulness, selfishness, ingratitude, immorality, cruelty, and finally, disregard of human life.

Character and intelligence of the Kurnai.

It should not surprise us that the Kŭrnai is superstitious. His belief that the dead survived as a ghost, in a form usually invisible, when taken in connection with the knowledge that during life his enemy was probably trying to destroy him by magic, is seen to produce naturally a belief that that enemy, when a ghost, may have power to work destruction, against which he is powerless. Nor is it strange that he should accept the statements of the Birraark, or

* The term Būllūm implies a duality, and I have heard it applied to Baukan, as Būllūmbaukan I may here note that the Kŭrnai numerals are Kūtūpan=one, Būlūman=two; three is Būlūman bata Kūtūk; four, Būlūman bata Būlūm

† [I expect to see this fact quoted by-and-by as a triumphant proof of the utter incapacity of savages in general to understand Christian teaching At least, I have seen that general incapacity asserted on no better grounds. Compare these two Kŭrnai with a young man, a native of Brooklyn, New York. He had long been lying sick in the Melbourne Hospital "They tell me," he said, "that Jesus Christ came into the world Is that true?" I replied, "Yes, it is true" A pause "They say He's coming again, eh?" "Yes, Tom, He will come again" A longer pause, while he lay apparently lost in thought And then, "Ha! anyway, I don't think He'll come to Australia"—L.F.]

that he should believe him able to communicate with ghosts, when we recall that he believes his own ancestral ghosts visit himself in dreams. We should be loth to reproach him with superstition when we reflect upon the extraordinary resemblance between the proceedings of the Birraark and the proceedings even now taking place in the midst of our highest civilization at "spirit *séances*"

I have found the Kŭrnai to compare not unfavourably with our own people in their narration of occurrences, or as witnesses in courts of justice as to facts Among them a person known to disregard truth is branded as a liar ("Jetbolan"). Selfishness and ingratitude may be considered together. There is no doubt that the Kŭrnai is selfish, and there is no doubt that he is ungrateful; but the former is restrained by family affection and by custom, and the latter sentiment probably does not arise with them under circumstances in which it might be expected to arise with us. It is inherent in human nature to desire that which will satisfy a want, or gratify a desire, or render life more pleasant and easy. Food is of essential moment to the Kŭrnai. It is often obtained with difficulty, and the amount may vary according to the degree of skill in the individual. Clothing, and other articles useful to him, attract him; but I have shown that the food obtained by the hunter is shared according to customary law with his family group; and, when earning money, I have known instances of the Kŭrnai parting with it to purchase presents for his wife and children, or his nephews and nieces. The gratification of self is, therefore, checked in them as in us by a sense of duty or by affection.

Speaking to a Kroatŭn young man about the food prohibited during initiation, I said, "But if you were hungry and caught a female opossum, you might eat it if the old men were not there" He replied, "I could not do that; it would not be right." Although I tried to

CHARACTER AND INTELLIGENCE OF KŬRNAI

find out from him some other reason, he could give no other than that it would be wrong to disregard the customs *

The sentiment of gratitude may be defined as a feeling of obligation towards some one who has performed a beneficial action towards us without having been under any obligation to perform that action It follows from such a definition that gratitude should not be expected where an obligation to perform the action exists. I attribute the want of gratitude among the Kŭrnai for kindnesses shown them by the whites, which usually take the form of food, clothing, or attention during sickness, to the principle of community which is so strong a feature of the domestic and social life of these aborigines For a supply of food, or for nursing when sick, the Kŭrnai would not feel grateful to his family group There would be a common obligation upon all to share food, and to afford personal aid and succour. This principle would also come into play as regards the simple personal property they possess, and would extend to the before-unknown articles procured from the whites The food, the clothes, the medical attendance which the Kŭrnai receive from the whites, they take in the accustomed manner; and, in addition to this, we must remember that the donors are regarded as having unlimited resources. They cannot be supposed by the Kŭrnai to be doing anything but giving out of their abundance

The charge of immorality would vary much in its force if we regarded it from the point of view of our belief, or from theirs. But many actions which would appear even highly immoral when viewed by us without complete know-

* The Kroatŭn were not initiated, but this young man had lived much with the Brabrolŭng and Tatŭngolŭng, and was well acquainted with their customs We were at the time talking about his being initiated, were the ceremony ever repeated

[This is a striking instance of that "moral feeling" which Sir John Lubbock denies to savages —L F

ledge, would have a somewhat different aspect when viewed by the light of more knowledge. For instance, the punishment inflicted for infidelity in the wife, under which it would seem that a number of men had some one woman in common, would at first sight appear only explicable by the belief that the tribe was utterly immoral, and without any conception of fidelity between the sexes; but on further knowledge it would be found that it was a punishment for infidelity. With us marital fidelity is guaranteed, independently of moral considerations, by public opinion. A woman guilty of infidelity to her husband risks the punishment of public reprobation and the divorce court. Among the Kŭrnai such a woman risked death, and probably became common to those who found her.* The punishment differs in these cases, and in the latter takes a savage form.

That which is immoral in one state of society, is moral in another state of society. The missionaries who first went among the Polynesians were highly shocked at their immorality; but we know that a woman who was living with one man one day, and with another man the next day, was only following out the "Turanian," or even perhaps the "Malayan," family system which obtained with them.†

Cruelty and disregard for human life may be charged against the Kŭrnai with some truth. They were cruel as against their enemies, but their enemies were equally cruel as against them. They treacherously sneaked upon each other, and blotted each other out of existence whenever possible, and even ate portions of the slain. They were often cruel in intention in devising and carrying out forms of incantation intended to cause pain, suffering, and death

---

* Lo-ŭngil rŭkŭt is a term of reproach. Lo-ungil = to entice or seduce away; Rŭkŭt = woman.

† [More than one of Mr. M'Lennan's instances of so-called *polyandry* are nothing more than instances of this system —L F]

to the victim. But towards those near to them, of their own family, clan, or tribe, the Kŭrnai were not cruel so far as I know. They did not inflict the terrible tortures during initiation which many other tribes caused their young men to undergo They were not, so far as I know, cruel to their women except in isolated cases, and no parents could be more indulgent than they are to their children. Yet the new-born infant was left to perish, and the daughter, when she had married the man of her choice, in accordance with tribal custom, was speared or beaten "within an inch of her life" by her father, mother, and brothers. The first they explain as being done under the exigencies of their life, and the latter as being not intended as cruelty but simply to follow an ancestral custom.

In one respect the life of the Kŭrnai was a life of dread. He lived in fear of the visible and of the invisible He never knew the moment when the lurking Brajerak might not spear him from behind, and he never knew the moment when some secret foe among the Kŭrnai might not succeed in passing over him some spell, against which he could not struggle, or from which even the most potent counter-charms given him by his ancestors could not free him. We can scarcely feel surprise that he should be pitiless against the prowling Brajerak, or should endeavour to forestall the suspected magic of some Kŭrnai by his own.

I think, therefore, that the indictment must be somewhat modified as regards the Kŭrnai ; and it is quite possible that were we able to examine the evidence in support of it as regards other tribes, even so imperfectly as I have been able to examine it as regards this, we should in those instances also find explanations, and extenuating circumstances now unsuspected, which would modify its force.

The idleness, incapacity, and want of energy shown by the Kŭrnai in most of our occupations are not to be wondered at* We could no more expect that the descendants of countless generations of wandering hunters should possess those qualities which our ancestors have transmitted to us together with pastoral pursuits, agriculture, commerce, arts, and sciences, than we could expect the young of the dingo, if brought up by us, to become a sheep dog.

As to the mental qualifications of the Kŭrnai, a few words may suffice. When trained in the mission schools the children have shown quickness to learn, and at Ramahyuk have even gained the highest results attainable in the examination of the State schools This is a circumstance of great weight in estimating the status of intellect and brain-power of the Kŭrnai The Rev. Mr Kramer, who trained them to this point of excellence, told me, however, lately, that the labour required to bring them up to the necessary standard, and to keep them there, was so great, that no possible inducement would cause him again to undertake it.

According to my experience, the young Kŭrnai can learn with great facility. He has great imitative powers, and, therefore, often acquires an excellent handwriting; but he also unlearns with great facility. In this we may recognize mental qualities naturally good, but not fixed by hereditary training. We may say, I think, that his mind develops quickly, and perhaps fully up to the standard of that of a white child of twelve or fourteen, but there stops.

* Like other Australian aborigines, the Kŭrnai have a natural aptitude for stock-riding. I have also known among them good shearers and reapers. This must be the exception to my general statement.

APPENDIX D.

THE DISTRIBUTION OF FOOD

Kŭrnai Tribe I.

IN illustration of the statement made as to the community in food, and the obligation to supply certain persons with food, the following particulars are now given in addition to those noted. They apply to the Kŭrnai.

Kangaroo.—It is assumed that a man kills a kangaroo at a distance from the camp Two other men are with him, but are too late to assist in killing. While the first man lights a fire, they cut up the game. The three cook the entrails and eat them. The distance from camp being considerable, the kangaroo is cooked. The following distribution is made:—Men No. 2 and No. 3 receive one leg and the tail, and one leg and part of the haunch, because they helped to cut the game up. Man No. 1 receives the remainder, which he carries to camp, and deals with thus:—The head and back are carried by his wife to her parents; the remainder goes to his parents. If he has no meat, he may keep a little; but if he has, for instance, an opossum, he gives all away. His mother, if she has caught some fish, may probably give him some. If the man has no other meat, his wife's parents may give him some; but they will give her a supply next morning. The children are well cared for in any case by their grandparents.

The giving of food on the following morning by the wife's parents is grounded upon the assumption that the son-in-law provided for her family on the previous day, but may want some food before going out to hunt afresh.

The food received by the husband's parents and the wife's parents is shared by them with their family.

Black wallaby.—We suppose two to have been killed. They might be cooked, or not, in the bush, according to distance. One would be given by the man to his father, the other sent by his wife to her parents.

Wombat.—A wombat being killed, would be, if far from camp, cut open, the intestines taken out, and the animal skewered up and carried home. Or, if close at hand, help might be obtained, and the game carried in whole. All the animal is sent to the wife's parents, being regarded as the best of food. The wife's father distributes it to the whole camp, but he does not give any to the hunter, who is supposed to have eaten of the entrails in the bush, and therefore not to be hungry. On the following morning, however, he sends some by his daughter to her husband.

Native bear.—This is either cooked where caught, or carried home raw, according to distance If one is killed, it is given to the wife's parents; if two, one to the wife's parents, and one to the man's parents If three, then two to the wife's parents, and one to the man's parents, and so on. The hunter will probably keep the liver for himself and his wife. On the following morning the wife's parents will give her some if she has no food.

Emu.—An emu is cooked where killed, unless close to camp. The intestines, gizzard, and liver are eaten there by the hunter. He will give the legs to his wife's parents, and the body to his own parents.

Iguana.—This lizard is divided with all who may be in the camp.

Opossum.—We can assume that more than one are killed. The hunter keeps one, which is enough for himself and his wife, or perhaps two, if he has children. The remainder goes to his wife's parents.

Swan.—If several are killed, the hunter may keep one or more, according to the wants of his family. The remainder goes to the wife's parents; or, if many have been procured, the most to them, and the less number to his own parents.

Conger eel.—This should be sent to the wife's parents, who will probably share it with their family.

In all cases the largest supply and the best of the food is sent to the wife's parents. The grandchildren are fed by their grandparents. The supply of vegetable food procured by the woman is all devoted to her husband, her children, and herself.

The above instances have been given on the supposition that the man's parents and his wife's parents were alone living with him in the camp.

I now give a few instances to show what would be the distribution when other members of the group were present.

DISTRIBUTION OF FOOD.
Kŭrnai Tribe II.

KANGAROO—Supposed to have been killed by a man (married), assisted by an unmarried man (Brewit):—

Wife's parents.—All; except to
Brother.—The left leg; to
Brewit.—The right leg.

NATIVE BEAR—Supposed to have been caught by a man, alone :—

Parents.—Right side, with two legs.
Wife's parents.—Left side, with two legs.
Self.—Head and liver; he gives his
Wife.—Part of the head; she gives her
Sister.—The ears.

FISH—If of medium size, to the
    Man.—Tail half; to his
    Wife.—Head half.

If of large size, or if many have been caught, the following division might be made. (It is supposed that six river eels have been captured—four large, and two small ones)—

    Man and wife.—Large eel.
    Mother's brother and wife.—Large eel.
    Elder and younger brothers.—Large eel.
    Elder and younger sisters.—Large eel.
    Children of mother's brother.—Small eel.
    Married daughter and husband.—Small eel.

These instances may suffice as further illustrations of the food division among the Kŭrnai.

There was a similar custom among the aborigines of Maneroo, but the details show considerable variation from those just given. I now subjoin a list given me by a Maneroo blackfellow a little time ago.

He informed me that in all cases the food was cooked before being divided. The relationships given are those of the persons who are supposed to be in the camp. The informant is unmarried.

DISTRIBUTION OF FOOD.

Maneroo Blacks.

KANGAROO:—

    Self.—Piece along the backbone near the loin.
    Father.—Tail, backbone, ribs, shoulders, and head.
    Mother.—Right leg.
    Elder brother.—Left leg.
    Younger brother.—Left fore leg.

Elder sister.—Piece alongside backbone.
Younger sister.—Right fore leg.
The father shares his portion thus:—
His parents.—Tail and piece of backbone.
The mother shares her portion thus:—
Her parents.—Part of the thigh and the shin.

WOMBAT is cooked; then opened and skinned. The skin is cut into strips, which are shared among the group:—

Self—The head.
Father.—Right ribs.
Mother.—Left ribs and backbone.
Elder brother.—Right shoulder.
Younger brother.—Left shoulder.
Elder sister.—Right hind leg.
Younger sister—Left hind leg.
Young men's camp.—Rump and liver.
The father shares his portion:—
His parents—Skin.
The mother shares her portion:—
Her father.—Backbone.
Her mother.—Some skin.

NATIVE BEAR:—

Self.—Left ribs.
Father.—Right hind leg.
Mother.—Left hind leg.
Elder brother.—Right fore leg.
Younger brother.—Left fore leg.
Elder sister.—Backbone.
Younger sister.—Liver.
Father's brother.—Right ribs.
Mother's brother.—Piece of flank.
Young men's camp.—The head.

APPENDIX D

Opossum:—

 Self.—Backbone.
 Father.—Left leg.
 Mother.—Neck and head.
 Elder brother.—Left ribs.
 Younger brother.—Part of backbone.
 Elder sister.—Part of right thigh
 Younger sister—Right shin and foot.
 Young men's camp.—The remainder.

Emu :—

 Self.—Backbone.
 Father.—Left leg, left shoulder, and left flank.
 Mother.—Neck and head, right flank, and right ribs.
 Elder brother.—Left ribs.
 Younger brother—Part of the backbone.
 Elder sister.—Part of right thigh.
 Younger sister.—Right shin.
 Young men's camp.—Left thigh and left shin.
The father and mother share theirs with their parents.

Iguana :—

 Self.—The left leg.
 Father } The upper half of the body.
 Mother
 Elder brother } The right hind leg.
 Younger brother
 Elder sister.—Part of lower half of the backbone.
 Younger sister.—The tail.
The father and mother share their portions thus :—
 His parents.—The fore leg.
 Her parents.—The backbone.
 The young men's camp.—The remainder.

PORCUPINE. The skin is cut up in strips:—
Self.—The left hind leg and some skin.
Father.—The head and some skin.
Mother.—Part of the skin.
Elder brother.—The right hind leg and some skin.
Younger brother.—Some of the flesh and some skin.
Elder sister.—The right fore leg and some skin.
Younger sister.—The left fore leg and some skin.
Young men's camp.—Some of the skin.

The whole of the animal is not here disposed of, and as my informant omitted to mention the grandparents, it seems to me probable that the remainder went to them.

APPENDIX E.

THE TŬRNDŬN.

THIS instrument was usually made, in Gippsland, of the wood of the native cherry *(Exocarpus cupressiformis)*. It is about three inches long, by an inch and a half wide and an eighth of an inch thick. It narrows to one end, which is perforated and attached to a short stick by a piece of kangaroo sinew about thirty inches in length. When whirled round, or whisked backwards and forwards, it makes a peculiar and slightly humming noise, which also approximates to the sound of the word "whew." It much resembles, in general character, the wooden toy which I remember to have made as a boy, called a "bull roarer." The occurrence of such an instrument with us as a toy, and with the Australian savage as an object of mystery used in their ceremonies, suggests that the "bull roarer" is a survival.

The awe with which this tŭrndūn is even now regarded by the surviving Kŭrnai is so strong, that when, on lately meeting two of them, I spoke of the tŭrndūn, they first looked cautiously round them to see that no one else was near, and then answered me in undertones.

I learn the following from correspondents:—

This instrument is known to the aborigines of the Gwydir river (Kamilaroi-speaking tribes). It is used in the ceremonies of initiation. It is, with them, about eight inches long by four wide; flat on each side, and very thin. The widest end is rounded, and the sinew is put through a hole in the smaller end, or sometimes tied round it. It is made of some hard wood, generally either brigalow or bumble, these being hard, tough woods, and not likely to split. (Mr. Cyrus E Doyle, Kunopia, New South Wales.)

The Chepără tribe, living on the coast of Southern Queensland, and about the head of the Albert, Logan, and Tweed rivers, have a similar instrument. They call it "bribbŭn," and use it only at their "boras," at which the lads are made young men. It is not used for doctoring purposes. It is kept secret and hidden from light by the head chief, and is considered to possess some mysterious and supernatural power or influence. The women and children are not permitted to see it; if seen by a woman, or shown by a man to a woman, the punishment to both is *death*. After the young men have been initiated, each of them receives, to take home with him, a toy or miniature "bribbŭn," as a sort of guarantee of their initiation, and as receiving a small portion of the virtue which the larger and principal one is supposed to possess. This last, after the "bora," is scrupulously kept concealed.

The "boras" held by the Chepără tribe were very numerously attended in former days by aborigines coming to them from an extended circle even as far south as the

Richmond district in New South Wales (Mr. J Gibson, J P, Stanmore, Queensland)

Among the Lower Murray river aborigines, this instrument was used for "doctoring purposes," if not in their ceremonies For instance, "If a man used it to make his wife well, he would go to a sufficient distance to allow it to swing clear of the patient. After making much noise with it, he would bring it up to the sick woman, and hang it over her till it ceased to move; then he repeated the operation, each time allowing it to hang over his patient until it became at rest" (The Rev J Bulmer, Lake Tyers, Victoria)

I observe notices of this instrument in the following works:—In "Discoveries," &c. (Eyre), vol. ii, pp 315-320, as "Mooyumkar;" "Native Tribes of South Australia" (Woods), p. 216, as "Witarna;" "The Dieyerie Tribe" (Gason), p 270, as "Yundra;" "Kamilaroi and other Australian Languages" (Ridly), p 154; "The Aborigines of Victoria" (R B. Smyth), vol i, p 176, as "Perboregan"

Mr E B Tylor has written a most interesting chapter on "Historical Traditions and Myths of Observation"* It might be expected that such traditions and myths should be found to exist among the Kŭrnai, but I have failed to collect more than a few One of these relates to the tŭrndūn, and is to the effect that long ago there was land to the south of Gippsland where there is now sea, and that at that time some children of the Kŭrnai, who inhabited the land, in playing about found a tŭrndūn, which they took home to the camp and showed to the women. "Immediately," it is said, "the earth crumbled away, and it was all water, and the Kŭrnai were drowned."† A second

---

* "Early History of Mankind," 3rd edition, 1878.
† I note the following in the "Report of the Select Committee of the Legislative Council on the Aborigines, 1858-9," p 12 (Victoria). Mr William Hull, in his evidence, says, as to the Yarra and Coast tribes

statement is to the effect that the fathers of the Kŭrnai speared sharks where the Mitchell river now flows at Bairnsdale.

It may be interesting to consider whether there is anything in the geological history of Gippsland which may throw light upon the two legends I have mentioned.

Gippsland consists, to the north, of a high mountain region, mainly of Palæozoic age, rising to the height of 6,508 feet in Mount Bogong, and having between it and the sea a tract of country of Mesozoic and Kainozoic age. I am not aware that the former exceeds 2,000 feet in elevation above the sea level, and the latter, according to my measurements, is below 800 feet. In the greater part of this fringe of low-lying country the rivers flow through wide alluvial valleys at only a slight elevation above the sea level, and mostly empty themselves into the Gippsland lakes, which are only separated from the sea by a more or less narrow strip of sandy land and dunes. The rise and fall of the tide on this coast is so slight that its influence is not felt within the Lakes; and it is to this cause that the freshness of their water, and of that of the river embouchures, is due. A depression of the land to less than thirty feet below its present level would submerge most of the river valleys as estuaries, and much of the low-lying land now cultivated. A less depression would cause the sea-water to flow up the Mitchell valley to Bairnsdale, and thus enable sharks to again reach that spot.*

(Western Port, &c):—" The blacks . . . say that their . . . progenitors recollected when Hobson's Bay was a kangaroo ground " They say—" Plenty catch kangaroo and plenty catch opossum there ; " and that " the river (Yarra) once went out at the Heads, but that the sea broke in, and that Hobson's Bay, which was once a hunting ground, became what it is "

* I observe that the railway stations at Melbourne and Sale are stated to be each 32 feet above sea level ; Bairnsdale is on slightly higher ground. The levels of the rivers at these three places are approximately the same.

An examination of the geological evidence has shown me that the mountainous part of Gippsland has not suffered submergence since the Lower tertiary period,* beyond the limits to which the beds—subsequent in age to that period —extend upwards on the flanks of the Palæozoic mountain mass. This extreme height I estimate at 800 feet above sea level, and the mean may be 600 feet; and to this must be added the difference between the present elevation of the land and its maximum elevation during the period of time I have mentioned. The measure of that difference may be more, but cannot be less, than the depth at which the courses of the rivers of Middle and Upper tertiary age continue below the present surface This may be roughly estimated at a mean of 400 feet. We have, then, 1,000 feet as representing the minimum limit of probability as to the oscillations of the land since the Lower tertiary period; and I do not think that the maximum would reach 500 feet more. The oscillations have, no doubt, been numerous, but they seem to me—judging from the appearances I have observed over a large part of the southern coast, from Spencer's Gulf to near Cape Howe, and northwards nearly to the tropics—to have been widespread and equable in their character.

The following notes may roughly give an idea of the oscillations as indicated in Gippsland At the period of the Middle miocene limestones (Bairnsdale, &c), the land was depressed to, say, 300 feet below its present level.†

At the period of the Upper miocene or Lower pliocene sands and clays (Moitun Creek beds), a depression of some-

---

* The oldest formations of tertiary age known in Victoria are the Mount Martha and Schnapper Point beds, which have been referred by Professor M'Coy to the Oligocene ; "Prodromus of the Palæontology of Victoria "

† " Progress Report, Geological Survey of Victoria," ii pp 59-72, ; vi , p. 122.

what greater degree occurred, by which the hollows and inequalities of the Bairnsdale limestone were filled in and smoothed over. A subsequent period of depression is indicated by the Newer pliocene sandy limestones (Jemmy's Point and Lake Tyers). A final depression of great extent occurred when those clays and sands were laid down whose highest limits, as I have said, now reach to some 800 feet above sea level.

Corresponding to these principal depressions, there seem to me to have been three periods of maximum elevation. The first preceded the formation of the Moitun Creek beds, and on this land surface flowed those streams now known to us as some of the oldest of the deep leads, such as that of the Welcome Rush, at Stawell * I am inclined to class the Moitun Creek ferruginous sands and clays with those of Flemington and Stawell. It may be that the great "reef washes" of Ballarat are to be referred to the period of depression during which the abovementioned marine beds were laid down.†

The elevation of the land of which I have just spoken as antecedent to the formation of the Moitun Creek beds, must have been greater than that now existing, otherwise the then rivers (deep leads) could not, assuming the oscillations of the land to have been widespread and equable in character, have had sufficient fall to the sea.

A second elevation of the land I conceive to have preceded the formation of the Jemmy's Point and Lake

---

* The expression "deep lead" refers to those ancient river-courses which are now only disclosed by deep-mining operations, and whose trend has often no connection with existing surface features See also Mr Norman Taylor's "Report on the Stawell Goldfield," "Report of Progress, Geological Survey of Victoria," iii , p 250

† "Report on the Geology and Mineral Resources of Ballarat," by Mr. R. A. F. Murray "Report of Progress, Geological Survey of Victoria," i , p. 66.

Tyers sandy limestones. This land surface was also probably of long continuance, and of great extent. To this period I incline to refer a great number of the newer deep leads—such, for instance, as those of the Ovens district, or the Commercial-street lead at Stawell.

A third elevation of the land may perhaps be indicated by the break which I observe between the limestones of Lake Tyers and the succeeding clayey and sandy formations, with quartz gravels, which I have already mentioned as rising to some 800 feet on the flanks of the Palæozoic hills.

A land communication probably existed between Australia and Tasmania at the period which I have indicated as that of the newer deep leads, that is, preceding the formation of the Newer pliocene beds of Gippsland. It existed, I think, even subsequently—indicated probably by the break which I find between the Jemmy's Point beds and the succeeding series of clays, sands, and gravels. It ceased to exist during the great depression co-existing with their formation, and which continued until re-elevation of the land brought about the existing physical conditions of Southern Australia.

I have not seen any signs in Australia of any glacial or glacier epoch, such as that of the Northern Hemisphere. The continuity of the land surface has in South-Eastern Australia been unbroken as far back, at least, as the period of the Oolitic carbonaceous formations of Victoria.

Eastern Victoria during the periods of greatest subsidence was a mountainous island; Western Victoria an archipelago of islands, many of them having active volcanos. During the periods of greatest elevation, the continental character of the land must have been even more pronounced than now, owing to its greater extent to the south, to the north, and probably also to the east The climate, as shown by the Miocene and later marine and terrestrial fauna and flora was warmer than at present. There is nothing, therefore, in the past geological or physical history of South-Eastern Victoria, which would render the existence of man in it less probable than when it was first discovered by the early navigators. Through how much of geologic time the progenitors of the Australian savage have inhabited it cannot be postulated; but if these views are near the truth, the separation of Tasmania from the mainland may have occurred within the time during which the present aborigines have inhabited this continent.

I suspect that the two Kŭrnai legends of history refer to the time following the period when the Newer pliocene beds of East Gippsland were formed. To the same period may, perhaps, be referred also other tales told by the Kŭrnai of a great deluge which, they allege, once happened in South Gippsland. It is, therefore, possible that these legends are the recollection of actual occurrences handed down from one generation of the Kŭrnai to another, through periods of time during which even the physical features of the earth's surface have been less constant than the customs of the savages who roamed over it.*

APPENDIX F.

THE GOURNDITCH-MARA TRIBE.

THE following information has been kindly furnished to me by the Rev. J. H. Stähle, of the Church Mission, Lake Condah, Western Victoria.

---

* Since writing the above, I have mentioned to Professor M'Coy, of the Melbourne University, these conclusions, to which I have arrived by a consideration mainly of the stratagraphical evidence as seen in the field. He has stated to me his own conclusions, from palæontological evidence, and he has kindly permitted me to quote them here.

"At the deep lead period, extinct marsupial animals, such as wombats

The territory claimed by this tribe may be defined as extending from the Glenelg River on the west to the Eumerella River on the east, and from the sea coast as far north as Mount Napier and Hotspur.

Its members called themselves Gournditch-mara, from "Gournditch," the distinctive name of the tribe (as also of Lake Condah), and "mara" = man. Neighbouring friendly tribes were recognized as being "mara," but this tribe alone was "Gournditch."* The tribe was divided into four classes, named Kerŭp (water), Būm (mountain), Direk (swamp), and Gilger (river). There was no exogamous rule affecting marriage. Hence a man, for instance, of Kerŭp might marry a woman of Kerŭp, Direk, Būm, or Gilger,

---

(phascolomys pliocenus), occur; and in the clays mainly of the same age, where more widely extended about Colac, we find several other extinct mammals now confined to the continent of Australia, but mingled with a few remains of living species—notably the dingo and the Tasmanian devil *(sarcophylus ursinus)*, the former abundant on the continent at the present day, but the sarcophylus extinct on the continent before historic times; that is, not leaving any evidence of any sort of its existence in company with man. Nor are there any known traditions of the existence of the living sarcophylus on the continent

"I think that, at this period, Tasmania and this continent were connected by land (newer pliocene or pleistocene). Immediately after this period subsidence of the land took place, separating Tasmania from the continent as seen at the present time; while shortly before it, there was a still wider separation by continuous moderately deep sea, as shown by the community of Upper miocene and Older pliocene fossil strata of considerable thickness, extending from Tasmania to the Murray at the present day, full of shells, echinoderms, corals, &c

"Roughly, or approximately speaking, I should guess that 75 per cent of the living fauna of Tasmania is identical with that of Southern Continental Australia, but the 25 per cent remaining—peculiar to Tasmania—is composed of many very remarkable forms, often separated by generic as well as specific characters from their nearest analogues on the mainland. This may amount to nothing more than the natural result of geographical distribution due to climate, if even the land were continuous now."

* We have here an analogous case to that of the Kūrnai. The Gournditch-mara were, therefore, probably a division of a much larger group, recognizing common descent, and calling themselves collectively "men"

or *vice versâ.* Wives were also obtained from other neighbouring and friendly tribes. These friendly tribes were recognized as being related to them, and from the same stock. They were also " mara."

The child belonged to the father's class, and spoke his language, and not that of the mother, when she happened to be of another tribe.* There was individual marriage by exchange of sisters (not of daughters), and the consent of the girl's parents was necessary. It occasionally happened that a young man eloped with a girl without her parents' consent. Sometimes the parents pursued them, captured the girl, and brought her back; at other times, if the young man belonged to some neighbouring tribe, and the fugitives had gone away to a considerable distance, no pursuit was made. The girl, if caught, received a severe beating; the man sometimes also a beating, from the girl's relatives.

The man who captured a woman in war never kept her himself, but he was compelled to give her to whomsoever he chose. It was, however, necessary that he should first take her before a council of elders and the head man of the tribe, as it were for inspection † If the wife was unfaithful to her husband, he gave her a severe beating the first time. If she repeated the offence, he left her altogether. This was the severest penalty inflicted, as thereby she incurred the scorn and dislike of the whole tribe, with the exception, perhaps, of those who were as bad as herself. A man was not, however, restricted

---

* Here we have an instance of a savage tribe in which at least some of the men and women spoke different languages. Taken alone, it might support Mr M'Lennan's views as to marriage by capture Taken, however, together with Mr Stähle's other statements, it raises doubts whether similar cases on which much stress has been laid, for instance that of the Caribbeans, might not bear another construction had we fuller information.

† This ceremony is highly suggestive of adoption.

to one wife—he might have half-a-dozen if he could get them.*

Not only was fidelity expected from the wife, but those were considered very bad man who lent their wives to others. When such a case occurred, it always occasioned a fight between the better-thinking of the tribe and the offender.

The office of head man in the tribe was hereditary. When the head man died, he was succeeded by his son, or, failing a son, by the next male relative. This was the law of the tribe before any whites came into the country. The head man had the power of proclaiming war, and when he did this, all the men of the tribe were obliged to follow him. He settled all quarrels and disputes in the tribe. When he had heard both sides, and had given his decision in a matter, no one ever disputed it. In war all spoils were brought to him, who divided them among his men, after having reserved the best for himself. The men of the tribe were under an obligation to provide him with food, and to make all kinds of presents to him, such as kangaroo and opossum rugs, stone tomahawks, spears, flint knives, &c.

The Gournditch-mara did not in war eat any portion of the slain.

Although there was no individual property in land, all such things as were left by the deceased were divided among his nearest relatives.

Game killed in the chase was divided amongst those present. Supposing a kangaroo to have been killed, the hunter gave one hind leg and the breast to his most esteemed friend, and kept the other hind leg himself. The

---

* In reply to a special question, whether there was any such unusual license on special occasions as that noted by the Rev. Mr. Kühn in the Turra tribe (Appendix H), Mr Stähle says :—"There was no such license allowed among the Gournditch-mara on any occasion whatever."

remainder was divided among the other companions. There was, however, no rule as to the distribution of cooked food in the camp, for all eat together—that is, each family did so. Each wife was, however, obliged to sit beside her own husband, nor near any other man unless her husband sat between them. Each family camped by itself.

The Gournditch-mara believed that there was a future good and bright place, to which those who were good went after death, and that there was a man at that place who took care of the world and of all people. The good place was called "Mūmble-Mirring." There was also, according to them, a dark place where bad people were punished after death. This place they called "Bŭrreet Barrat." This belief they had before there was any white person in the country.

They believed that the spirit of the deceased father or grandfather occasionally visited the male descendant in dreams, and imparted to him charms (songs) against disease or against witchcraft.

There were also among the Gournditch-mara persons who professed to communicate with the spirits of the deceased, and to learn from them corrobboree songs and dances, and to inquire from them concerning future events.

This tribe had no ceremonies of initiation of the young men or young women to manhood or womanhood.

APPENDIX G.

THE GEAWE-GAL TRIBE.

I AM indebted to Mr. G W. Rusden, Clerk to the Legislative Council of Victoria, for the following interesting information in respect to a tribe speaking the Geawe-gal dialect, on the Hunter River, New South Wales. This tribe is, I believe, now extinct. Mr. Rusden was identified with it, and spoke the language as a youth. Geawe-gal belongs to that class of tribes whose language is described by its negative—in this case, Geawe = No. Mr. Rusden says :—" The territory claimed by them may be defined as being part of the valley of the Hunter River extending to each lateral watershed, and from twenty-five to thirty miles along the valley on each side of Glendon. These aborigines spoke the language of, and intermarried with, those of Maitland. Less frequently with those of the Patterson River, and rarely with those of Muswell Brook. They were always in dread of war with the Kamilaroi, who intruded down the heads of the Hunter across from the Talbragar to the Munmurra waters, and even occasionally made raids as far as Jerry's Plains. A section of the Kamilaroi occupied the upper sources of the waters flowing into the Hunter River —that is, those which form the heads of the Goulburn River, for instance, the Munmurra Creek. The Dividing Range between the Munmurra and Talbragar sinks down so that a traveller would not think he was crossing the boundary between any waters, much less those which divide the Darling waters from those of the Hunter River.

This probably facilitated the spread of the powerful Kamilaroi.

"The myall wood weapons made at Liverpool Plains were exchanged with the coast natives for others (myrtle, &c.) which were made on the Hunter, and the Kamilaroi were spoken of as Myall blacks by the Geawe-gal, so that myall was almost synonymous with fierce.

"Although I do not recollect all their class divisions, they had distinctly the great divisions, Yippai and Kombo.* Apropos of the generic names, the Geawe-gal had a superstition that everyone had within himself an affinity to the *spirit* of some bird, beast, or reptile. Not that he sprung from the creature in any way, but that the spirit which was in him was akin to that of the creature. I have often spoken of the superstition, and found my *causeur* incredulous himself, but not doubting that it was an ancient tradition of his people.

"Marriage was ordinarily by gift of the woman and by consent of both fathers, in case the future husband was a boy or a youth, and would be arranged years before the time for marriage. Girls were thus affianced, in childhood also, to men much older than themselves. Wives were also exchanged (swapped) by their husbands. Some strong men, or popular men, had a number of wives. Elopement of unmarried girls was occasional, and in such cases the man would have to fight the intended husband or her male relatives. If he proved to be the victor, he kept the girl. She, in such cases, ran the risk of being beaten by her relatives, or even killed. In the case of female captives, they belonged to their captors, if of a class from which wives might be legally taken by them. If of a forbidden class, then, I

---

* [It always struck me as remarkable that even young children knew and could state off hand, with regard to every soul in the tribe, whether he or she was Yippai or Kombo.—G.W.R.]

think that the captor might make an exchange with some one of the proper class who had a woman at his disposal. The class of the female captive would be known if she belonged to any of the tribes with which the Geawe-gal were familiar. If the class could not be ascertained, then there would not be any objection to her captor retaining her.

"As a man had power of life and death over his wife, so, in the process of violent seizure, he assumed the same power. The only risk he ran was from the rage of her relatives or friends.

"In all cases it was absolutely necessary that women should be married according to tribal laws. The contrary would be inconceivable to the Geawe-gal. For instance, were the question put, 'Could not so and so marry?'—mentioning some man and woman of forbidden degree or class—the reply would invariably be, 'It cannot be.'

"I have occasionally heard of a saturnalia taking place among them, whereat wives were exchanged or lent to the young men, so that intercourse was almost promiscuous (subject to the class laws). When they admitted this to me, they did so as if also admitting that they were ashamed of it. This occurred not in open daylight, but at night. It might not happen for years.

"The best man in war would be recognized by them as principal adviser, and would have authority by consent of the elders. I have known the office to be hereditary, when the son proved himself a capable warrior. Without such proof, there was no possibility of his being accepted.

"A koradji (*i e*, wizard, medicine man) might be such a leader. In every case, however, the leading or chief man would be only *primus inter pares*, and be liable to be set aside by the council of old men if his actions were disapproved. At this council the younger men (that is those having been initiated) might be present, but would not speak. Such councils were held at night. On ordinary occasions, for instance, in cases of disputes or of ordeal by battle, the old women had much to say.

"The principal social restraints in vogue were laws of satisfaction for injury done, by the offender submitting to an ordeal by which he exposed himself to danger. They did not, however, assume the form of the Saxon wehrgild, by which an injury could be compounded for; but they required that the offender should run the risk of a similar injury to the one he had done. According to the magnitude of his offence, he had to receive one or more spears from men who were relatives of the deceased person, or, when the injured person had recovered strength, he might himself discharge the spears at the offender.

"Obedience to such laws was never withheld, but would have been enforced, without doubt, if necessary, by the assembled tribe. Offences against individuals, or blabbing about the secret rites of the tribe, and all breaches of custom, were visited with some punishment. Such punishments, or such ordeals, were always *coram publico*, and the women were present. Not so the adjudication according to which the penalty was prescribed.

"They believed in the mysterious power of the koradji; but it is hard to say what special means of using it they ascribed to it as exercised in his own tribe. If one of them wasted away, his ailment was almost always imputed to the evil influence of some koradji of another tribe. Their own koradji would, after resort to seclusion or mystery, pronounce from what quarter the malign influence had come, and then the whole tribe was committed to feud or revenge. The koradji were supposed, in some undefined way, to have preternatural knowledge of, or power of communicating with, spiritual influences.

THE GEAWE-GAL TRIBE.

"In connection with the ceremonies of initiation of the young men, a wooden booming instrument, whirled round at the end of a cord, was used. It was used then, and then only. A particular 'cooee,' and a particular reply to it, were made known to the young men when they were initiated. Among the symbols used were the form of the cross mounded on the earth; a circle similarly formed, and sinuous parallel lines and other marks on the trees surrounding the site of the ceremony; which sites the women and children were never allowed to approach. The murramai, or rock crystal, was first seen by the young men at their initiation. It was held in reverence. Think of the defeat of tribal reverence which was brought about when a white man put a station close to one of these secret places, and it became a thoroughfare!

"A European who had gained the confidence of the tribe might be permitted to be present at the ceremonies of initiation; and a knowledge of them would be a safe passport for a traveller among a strange tribe, if by any means he could communicate the fact of his initiation. The wonder and the readiness to fraternize shown by strange blacks to an initiated white man seen by them for the first time are very great, accompanied by earnest entreaties not to reveal anything unlawful.

"The means of communication with adjoining, or even more distant tribes, was by persons having the character of heralds. Their persons were sacred even among hostile tribes From occasional residences in distant places, many of them acquired different dialects fluently. Other men, engaged in affairs of less moment, may be termed 'special messengers.' They also were respected scrupulously, I think; but I doubt whether their persons would have been so sacred as those of the heralds, under certain conditions. Their journeys were made in safer territories. A herald would be selected for dangerous latitudes.

"Infanticide was, I have reason to believe, permitted by the Geawe-gal tribe, though I never knew an instance. They alleged that while their food was abundant and their habits were simple, it was at least uncommon. They were very fond of their children, so far as I could observe.

"I have known the hands of enemies slain in a foray to be carried as trophies for weeks, and I have known cannibalism imputed to a tribe (guiltless of it) on the ground of these hands being found in a camp.

"All implements, the property of a warrior, were interred with his body, and, indeed, every piece of inanimate property he had possessed. The name of a deceased person was never mentioned after his decease; and when a white man carelessly or recklessly has spoken of a dead man by name, I have seen several blacks hang their heads sorrowfully, while one of them would remonstrate, if they had any respect for the speaker; otherwise they would endeavour to turn the conversation."

APPENDIX H.

THE TURRA TRIBE.

I AM indebted to the Rev. W. Julius Kühn, of the Boorkooyanna Mission, for the following important particulars.

The Turra tribe is located in York's Peninsula, South Australia. It is divided into the following classes and totems:—

WILTŪ (Eaglehawk), and MŪLTA (Seal).

Wortū = Wombat	Worrira = Wildgoose.
Woldla = Wallaby.	Worrimbrū = Butterfish.
Nantū = Kangaroo.*	Gatta worrie = Mullet.
Berūna = Iguana	Mittaga = Schnapper.
Gūtūbarū = Wombat—snake.	Papūs = Shark
Mata = Bandicoot.	Wittata = Salmon.
Worra = Black Bandicoot	
Gūa = Crow.	
Gerntū = Rock Wallaby	
Gari = Emu.	

The classes are exogamous, but any totem of one class may intermarry with any totem of the other class; the children take the father's class and totem.

Girls are given in marriage by their parents, whose consent is essential; wives are also obtained by exchange of female relatives. If the parents refused their consent, it might be that a young man would run off with a girl. The parents would search for him for the purpose of killing him, and the penalty as to the girl, if caught, was death, which was inflicted by the parents or nearest relatives. The man was generally protected by his class division. When opinion was divided as to this, a fight might take place to decide his right to keep the girl. For instance, if a Wiltū-wortū man were to elope with a Mūlta-worrimbrū woman, he would be protected by the Wiltū-wortū men. But a Wiltū-wortū man would not be permitted to keep a Wiltū-wortū woman as his wife. Even if he were to capture one she would be taken from him, and if she persisted in following him she would be killed. When a female was captured in war, she was the property of her captor;† but

---

* The word Nantū seems to have been carried from tribe to tribe into Central Australia, where it is used for "horse," just as the word "yarraman" has also been carried there from New South Wales, having the same meaning The Dieri or Yantrūwūnta word for kangaroo is Tchūkūro.

† It follows from the preceding statement that it would only be the case if she were of some class from which he might legally take a wife.

the section of the tribe to which she belonged would fight for her recovery. Failing to do that, they would endeavour to capture a woman from the other section of the tribe, and keep her.

Women were bound to be faithful to their husbands, also the husbands to their wives. Whoever was guilty of unfaithfulness was liable to be punished by death at the hands of the class of the offender.

When the two sub-tribes Wiltū and Mūlta met for a grand corrobboree, the old men took any of the young wives of the other class for the time, and the young men of the Wiltū exchanged wives with those of the Mūlta, and *vice versâ*, but only for a time, and in this the men were not confined to any particular totem. Yet at other times men did not lend their wives to brothers or friends.

In the ceremonies of circumcision they used an instrument which makes a humming noise, but no information can be got as to its shape, as anyone showing it to an uninitiated person is liable to be punished with death, as well as the one who saw it.

When a young man is to be circumcised, they take one of his male relatives, and, drawing blood from his arm, cause the young man to drink it. Two or three months afterwards he is circumcised, and is then free to marry. Some of the married men, after two or three months, undergo another operation. They are cut along the back, and receive the designation Willerū;* after this they are not permitted to go to their wives for two years.

In hunting, if, for instance, a man kills a kangaroo, he gives to the man on his right hand the head, tail, the lower part of the hind leg, some fat, and some liver; the second

---

* Among the Dieri one of the designations attached to the initiated is Wilyarū.

to the right receives the hinder part of the backbone and the left shoulder. The man to his left receives the right shoulder and some ribs from the right side, and the upper part of the left leg. His mother receives the ribs; his brother receives of his father's portion, and his sisters receive the flank The kangaroo is cooked before being distributed.

In camping, the place of the parents is to the right hand side of their son's camp; the brother's to the left side; sister-in-law to the right side, or near his father's. From whatever cardinal point the aborigines arrive, they accordingly fix their camps some distance from those already there

In the camp the husband sleeps at the right hand of the fire, his wife behind him, and her young children behind her.

There are doctors among these aborigines who profess to cure disease by charms and sucking the part of the body where the person suffers. When a doctor is old, or for some reason unable to practice, his son takes his place.

Men who profess to learn corrobboree songs and dances from departed spirits are called Gūreldres; they are taught songs for the dead, which are sung to make the departed happy, who are gone to another country to live for ever, but to return no more.*

---

* The totems of the Mūlta class divisions are perhaps not complete, and there is seemingly some confusion as to the rules given for camping. I have, unfortunately, not received replies from the Rev Julius Kühn to further questions I addressed to him on these subjects, up to the time of going to press.

APPENDIX I.

THE WA-IMBIO TRIBE.

THE Rev. John Bulmer, who, many years ago, was intimately acquainted with this tribe, has kindly furnished me with the following particulars.

The Wa-imbio called their language Maraura. Their territory extended from the junction of the Darling and Murray Rivers down to the Rufus. It did not extend up the Murray, for the blacks at Mildura—twenty miles above the junction—were called Kerinma, and their language was totally different; while the tribe below the Rufus was called Pomp-malkie. I believe the Maraura language extended up the Darling to Menindie—at least, our missionary, Holden, could converse with blacks of that locality in that language; and I recognize their totemic names (animals) as Maraura; for instance, Karnie (a large lizard), which belonged to Muquarra, and Namba (the bonefish), which belonged to Kilparra.

The Wa-imbio were divided into two primary classes, Muquarra (eaglehawk) and Kilparra (crow). Muquarra married Kilparra, and Kilparra married Muquarra

With respect to the conditions of marriage, I think that the parents' consent was usually required. I remember a case where a young man named Na-withero married a girl named Malukra. She had been promised to him when he was a young man, and she was given to him when of sufficient age. Malukra was a member of the tribe living at Tapio, on the Darling, and Na-withero belonged to the junction of the Darling and the Murray I think it probable that the Tapio people were merely a division of the same tribe.

Marriage was brought about by elopement If the woman was caught, her female relatives gave her a good beating Fights took place over these cases between the girl's relatives—both male and female—and those of the man. The women were generally the most excited; they would stir up the men, and then assist with their yam-sticks If the girl was first caught by others than her own relatives, she would be abused by all the men; but this never occurred when her parents or her brothers were present to protect her

I do not think it would happen that a man would persist in keeping a woman of the same class as himself; but, at any rate, the blacks would never hesitate to kill a man who would break that rule. If the woman were of the proper class division, and she wished to remain with the man with whom she had eloped, she would be given to him after a little bother Under such circumstances he would stand and allow all her male relatives to give him a knock on the head, after which they would be satisfied, and the man would be recognized as her husband.

If a man captured a woman, he would not be permitted to keep her unless she were of some class from which he might legally take a wife A man would as soon think of marrying his own sister as a woman of the same class as himself I remember, when I first went among the Murray blacks, one of the young men attached himself to me He said we must be brothers; and as he was a Kilparra man, I was, of course, the same. I one day said to his wife—" I am John's brother: you are my sister." The idea was, to her, most ridiculous. With a laugh she said—" No; you are my husband." This shows how strict they were to keep up

APPENDIX I.

class rules ; and, also, that they would never allow a captured maiden to be kept by a man of her own class.

I do not think that, among the Wa-imbio, brothers usually occupied any other position, as to their brothers' wives, beyond the right of having the brother's widow Yet I remember that these relatives were very free and easy in their intercourse with each other, and, generally, that the men were also much more so as to the women than was the case in Gippsland. I know that one of them did not think that he had done anything wrong when he took his brother's wife I have known, when a man and his wife quarrelled, the brother would take the wife, and send his to the sulky husband This was very common, and, no doubt, was the remnant of an old custom

I have known men to have two or three wives, but I have been told that some had four or five. Sometimes the parents had a difficulty in getting their daughters married to a proper person, within class limits ; so that they would give her to a man who had one already, to obviate the difficulty I think one wife was the rule, and the plurality the exception.

At times, when there was a great gathering at corrobborees, wives were exchanged, but always within class limits. But they also resorted to this practice to avert some great trouble which they fancied was about to come upon them. For instance, they once heard that a great sickness was coming down the Murray, and the cunning old men proposed exchanging wives to ensure safety from it.* Yet, at all

---

* I suspect that this suggestion made by the old men as to the exchange of wives, may receive another explanation, if we assume that it was suggested as a means of averting impending evil, supposed to be consequent upon disregard of ancient customs by the tribe generally The occasional exchange of women, which is a custom common to many Australian tribes, especially at their great social gatherings, is clearly a survival of those old communal matrimonial rights of the class divisions, which we have shown

other times, the men expected wives to be faithful to their husbands, unless by their consent and command. This was often given, as the husband was liable to fancy the wife of some other man, and effected an exchange I remember a case where two men exchanged wives for a month ; this was called *be-ama*, but I am unable to say whether it was done frequently. In every case, they were careful to keep within the class limits

Children were always of the same class as their mother. As to this point I am most confident, as I was so familiar with the whole affair in my early days.

These blacks often talked to me of Captain Sturt and Major Mitchell. Many old men were there who had, no doubt, been among those who opposed the former near the Junction.

to underlie the whole present social structure of these aborigines, and to be preserved in their kinship terms In tribes such as the Wa-imbio, where individual marriage had largely supplanted group marriage, the ancient communal customs had been in so far abandoned That personal misfortunes are supposed to follow upon breach of ancestral custom is undoubted For instance, in the tribe at Roebourne, Western Australia, it is believed that a man's hair will turn grey if he knowingly looks at his wife's mother (tūa)—(Mr A R. Richardson, Roebourne, W A) The explanation I suggest, is to me strengthened by a statement made to me by a man of the "Majauka" tribe (Menindie), Darling River, that "he believed the dying out of his race to be in consequence of their disregard, since the arrival of the white man, of the customs and laws of their fathers "—A W.H.

APPENDIX K.

DINNA BIRRAARK.*

THE following further particulars as to the Birraarks of the Kŭrnai are worth noting :—It appears, from inquiries which I have lately made, that there was one Birraark to each clan, more rarely one to a division. For instance, of the last Birraarks one belonged to each of the following places:—Wūrnŭngatti (Kroatŭn), Brūthen (Brabra), Būnjil Kraura (Braiaka), Būnjil Nellŭng (Braiaka), Dairgo (Brabra), Delin (Brataua), and Ngarrawŭt (Tatūng). The stories told of these men all agree in certain particulars, namely— a professed intercourse with the spirits of the departed Kŭrnai, and a power to call down these spirits to *nocturnal* converse with their descendants. The following instance is highly typical of all the stories respecting them. I give it, as nearly as possible, in my informant's words :— " I was once at Yūnthŭr. The Dinna Birraark Brewin was there with his wife In the night she woke and shouted out that he was gone up to the mrarts. We all got ready, and some one shouted out, 'Where are you?' He replied, 'Here I am—I am coming down!' He said he had heard the mrarts having a corrobboree (gounyūrū), and making a great noise, and had gone up to them. Then the mrarts came down with him, and conversed with us about where the other mobs of Kŭrnai were, and whether any Brajerak were coming after us. When the mrarts went away, we found Brewin lying, as if asleep, where we had heard them speaking to us. The mrarts talked in very curious voices This Birraark was once away with the mrarts for two nights and a day, and the Kŭrnai therefore gave him the name of Brewin." †

* *See ante* p 253
† For Brewin, *see* p 254

THEORY OF THE KŬRNAI SYSTEM

OF

MARRIAGE, DESCENT, AND RELATIONSHIP.

BY

LORIMER FISON.

THEORY OF THE KŬRNAI SYSTEM.

DURING the course of my investigations among the Australian tribes, information reached me from time to time which seemed to point to a system widely different from that which, for brevity's sake, I have called the Kamilaroi It appeared to reckon descent through the father, and such glimpses of its marriage regulations as I could catch in the details furnished by my correspondents showed that they did not coincide with those of the Kamilaroi. For several years I strove in vain to get such information as would enable me to determine the system; but when the MS of my friend Mr Howitt's memoir on the Kŭrnai tribe came into my hands, I had not read many pages before it became clear to me that their system of marriage, descent, and relationship is that of which indications had presented themselves here and there in the information supplied by my correspondents, but which I had been unable to ascertain. On several important points it appears at first sight to be directly at variance with the Kamilaroi, but I think it may be shown that this variance admits of a very simple explanation

Mr. Howitt's monograph shows the following characteristics of the Kŭrnai system:—

1. The Kŭrnai have, to a certain extent, descent through the father.
2. They have marriage with consent of the woman.

3. So far from marriage being communal, the strictest fidelity is exacted from the woman.

4 Each of the divisions, or gentes, can marry anywhere beyond its own limits, with certain restrictions to prevent marriage between persons who are too near in blood.

5. They have, at least, the germ of inheritance by the individual to the exclusion of the group, as shown in the exclusive ownership by inheritance of the swans' eggs at the breeding place on Lake Kurlip —(*Ante* p. 232)

All this is so astonishingly far in advance of the Kamilaroi system, that, if we look upon it as the result of a gradual orderly development without special disturbing causes, we must reasonably expect to find a parallel advance in other respects This, however, we do not find. Neither in the arts of peace nor in those of war did the Kŭrnai exhibit any marked superiority over other tribes Their huts, their canoes, and other articles of their rude manufacture were no better than those which were made elsewhere. In no respect, as far as I am aware, did they give any token of an intelligence higher than that of their neighbours; nor do I know of any reason why we should expect such tokens from them. And yet their almost complete isolation from external impulse, so ingeniously shown by Mr. Howitt, forces upon us the conviction that their system must have been, to a certain extent, of indigenous growth. In the Kŭrnai, therefore, we have an isolated tribe which has gone very far in advance of its neighbours as regards marriage and descent, but is no more than on a par with them as to other respects; and the problem now before us is to account for this apparent anomaly.

That, "when the Yeerŭng or Djeetgŭn family first occupied Gippsland they were in an early stage of the Turanian family," as Mr. Howitt observes, appears to me to be almost a certainty; and his supposition that "the passage of their descendants from that family to the status of the pairing family has been comparatively rapid," is fully borne out by the present status of the Kamilaroi, with whom the Kŭrnai can be shown to be connected The difficulty is to account for that rapid transition. For the isolation of the Kŭrnai must have tended to conservatism, not to change; and, other things being equal, we should naturally expect them to be in the rear of those tribes which have been easily accessible one to another, rather than so very far in advance of them. We must therefore, as it seems to me, look for the motive power of that advance in some disturbing cause which forced the Kŭrnai out of the old groove, as far as the inter-sexual relations are concerned, and compelled them to make new arrangements. Of such a disturbing cause their system affords strong internal evidence.

A careful study of Mr. Howitt's valuable monograph has convinced me that—

The Kŭrnai are the descendants of an isolated division of a tribe which formerly consisted of two exogamous intermarrying divisions, such as the Kumite and Kroki of Mount Gambier, and that their regulations as to marriage and descent are such as would arise from an endeavour to follow the regulations of such divisions under circumstances of peculiar difficulty.

Statement of the theory.

At all events, this theory gives a reasonable explanation of the points of difference between the Kamilaroi system and the Kŭrnai: it shows how this tribe might come to be far in advance of its neighbours, as regards the inter-sexual regulations, without surpassing them in other respects: the facts supplied by several of my correspondents fit in with it: and, as Mr. Howitt justly observes, "that hypothesis must be provisionally accepted which best explains the facts observed." Let us now take the most important points of difference between the two systems, and test my theory by them. They may be arranged in parallel columns as follows:—

KAMILAROI SYSTEM	KŬRNAI SYSTEM.
1. The classes include both males and females	1 Yeerŭng consists of males only, Djeetgŭn of females only
2. All children take their mother's totem—*i e*, descent is through the mother	2 Boys are Yeerŭng, like their fathers ; girls are Djeetgŭn, like their mothers : that is to say, descent is through the father as to males, and through the mother as to females
3. Marriage is, theoretically, a matter of status, not of contract Consent of neither party is requisite There is no secrecy Parents and friends are acquiescent.	3 Marriage is a matter of contract between the parties, founded on mutual liking The woman has a power of choice Secrecy and elopement are indispensable Parents and near kinsfolk of the woman are furious, and inflict cruel punishment
4. Marriage is, theoretically, communal, and is still practically so to some extent Certain gentes have mutual conjugal rights These rights are claimed by, and granted to, guests from other tribes of like organization	4 There is nothing approaching communism *after marriage*, though there is unmistakable evidence of its former prevalence All marital rights, after the consummation of marriage, are vested in the husband He exacts strict fidelity from his wife ; does not lend her to friendly visitors.
5 A gens can only intermarry with the gentes in a phratria other than its own	5 Each division can marry into any other division within certain limits, drawn to prevent a too close intermingling of blood

We may now inquire whether my theory can account for the facts.

Say that by some means or other—which we may consider by-and-bye—the two phratriæ,* Kumite and Kroki, are driven asunder, and that the Kumite phratria, or a gens belonging to it, settles in Gippsland, and becomes the Kŭrnai tribe. What will be the logical consequences of this event?

* *Phratria*—I use this term for the sake of convenience

STATEMENT OF THE THEORY. 299

I. In the first place, what is the organization of this band of Kumites? All the adult males are Kumite. We may suppose that their wives accompany them. All these women are Krokigor. There can be no Kumitegor among them, for the Kumitegors are with the other phratria as the wives of the Krokis—(*See* Table A, p. 34). Hence all the men are Kumite and all the women are Krokigor. For these names substitute Yeerŭng and Djeetgŭn, and we have precisely the Kŭrnai system.

II. In the second place, what will be the status of their children?

If the whole tribe were still united, all these children would pass over to the other phratria. All the boys would be Kroki and all the girls Krokigor, because all the mothers are Krokigor—(Table A) But this is no longer possible, for the simple reason that the other phratria is no longer within reach. And, besides, if the Kŭrnai were still to follow the old rule, there would be no Kumite among those children; and, what is more, there could never again be a Kumite in any subsequent generation, if descent continued to be reckoned entirely through the mother The son in the first descent would be Kroki, after his mother Krokigor, but his son could not be Kumite, because there are no Kumitegors; and, under the old rule, without a Kumitegor mother there could not be a Kumite son.

The Kumite, therefore, would be compelled to break the old rule, as far as regards their sons: firstly, in order to prevent their name from becoming utterly extinct; and secondly, because, if the rule were not broken, it would for ever afterwards bring husband and wife under the same class name, for all men would be Kroki and all women Krokigor. And this would be an utter abomination to minds which had become hard set in the Kamilaroi mould. My theory is that the Kŭrnai *feigned* their sons to be of the father's class, in accordance with the well-known habit of such hard-set tribes, who, when they are compelled to accept new arrangements, invent fictions to bring them under the sanction of ancient usage. There would be no difficulty about the girls. Their mothers being Krokigor, they also would be Krokigor throughout all generations, as may be seen at a glance by referring to the diagram of descents given in a note at the end of Kamil. Mar., chap. iii.

In the first descent, therefore, the male children would be Kumite by an absolutely necessary breach of the old rule, while the girls would be Krokigor in accordance with that rule; and this would apply to all succeeding generations. Once more substitute Yeerŭng and Djeetgŭn for those class names, and again we have precisely the Kŭrnai system.

This arrangement seems to be all the more probable because it simply perpetuates that which was the organization of the phratria at the date of separation, when all the adult males were Yeerŭng and all the females Djeetgŭn.

III. In the third place, what will be the marriage regulations?

Had the tribe remained united, the young men would have taken wives from the other phratria, and the girls would have been taken to wife by its youths. That is to say, Kumite would have married Krokigor, and Kroki Kumitegor, and no man would have said them nay. This being now impossible, some other arrangement must be made; and none other can be made which does not involve marriage within the phratria.

But this is abhorrent to the old rule. It has been shown that, among tribes organized on the Kamilaroi system, such marriages are strictly forbidden, and sternly punished when they occur. The prohibition extends even to cases of forcible abduction, and to captives taken in war. Nevertheless, mutual liking proves stronger than ancient custom, and sometimes leads to connections of the forbidden kind. In such cases the only way in which the young people can effect their purpose is by elopement, and hiding themselves away in the bush. Great indignation is shown by their kinsfolk, and the runaway couple are followed by a hot pursuit. If taken, they are severely punished, perhaps even put to death.—(*See* Kamil. Mar., chap. iii)

And this, which is the custom under the Kamilaroi system in cases of illicit cohabitation within a phratria, is precisely the Kŭrnai usage in all cases, for the reason (if my theory be correct) that every Kŭrnai marriage must be of that kind.

Excepting in the rare cases noted by Mr. Howitt, where the consent of the girl's father could be obtained—together with the case of the deceased brother's widow, and that of the wife's younger sister, both of which are in strict accordance with ancient rule—marriage among the Kŭrnai was invariably by elopement Secrecy was indispensable. As Mr Howitt tells us, " it was indispensable to success that the parents of the girl should be utterly ignorant of what was about to take place " When the elopement occurred, the friends of the girl were furious If the runaways were caught, the man had to stand as a target for the spears, boomerangs, and *kulluks** of her near kinsmen, while the poor girl was "speared, or beaten within an inch of her life, by her father, mother, and brothers." This is precisely what would take place among the Kamilaroi if a man ran off with a woman of a forbidden class. Compare Mr Howitt's account with that given to Mr. Reeve by Dora, of the Herbert River tribe, of how her

* [Kulluk = gallak = wood, or tree —A W H]

brother slashed " under the left breast and over the back " the woman whom he found in the bush with her disqualified lover.*

Again, my correspondents agree in stating that among the Kamilaroi, if the eloping couple can elude pursuit " for a certain time," their offence may be condoned; and this, also, is in accordance with the usage of the Kŭrnai, of whom Mr. Howitt tells us that, " if the couple can remain away until the girl is with child, it is said that they will be forgiven" Very significant, too, is the Kŭrnai's defence of their usage against the accusation of cruelty, on the ground that " it was not intended as cruelty, but simply to follow an ancestral custom "

It is manifest that both the elopement of the young people, and the cruelty of their kinsfolk, are in accordance with the "ancestral custom" which still prevails among the Kamilaroi, and I venture to say that my theory is very strongly confirmed by its affording what seems to be the only possible explanation of the Kŭrnai usage Their marriage by elopement cannot by any possibility be looked upon as a survival of an older custom of marriage by capture; for this kind of marriage is co-existent with it among the Kŭrnai, is openly practised, and brings no penalty upon the man or the woman at the hands of their own kinsfolk. The cruel punishment of the lovers is satisfactorily explained by the theory now advanced, and I cannot see that it admits of any other explanation.

IV. In the fourth place, how do we account for the fact that the Kŭrnai husband has an exclusive right to his wife ?

Under the old regulations, his wife would be "of the other phratria," and every one of his tribal brothers would

---

* *Ante*, p 65.

STATEMENT OF THE THEORY.

have, at least theoretically, marital rights over her. But now, when the elopement has been successful, there is no one to share his right, for the conditions under which the old regulations worked no longer exist. His wife is his own, not by right of a status in which others share, but by special contract between himself and her. He has made her his own by elopement, risking death from the weapons of her kinsmen, while she, on her part, risked dangerous spear wounds and a savage beating with clubs and sticks She cannot be of a gens over which his tribal brothers may have marital rights, for all those gentes must belong to that other phratria, of which perhaps even the very tradition has been forgotten by his tribe She is his own, and no man can share in his right after he has fully acquired it.*

Still more clearly do we see why it should be no longer a part of the rights of hospitality to lend the wife to a friendly guest This accommodation is afforded by tribes who have the Kamilaroi system, not as a matter of favour, but in accordance with a mutual obligation binding upon them all That it is commonly claimed and granted is beyond dispute Of this we have a striking proof in the fact made known to us by Mr Howitt, that their gesture language has a special sign for it; "a peculiar folding of the hands" indicating "either a request or an offer, according as it is used by the guest or the host" This is so among those tribes, because their common organization gives them a common privilege. But the Kŭrnai have no longer that

* Mr Howitt's Latin note shows plainly that the exclusive right is not acquired until the dangers of elopement have been successfully encountered The man is one of a group, each member of which has as much right to elope with the girl as he has The secret meeting in the forest seems to be a compounding for that right, which, however, must be distinguished from the marital right of the Kamilaroi Such a right may, to a certain extent, have grown up among the Kŭrnai since the "dispersion," but it is manifest that it was subject to the ancient law.

organization in common with them; and, therefore, they are no longer under its obligation. They stand alone A stranger, unless he come into one of their "divisions" by adoption, can have neither part nor lot with them. Other tribes call themselves after their languages—the Unghi-speakers, the Kamilaroi, the Wiraithari, people who say "Kamil" or "Wirai,"* as the case may be. But the Gippsland blacks are Kŭrnai—MEN; while their enemies, of all tribes, are Brajerak—wild men, savages, βάρβαροι

V. How comes it that each "division" of the Kŭrnai can marry anywhere beyond its own limits, though not within those limits?

According to my theory, the "divisions" were formerly exogamous gentes, belonging to an exogamous phratria.† But now this phratria can no longer be exogamous, because all marriages must be within its boundaries; and the old law being of necessity broken, there is no reason why it should not be broken as regards any part of the phratria, provision being made against the union of relatives too near in blood.

"But, if this be so," it may be asked, "why should not marriage take place within a division?"

The reason seems to be that the Kŭrnai still *recognized* the old law of exogamy to its full extent, and they *obeyed* it

---

* Kamil, or Wirai These are the negative There are other tribes which call themselves MEN as their distinctive title; but information as to their marriage customs is coming all too slowly in

† The "divisions," as now existing, may perhaps have been formed since the "dispersion" Several facts point to this as probable

[I do not think that the "divisions" of the Kŭrnai clans were formerly exogamous gentes It seems to me that, granting the original occupation of Gippsland by a group such as that suggested by Mr Fison's theory, the natural growth of the population as to numbers spreading over the country, along the lakes and rivers, would cause that population to break up into related groups, which, following the form of the ancient rule, would be exogamous —A W.H.]

STATEMENT OF THE THEORY

as far as they could. They forbade marriage within the gens, for this was still possible to them; and they refused to *legalize* marriage within the phratria, though it was impossible for them to avoid it They showed how strong a hold the law had upon them by punishing every breach of it with cruel severity, although it was no longer possible for them to keep it; and in so doing, if my theory be the true one, they followed an "ancestral custom" which obtained among their forefathers in the days when marriage was not of necessity a breach of law

The separation of a phratria, or a gens from the tribe to which it belonged, will not, I think, be deemed an event so improbable as to weaken the hypothesis on which I have endeavoured to explain the peculiarities of the Kŭrnai system The event might have come to pass in any one of the following ways:— *Disruption of a tribe*

1. By the voluntary withdrawal of a part of the tribe, or a separation by mutual consent

2 By the inroad of a stronger tribe, breaking up the weaker, and scattering it in various directions.

3 By the expulsion of an offending gens from the tribe.

4 By an angry blood feud between the two phratriæ resulting in war, and the conqueror driving the vanquished away from the common hunting grounds.

I do not think it likely that the separation was a peaceful one; for the two phratriæ are so woven together, as it were, that nothing short of a very powerful force would be strong enough to rend them asunder.

Segmentation of a tribe by mutual consent must have been of no uncommon occurrence—the identity of the classes in so many widely distant localities seems to make it certain that this was how the natives spread themselves over the continent—but in all such cases each segment had its due proportion of both phratriæ The movement was simply a migration of a part of the community to new hunting grounds, and we have seen that the old tribal bond remained unbroken. Hence it could not account for the Kŭrnai peculiarities. An overwhelming hostile inroad, though it might break up the tribe, would scarcely be likely to effect the complete separation of the two phratriæ. Still, it is a barely possible cause. The expulsion of an offending gens from the tribe we know to have occurred elsewhere; and such a gens settling in a country like Gippsland, where it would be completely isolated, might account for the Kŭrnai. But, on the whole, the most likely cause of separation seems to be a bloody quarrel between the two phratriæ, which had gone too far to be appeased. Blood feuds between them are of common occurrence, the mode of expiation being that described by Mr. Howitt. If in any case the atonement for blood were refused by a man, and his kinsmen backed him up in his refusal, a bitter quarrel might ensue, in which every member of the tribe would soon be involved. So easily, indeed, might such a feud arise, that we can but admire the strength of the tribal bond, and wonder that it has ever sufficed to hold together such materials without chiefs or executive, or any basis of authority other than public opinion based upon ancient custom.

In any case, if my theory be correct, the "other phratria" must be somewhere, unless it were either completely blotted out—which is unlikely—or absorbed into some other tribe of like organization. Hence we should expect to find, somewhere or other, a tribe answering to the phratria which was formerly the complement of that which is now the Kŭrnai. I think it probable that we shall find a number of such tribes, because, if the history of the Kŭrnai was what I suppose it to have been, it has, doubtless, repeated itself elsewhere. There is one tribe within my knowledge

—the Narinyeri, of South Australia—who appear to bear a strong resemblance to the Kŭrnai. They, too, arrogate to themselves the title of MEN, this being the meaning of their name; and they contemptuously brand all other tribes as Merkani, a word which has exactly the meaning of the term Brajerak, used by the Kŭrnai. The designations of their clans are not totems like those of the Kamilaroi (and other clusters of tribes who call themselves after their languages), but names of places like those of the Kŭrnai. Each clan has a totem, but it calls itself by the name of its *habitat*. They also appear to have, to a certain extent, descent through the father. This information I received, more than six years ago, from the Rev. George Taplin,* of the Aboriginal Mission at Point Macleay; but he was unable to give me the particulars which are necessary to fix the exact status of the tribe, and all my subsequent

---

* At the eleventh hour, just before sending my MSS. to the printer, I have received a copy of the "South Australian Aboriginal Folklore," edited by Mr. Taplin. It contains communications from some of my own correspondents, and much material which, when collated and systematized, will be of great value.

The information as to marriage and relationship in most cases needs further inquiry and explanation. Thus, the oft-recurring statement, "Blood relations are not allowed to marry," is perfectly useless, unless we can ascertain what the informant means by blood relations. Quite enough, however, is shown to strengthen my conviction that there is another system of marriage and relationship in Australia, differing from the Kamilaroi; that the Kŭrnai system, or one nearly approaching it, will be found in other tribes; and that South Australia is where we shall find it.

The tables of the kinship terms given in the work are not full enough to be of much practical use. I have had nearly all of them in my possession for several years, but have never been able to get them completed. It was at my instance that Mr. Taplin first began to collect the terms, and he has done Mr. Howitt and myself the honour of using the methods of obtaining them which we gave him. He disposes of my interpretation of the "Tamil System" in a rather summary manner; but, doubtless, owing to my own deficiencies as to clearness of expression, I signally failed to make him understand what that interpretation is. After much correspondence with him on the subject, he came to the conclusion that I supposed the Tamil system to be the result of polyandry.

efforts to ascertain them were of no avail. Hence I cannot say positively what the Narinyeri system is, but I have little doubt that it will be found to resemble the Kŭrnai, though it may not have taken precisely the same form ; for the Kŭrnai were an isolated tribe, while the Narinyeri, as far as I know, have not been shut out from external impulse.

The Kroa-tungolung.
All the Kŭrnai peculiarities noted by Mr Howitt appear to be satisfactorily accounted for by my hypothesis, with one exception. And this is the fact that the Kroatŭngolūng clan, alone of all the Kŭrnai, do not join in the ceremony of "initiation." This seems to be a fact of considerable importance—at least it is so if they do not join in that ceremony because they are not *qualified* For the "Brogan" are not brothers because they have a common initiation: they have that initiation because they are brothers—that is, none but tribal brothers can be Brogan. They are all Yeerŭng: and since it appears that the Kroatŭngolūng males also are all Yeerŭng, it is not easy to see whence their disqualification can arise

Objections to the hypothesis
To my theoretical explanation of the curious usage as to marriage among the Kŭrnai on the supposition that both the elopement and the punishment which followed were forced upon the tribe by the circumstances in which they were placed, and by the hold which ancient custom had upon them, it may possibly be objected that, even if the Kŭrnai were a fragment of a broken tribe, they would not have been compelled to marry within their own bounds, because they could have stolen women from other tribes—in other words, that they could have supplied their needs by what Mr. M'Lennan calls marriage by capture

But, in the first place, Mr. Howitt has shown that the Kŭrnai were not easily accessible to other tribes, and, consequently, other tribes were not easily accessible to them ;

whence it is impossible that they could have stolen a sufficient number of women.

In the second place, they did what they could in that line. They stole women from their enemies whenever they had the opportunity.

And, in the third place, marriage by capture, however successful, could not have met their case. Even if they had been able to help themselves to Brajerak women whenever they pleased, this could not have prevented the forbidden marriages, unless they had stolen husbands for their daughters as well as wives for their sons. Those young ladies would most certainly never have consented to devote themselves to a single life for no better reason than that an old law stood in their way. Mr. Howitt has told us how ready they were to brave spear-thrusts and club-strokes rather than remain unmarried, and how vigorously they battered the tardy swains of their tribe into a proper matrimonial spirit.

The Kŭrnai stole women, not from their enemies only, but from one another also—Tatūngolūng from Briakolūng, and so forth. In this, too, they followed ancient custom— the custom which still prevails among the tribes which have the Kamilaroi organization. Among these tribes, however, the capture of women is not a mere act of robbery. It is only a violent assertion of the communal right extending over all the tribes so organized. The captors have a *right* to the women whom they abduct; and if any one of them be so unlucky as to drag away a damsel of a class over which he has not that right, he dares not take her to himself.* Hence we see that marriage by capture falls in with the regulations of tribes which are divided into exogamous gentes and held together by a common organization. The feigned wrath of the bride's

---

* See the instances given by Mr Howitt, which prove that this prohibition was in force among the Kŭrnai also.

relatives, which is customary in many tribes at the present day, and which has been brought forward as evidence of the former prevalence of that kind of marriage, may well (in some cases, at least) be a survival of a usage like that of the Kŭrnai. Not a few such cases point to marriage by elopement even more clearly than to marriage by capture.

Former prevalence of communism There is strong evidence that communal marriage formerly prevailed among the Kŭrnai ancestors. The practice set forth in Mr. Howitt's Latin note is not otherwise to be explained. It is a valuable piece of evidence in support of what Sir John Lubbock calls expiation for marriage, and it affords precisely those conditions which Mr M'Lennan justly requires as necessary to make such evidence of value:—

"The privileged persons should be of the bridegroom's group only, and the cases should be capable of no simpler explanation" ("Studies," &c., p. 436)

Note also the remarkable significance of the fact recorded by Mr. Howitt, that, when a woman elopes from her husband, she becomes for the time being the common property of her pursuers if they can catch her. By her own act she has severed the tie which, binding her to her husband, guarded her against the old communal right, and forthwith that right asserts itself.

The Kamilaroi system could not have been evolved from the Kurnai. Although the Kŭrnai system appears, at first sight, to be directly at variance with the Kamilaroi, the connection between the two systems has been shown to be so close as to lead irresistibly to the inference that one of them was developed from the other According to my hypothesis, the Kŭrnai system was developed from the Kamilaroi under exceptional circumstances. Can we entertain the supposition that this order should be reversed, the Kamilaroi system having been developed from the Kŭrnai? I think not, and that for the following reasons:—

IMPORTANCE OF MR. HOWITT'S MONOGRAPH.

1. From the Kŭrnai to the Kamilaroi would be a retrogressive movement, and would therefore require strong *primâ facie* evidence to entitle the theory to consideration. As far as I am aware, there is no such evidence.
2. It would involve a change in the line of descent from the male line to the female, which is a reversal of the known order.
3. It would involve the development of communal marriage from the pairing family, which is a reversal of the natural order.
4. It fails to explain the Kŭrnai marriage by elopement, followed by severe punishment
5. The Kŭrnai system bears evident traces of former descent through the mother, and of other Kamilaroi characteristics which are the direct result of the Kamilaroi organization
6. The Kamilaroi system has been shown to be the logical outcome of the division of a tribe into two exogamous intermarrying phratriæ, and its development has been traced step by step
7. The Kŭrnai system cannot account for the Kamilaroi, whereas the Kamilaroi system satisfactorily accounts for the Kŭrnai.

If my theory of the Kŭrnai system of marriage and descent be the true one, the importance of Mr. Howitt's monograph can scarcely be exaggerated. It is a faithful portraiture of a savage tribe, drawn, not by a passing traveller, but by an experienced observer who has an intimate acquaintance with the people he describes, and has thoroughly gained their confidence. Were it no more than this, it would be of considerable value But, in addition to this, it is perhaps the most striking illustration on record of the tenacity with which ancient custom keeps its hold upon the savage mind, even under circumstances

The importance of Mr. Howitt's monograph.

which make obedience to the old law an utter impossibility. It shows how exclusive marital rights could be established in the midst of surrounding communism without a parallel advance in other respects. It exhibits the germinal idea of the personal acquisition of property, and its transmission by inheritance to individuals in a tribe apparently saturated with communal ideas. It shows us such a tribe, the communal bond being suddenly broken, dragged rapidly by the irresistible force of circumstances along the very path by which others have slowly advanced, and struggling vainly to conform itself to the old law from which these others struggled successfully to free themselves. It affords what seems to be a novel form of marriage; and, above all, it shows the line of descent *in process* of change from the female to the male, together with the cause and the manner of that change. Many tribes bear manifest tokens of having made the change, but they do not tell us how they made it.*

But though the Kŭrnai was in the direct line of progress, he seems to me to have got there by accident, against his will and before his time. He did not *grow* out of the old groove—he was *thrown* out of it; and he appears to have

---

* In one or two instances we may note the change in course of progress. Thus, Campbell tells us that, among the Limbu, a tribe of North-eastern India, the father *buys* his sons into his own gens by payment to their mother. (Campbell's Statement, quoted by Lubbock, "Origin," &c., p 123)

In Mota, one of the Banks group, where descent is through the mother, the Rev R. H Codrington informs me that the heirs to the real estate are the sister's children, but the agnates redeem the inheritance by payment out of the personal property. A landowner, when dying, gives directions as to the amount to be paid for the redemption of the land from his sister's children. When a tribe reaches this point, it is not far from descent through the father. Instances have occurred, not long ago, of rebellion against the old custom at Mota The son insisted on inheriting from his father, and shot the heirs in defence of his claim. Landed property and settled abodes are sure to be fatal, sooner or later, to uterine succession. (*See* "Transactions of the Royal Society of Victoria, 1879.")

been utterly unable to free himself from its traditions, though he was forced into acts which were directly antagonistic to them. Nevertheless, if he had not been brought to an untimely end by the invasion of the white man, it seems not improbable that he would have fitted himself to his altered surroundings. For instance, the practice of marriage by elopement, followed by cruel punishment, would, doubtless, have been abandoned. Already, as Mr. Howitt tells us, there were rare instances of marriage with consent of the girl's father; and if time had been allowed for this to become the rule, instead of the exception, the system of pairing marriage with consent of the woman and her friends, exclusive marital rights, and descent in the male line would probably have been fully established among the Kŭrnai.

The fact, however, remains that—granting my theory—the original impulse of their advance was what may be called an accident. But it was an accident which must have been of not unfrequent occurrence elsewhere. Many a tribe, organized like the forefathers of the Kŭrnai, must have been broken up in the old, wild, stormy times, either by blood feuds at home or by invasion from abroad; and, in some cases, the scattered fragments must have been forced away from the old regulations. And if one of these scattered groups, falling into favourable circumstances, grew into a conquering race, it must have had a powerful influence in breaking down old customs and introducing new ones.

Say, for instance, that the Kŭrnai had been permitted to develop undisturbed in their Gippsland fastnesses. Mr. Howitt has shown that their country was exceptionally favourable to the growth of population. It abounded in nourishing food, and was exempt from the terrible droughts which periodically devastate other parts of the continent

If, under these circumstances, the Kŭrnai had grown into a tribe strong enough to overrun the surrounding country, they might have imposed their system on the vanquished tribes, making communal marriage give way to the pairing family, changing the line of descent from the female line to the male, and introducing the new idea of the personal acquisition of property, with inheritance by the individual to the exclusion of the group, which seems to have been the most powerful agent in the breaking up of the old commune

We cannot put aside these cases as not worth counting among the agents of human progress on the ground that they are "exceptional" They are so only in the sense that they are not the result of orderly development; but they must have been of frequent occurrence, and they could not have been without effect. Our own experience, and the records of history, have so accustomed us to orderly growth that we are apt to look upon it as the only process worth recording, and to lose sight of the fact that it is order, and not disorder, which must have been exceptional in the old times when "the earth was filled with violence." Our experience is only of society as it has presented itself to us, and history begins for us with great nations fully organized, and with orderly processes "shaping their ends" But the study of savage life takes us back to the days before the tribes had consolidated into nations. In those days the "ends" of society had to be "rough-hewn;" and broken tribes, flung out of old grooves, and forced into breaches of old law, may have done much of this preliminary work. And so, here as elsewhere, that which seemed to be disorder falls into its place among the marshalled forces which have been working together in the accomplishment of one Great Design.

LORIMER FISON.

SUMMARY AND GENERAL CONCLUSIONS.

BY

A. W. HOWITT.

SUMMARY AND GENERAL CONCLUSIONS.

FROM the facts stated in the preceding pages, it is, I think, clear that the Kŭrnai, when Gippsland was first discovered, were in that social condition which is defined by individual marriage in its form of the pairing family.* The restriction which is the essence of individual marriage applied, however, only to the woman. The man recognized no restriction, excepting that which prohibited his intermarriage, or cohabitation even, with a woman of certain forbidden degrees or classes The forbidden degrees included, among others, all those of the contemporaneous generation whom we should regard as brothers, sisters, or cousins.† The forbidden classes had not that precision which is given by the class names or totems of other Australian tribes, but they were sufficiently defined by the limits of those social aggregates which I have termed "divisions;" and these "divisions," being local, indicate common descent. Many customs co-existing with the pairing family of the Kŭrnai appear at first sight to be unmeaning or inexplicable. The curious temporary license attending marriage by elopement, the penalty inflicted upon the unfaithful wife, the right of the widower to his deceased wife's unmarried sister, the occasionally-admitted claim by the husband to the unmarried sister of his wife, and the right of the surviving

margin note: The present condition of the Kŭrnai is that of individual marriage.

---
* Pairing Family, see p 236
† Including even father's sister's children and mother's brother's children, Ego being male or female

brother to his deceased brother's widow—all seems at first sight incompatible with individual marriage, in which the woman's faithfulness is ensured under severe penalties.

The kinship terms have been developed and not invented

These seeming inconsistencies disappear, however, upon a careful consideration of the terms used by the Kŭrnai to define the inter-sexual relations. I have already pointed out what, as it seems to me, that meaning is, and I need only now briefly state that it raises a strong presumption that at some former period the terms were accurately fitted to a social state in which there was group marriage regulated by class laws. From this point of view the various terms and their reciprocals are seen to follow logically, or, where they apparently do not do so, the discrepancy is capable of explanation. On the assumption that these terms have been invented, as suggested by Mr. M'Lennan, as "a code of courtesies and ceremonial addresses," we might certainly expect some logical sequence, but scarcely that there should be exceptions which are only explicable upon the assumption that they have been gradually developed, but not deliberately invented. This is of itself a strong ground for regarding them as having been developed gradually, as language is, to meet the wants and requirements of the time.

To my mind, Mr. M'Lennan has taken up an untenable position in respect to those terms which he calls a system of "ceremonial addresses," and which Dr. Morgan has named the classificatory system of kinships.

He admits that the terms "in the Malayan form illustrate a very early social condition of man;" "that the phenomena presented in all the forms of the classificatory system are ultimately referable to the marriage law, and, accordingly, its origin must be so also." He also says that "the system of blood ties and the system of addresses would begin to grow up together, and for some little time have a common

KINSHIP TERMS HAVE NOT BEEN INVENTED. 319

history."* The distinction between the two systems appears, therefore, according to Mr. M'Lennan, to arise only after "some little time," and this undefined period he afterwards fixes as being when polyandry of the Nair type was instituted † The evidence in this work shows that his hypothesis that polyandry was the first form of the family is utterly untenable, at any rate as concerns the Australians. But even without this, the statements I have quoted convey serious doubts as to the soundness of his conclusions

It follows from the above quotations that, admitting this hypothesis of a system of "ceremonial addresses," his other system of "blood ties" must either be yet extant, or have died out

That a "system of blood ties"—that is, terms of kinships—should have totally died out while conditions requiring such definitions existed, is to me as utterly inconceivable as that no system of kinships should have ever arisen That a system of "blood ties," having a common origin, and for some little time a common course, with that which Mr M'Lennan is pleased to call a "system of ceremonial addresses," yet exists, must be left to him, or to those who hold his views, to prove All I feel myself called upon to show is, that no such system exists among the Australian savages, excepting that classificatory system whose origin and development have been demonstrated in this work.

I cannot but think that if Mr. M'Lennan had had as much personal acquaintance with savages as we have with those of Australasia, he would have seen, as clearly as we see, that the classificatory system is to them as truly a system of "blood ties"—that is, of kinships—as our own descriptive system is to us.

After twenty years of observation of the Australian

---
*"Studies in Ancient History," &c , p. 372, *et infra.*
† *op. cit* , pp. 373-379.

savages, I have no hesitation in saying that neither they nor their progenitors, to judge of them by their descendants, are or were capable of inventing so complete and logical a system of terms

At any rate, that hypothesis must be provisionally accepted which best explains the observed facts The hypothesis which suggests to us that the terms of kinship and relationship used by the Kŭrnai are survivals from a time when they accurately defined the then existing conditions, is also able to explain to us why they should still very often express those feelings which would naturally arise under such a state, and which have partially survived till now. On the other hand, the hypothesis which regards those terms of kinship and relationship as mere "ceremonial addresses" fails to explain why it is that we find the feelings of parental and filial affection spreading widely beyond those bounds which are indicated by the pairing family and individual marriage. Of these two hypotheses, it is the former only which is in harmony with that which we know of the social and domestic condition of the Australian aborigines.

The class divisions of the Kurnai. It is universally the case, so far as my experience goes, that class divisions exist in the Australian tribes.* The origin of these class divisions was probably connected with the segmentation of an undivided commune They differ to some degree locally in the extent to which the subdivision of classes has been carried out. In those tribes having group marriage the classes have both male and female members. In the Kŭrnai tribe, having individual marriage, one class is wholly male and the other wholly female. The former class is Yeerŭng and the latter is Djeetgŭn. We

* Since writing this, I learn from the Rev. C W. Kramer, that the Wimmera tribe in Western Victoria had no class divisions This is the only exception I know of to the general rule.

THE CLASS DIVISIONS OF THE KŬRNAI. 321

may infer that the Kŭrnai ancestors, by whom Gippsland was first occupied, formed such a group as that I have mentioned bound together by communal intermarriage of exogamous classes.* The classes being exogamous, Yeerŭng

---

* In adopting Mr M'Lennan's convenient terms Endogamy and Exogamy, it is necessary to define clearly the sense in which I use them I may do this by saying that the Kŭrnai tribe is endogamous as to the tribe (plus marriage by capture as regards alien tribes), and exogamous as to all those social aggregates which I have named "divisions" I take this opportunity of making a few remarks on the sense in which Mr M'Lennan uses his own terms. In "Studies in Ancient History," &c , p 37, he defines "endogamous families or tribes as being those whose members are forbidden to intermarry with members of other families or tribes " Exogamous tribes he defines as being "organized on . . the principle that prohibited marriage within the tribe, and which * were then dependent upon other tribes for their wives " He says that it is "obvious that intertribal marriages could only be peaceably arranged between tribes whose relations were friendly But peace and friendliness were unknown between separate groups or tribes in early times, except when they were forced to unite against common enemies The sections of the same family, when it fell into sections, became enemies by the mere fact of separation ; and while this state of enmity lasted, exogamous tribes never could get wives except by theft or force" (p. 42) There is some looseness here in the use of the terms "tribe" and "family ;" and the expression "tribes in early times" is clearly convertible with that of "existing savage tribes" Some light may be obtained as to the probability of Mr. M'Lennan's statements by taking the Kŭrnai as an example Any other Australian tribe with which I am acquainted—excepting, perhaps, the Gournditch-mara, which appears, according to the Rev J H Stähle, not to have been an exogamous tribe (*see* Appendix F, p 274)—might serve equally well as an illustration Mr M'Lennan's statements apply, almost word for word, to the Kŭrnai, merely substituting the word "clan" for "tribe" The clans, which are sections of the same "family"—to use the author's synonym for tribe— were, as I have shown in this work, habitually more or less at war with each other; and while that state of enmity lasted between any two, they might perhaps only have obtained wives from each other by capture. But, as regards each such clan, the table I have given at p. 227 shows that the other Kŭrnai clans who remained friendly would still be open to it Even when the whole community was divided into two hostile moieties—as, for instance, by a great blood feud such as that arising out of the death of Kaiŭng (p 218)—the state of war was interrupted by times of peace, in which the exogamous practice would revive in the ordinary form of marriage by elopement However that may have been, this is certain— that the Kŭrnai, as repeatedly insisted upon to me by themselves, did not,

* "The tribes"

and Djeetgŭn would then represent, perhaps, one totem of each class. The original class names are seemingly lost to the Kŭrnai, and we cannot do more than conjecture that they may have been "Eaglehawk," and, perhaps, "Crow."

In its various local dialectic forms, such as "Mūquarra" or "Merūng," "Eaglehawk" is found as one of the two primary class names throughout much of the watershed of the Murray and the Darling rivers. The second name is usually "Crow"—for instance, "Kilpara" at the Darling River, and "Yŭkembrūk" at the Upper Murray River and at Maneroo. In South Australia I find, however, that "Eaglehawk" is associated, not with "Crow," but with 'Seal" (the Turra tribe, York's Peninsula, according to the Rev. W. J. Kühn). The Brajerak and Bidwelli, near neighbours of the Kŭrnai, have both "Eaglehawk" and "Crow." Among the Kŭrnai, the Eaglehawk ("Gwannŭ-

excepting on rare occasions, capture women of alien tribes (Brajerak); and it is equally certain that they did not obtain wives from them by exchange, gift, or elopement. It is, therefore, self-evident that the Kŭrnai were exogamous, that their clans were in a state of enmity amongst themselves, and that they did not obtain wives from other (alien) tribes unless in rare cases Yet this tribe did not die out, as it ought to have done under such circumstances according to the conditions laid down by Mr M'Lennan's theory, but married and perpetuated itself until our times. It is, therefore, clear that the Kŭrnai tribe was composed of sections of the same "family," and that those sections were habitually in a state of hostility with each other. Further, that, in spite of this, they did obtain wives from each other, and not from the section of any other "family" (tribe); and that these wives were, unless in exceptional cases, obtained in the ordinary course by elopement, which was the recognized form of marriage. Here we have those conditions which Mr M'Lennan declares are incompatible with each other.

This being the case, then, the grounds upon which he has based his theory of marriage by capture are insecure; and as this theory is, in fact, the keystone of his arch, his whole structure is in danger of collapse.

It appears to me that the fallacy in Mr. M'Lennan's argument is due to the looseness with which he applies the words "horde," "tribe," and "family," and to his overlooking the fact that the aggregate, which he calls a "tribe," is not in fact a community—*totus, teres, atque rotundus*—but merely a segment of such a community. See also *ante* p. 138, where Mr. Fison has referred to this subject.

mŭrŭng") is greatly reverenced. He is regarded as the type of the bold and sagacious hunter. His plumes and talons played a part in their necromancy. He figures in their tales in company with "Ebing," the Little Owl. It is possible that in "Ebing" we have the second class name, and were it not, perhaps, too fanciful, might see in the quarrels of "Gwannŭmŭrŭng" and "Ebing" a trace of the severance of the original commune into two classes, or of a social disruption which may have impelled the Kŭrnai ancestors into Gippsland.

It is not easy to conjecture from what tribe the original Kŭrnai were an offshoot I know of no tribe in which the birds Yeerŭng and Djeetgŭn are totems; but it must have been located in some district where the Superb warbler and the Emu wren are found The former is met with in some of its varieties over the Australian continent, but the latter is, so far as I know, confined to the cooler parts of the south-east. This suggests that the migration took place along the coast, either from the direction of Twofold Bay or from Western Port. Access from either place would be attended with much the same difficulties. Theie are but few facts upon which an opinion may be formed. In the Western Port tribes the word Būnjil was Eaglehawk; and, also, as I have pointed out (p. 210), Būnjil was regarded as a supernatural being living at the sources of the Yaira. An explanation may be suggested as to the present signification of the word among the Kŭrnai. With them Būnjil means an elder. It does not merely imply age, for Boldain is "old man"—it implies age, and, I think, some special qualities belonging to the individual. It might, therefore, have been attached to the early Kŭrnai in its signification among the Western Port tribes of "Eaglehawk," in other words, as the class name of the male ancestors of the Kŭrnai. In this case Yeerŭng would have been a totem of the Būnjil (Eaglehawk) class. Hence, every descendant under the partially-changed descent in the male line would be Yeerŭng, and also Būnjil. We might thus understand how Būnjil, meaning Eaglehawk in the Western Port tribes, would appear as the supernatural being living in the mountains at the source of the Yarra River—the eponym, as it were, of their tribe.* The customs of the Port Phillip tribes, as recorded by Buckley, the "wild white man," have a remarkable resemblance to those of the Kŭrnai, especially as regards marriage by elopement. I note, also, though little stress can be placed on this, that he uses the word "mŭrrawŭn" for throwing-stick, which is that still used here.

On the other hand, the word Gwannŭmŭrŭng (Eaglehawk) of the Kŭrnai is clearly the "merŭng" of the "Ngarrego" tribe of Carrawong, on the Maneroo tableland, and of the Wakerŭk tribe (Bidwelli) east of the Snowy River. It may, however, be that that word has been acquired from them by the Kŭrnai, and has thus superseded the original term. Moreover, the Kroatŭn Kŭrnai, whose most eastern division (*see* Table A, p. 227) intermarried with the Twofold Bay tribe, tell me, in their acquired English, that the latter were "their cousins." If they regarded them as "their cousins," and intermarried with them, it would be some evidence pointing to a former class connection.

Starting, however, from such a settlement by a communal group, it would have, during its expansion within the natural boundaries of Gippsland, a homogeneous social development free from external influences. The simplicity of system embodied in the Kŭrnai terms of kinship is archaic, and strongly contrasted with their actual and

---

* In the Mŭk-jarawaint tribe of Western Victoria, Būnjil seems to have been similarly regarded as a supernatural being. The eaglehawk was one of their totems, but it was called Wŭrpl.

advanced condition of family. It seems to me most probable that when the Yeerŭng and Djeetgŭn group first occupied Gippsland they were in an early form of communal marriage, and that the passage of their descendants from that to individual marriage and the pairing family has been, comparatively, very rapid. Their domestic and social organization is, in fact, strongly leavened by the fundamental idea of a pair, with partial descent through the male, while their language bears testimony to the former existence of group marriage and descent through the female.

As might be expected of a community in this condition, authority is in the husband and father, and thence, by a natural extension, it passes in the aggregate of families to the elders of the division.* The wide extension of the group over Gippsland has caused it to break up into clans which, although recognizing common descent, differ more or less from each other in language ; and those which are most distant differ most. Looking at all the evidence, I think it may be assumed, with confidence, that the domestic and social condition of the Kŭrnai has undergone a slow process of development from earlier conditions less advanced than those now existing. That it has been a slow process, if we reckon by years, we may justly infer on considering that, owing to extreme isolation, the changes would be induced by internal rather than external influences. The progressive change in the family has evidently been slowly followed by an adaptive change in the language, and in this we may perceive another instance of the tenacity of hold which custom has upon savages.

It has been shown, in the earlier part of this

* Mr. Fison has suggested to me a just doubt whether this authority of the individual husband and father is a natural development of *patria potestas*, or whether it is not rather a survival of the older form of authority when the elders were the rulers of the communal group.

326 SUMMARY AND GENERAL CONCLUSIONS.

The present social condition of the Australian tribes lies between communal and individual marriage

work, that the theoretical domestic condition of tribes, such as those which have the Kamilaroi organization, is that of group marriage in its typical form of two exogamous communes, each having sub-classes, totems, and the classificatory system of relationships developed therefrom. But the actual family condition of these tribes varies with each community, and it does so according to the slightly different conditions under which each particular society has been developed I am not aware that any tribes having the typical communal structure still exist in Australia at the present time. It is, however, premature to say positively that they do not until full information has been collected as to all the aboriginal communities. Yet some tribal organizations approach near to it. The following instances are, I think, typical.

In many other tribes than that mentioned by Mr. T. E. Lance (p. 31) the women are, more or less, monopolized by the elder men. Yet, on certain occasions, the communal rights revive in favour of the younger men, and are also extended to friendly strangers visiting the tribe (*e g.*, Dieri and Yantrūwŭnta of Cooper's Creek, and the Turra of York's Peninsula). These rights arise out of, and are exercised under, the class rules. Elsewhere a man of any one class may claim marital rights over a woman of the corresponding class wherever he may meet her, although he never saw her before, and his right will not be questioned (Kamilaroi—Mr. Cyrus E. Doyle, Kunopia, N S.W.; *see also* p. 53). In other tribes women are betrothed when merely infants, but in accordance with stringent class rules (Geawegal tribe, *see* Appendix G) In tribes of this organization women are not generally "lent." Yet in others, it may be said that "Brothers have their wives in common" (Waimbio tribe, Lower Murray—Appendix I), and the Levirate generally exists (Kŭrnai tribe, &c.)

Again in other tribes, and, so far as I know, especially in south-eastern Australia, individual marriage has become established; an extreme case being that of the Kŭrnai, amongst whom selection rested with the woman, who became a wife by elopement with her future husband, but still under well understood, although modified, class laws.*

In all this there is a gradually progressive series, commencing at a society nearly approaching to the divided exogamous commune, and extending upwards to a society based upon individual marriage. Taking two extreme instances—namely, the Queensland tribe, having the Kamilaroi organization, and the Kŭrnai—it is plain that the social condition, as shown by actual customs, is always in advance of the theoretical social condition to be inferred from class rules and the kinship terms.

The tendency of the class and totemic divisions has been to restrict the exercise of marital rights, and thus to prepare for the establishment of individual marriage.

Mr. Fison has clearly demonstrated that the totems, sub-classes, and class divisions of the Australian tribes point to the former segmentation of an undivided commune. Starting from the segmentation of an original commune, produced by influences such as those alleged by the Dieri legend, all the subsequent steps are such as might readily follow under the laws of social development. The rules regulating marriage are directly in accord with such a segmentation, and it is out of the action of such rules that the classificatory system of kinship has arisen. If any system of kinship did arise under such

The primitive social condition of the Australian savage is that of the commune,

---

* The Gournditch-mara tribe (Appendix F) was, according to Mr Stähle, an exception to the general rule, as there was no restriction upon marriage within its four classes, other than that based upon forbidden degrees of relationship. According to Mr J. Gibson, the Chepara tribe of Southern Queensland was similarly constituted.

rules—and the contrary is inconceivable to me—it would be just such a one as the classificatory that the circumstances would have developed. No people have ever set themselves to deliberately invent a complete system of designations for kinships and relationships. The process has been one of adaptation of language to wants as they arose. Even the elaborate extension and amplification of terms under the Roman law is a direct case in point. They were invented by the civilians to meet an imperative want, and do no more than complete a code of relationships which already existed.

Such an undivided commune, if it existed, must logically be one in which cohabitation would be, to a certain extent at least, promiscuous. Terms implying this, as regards each contemporaneous generation, are found in many Australian tribes. Thus, inferentially, such a commune might be suspected; and there is some direct evidence in the Dieri legend, given by Mr. Gason, of its former existence.*

Relationship among the Australians is to the group.

In connection with group marriage and the exogamous class divisions, we find the recognition by individuals of one tribe and class, or totem, of their relationship to other individuals, members of an alien tribe, but of analogous class or totem. We find that this recognition is not merely of individual to individual, but of class to class, and group to group.

The communal principle is strongly evident in Australian aboriginal society.

The communal principle is a strongly-marked element in the structure of aboriginal society. With the Kŭrnai, it shows itself in the division of food, in curious customs attached to their marriage state, in their recognition of

---

* In communications received while this work is going through the press, concerning another tribe of Cooper's Creek, the Kūnandabūri, I find that the terms of relationship and some exceptional customs attending marriage point strongly to the above conclusions. The important evidence derived from a study of this tribe must, however, necessarily wait for a future opportunity.

relationship to the group, and in the liability of the whole group for the crimes of its members.

Evidence has been given in support of this position, and I may now particularly instance the case of Billy Blew (p. 218), and also the case of Bŭnbra (p. 216) and the kin of Barney. These show clearly that a wrong done to the individual was done to the community of which he was a member. The extent of this principle has, I think, been generally overlooked and misunderstood.

Sir John Lubbock, in his work, "The Origin of Civilization and the Primitive Condition of Man," 1870, quotes (p 318) three instances from which he draws this conclusion. "Since, then, crimes were, at first, regarded merely as personal matters, in which the aggressor and the victim alone were interested, and with which society was not concerned, any crime, even murder, might be atoned for by the payment of such a sum of money as satisfied the representatives of the murdered man." The premises from which this conclusion is drawn appear to be embodied in three quotations, which Sir John has previously made. The first, taken from the Carribbeans, is that "the individual redresses his injury without the public concerning itself at all." The second is from the North American Indians, to the effect that "the family of the murdered man only have the right of taking satisfaction." The third is a statement made by Grey ("Travels in North-west and Western Australia," vol. ii., p. 243) that, among the Australian aborigines, "crimes may be compounded for by the criminal appearing and submitting himself to the ordeal of having spears thrown at him by all such persons as conceived themselves aggrieved." This instance is on all fours with the case of Bŭnbra. The conclusion is not very clearly stated, but I think it contains the following propositions:—

1. Crimes only concerned the victim and the aggressor.

2. Society did not concern itself with them.

3. Even murder might be condoned by payment to the representatives of the murdered man.

The first and second propositions I refer to now only. The third is not disclosed by either of the first two instances quoted, and can only be doubtfully inferred from the third in its concluding portion, which I have omitted as unnecessary to my argument. I do not dispute, however, that other evidence exists, even in the past history of our own race, in support of it; but it is beyond the point I am now considering.

Sir John Lubbock does not define "society" in the above conclusion, but I gather that it may have a twofold meaning; one implying the social aggregate of the savages instanced, and the other the social aggregate of primitive mankind. Looking at "society," as implied in the first definition, by the light of Bŭnbra's case, it becomes apparent that "society" and the "representatives," in other words "relations," are one and the same. There is no other "society" possible; for I have shown in this memoir on the Kŭrnai that their "society" includes those only who recognize a common descent, language, and country.

It is, therefore, erroneous to say that in such cases "society" does not concern itself. The case of Bŭnbra clearly illustrates this position. Bŭnbra and Barney belonged to two "societies," which, together, formed a larger "society." Each "society" was a body corporate. One was the victim by the supposed murder of its member, Barney; the other the aggressor, through its member, Bŭnbra. Every member of such a body would be supposed, in the first place, to instantly redress his own wrong, but this would not, in the least, prevent all his co-members from also revenging it, and not only upon the individual aggressor, but also upon all and several of his co-members. Such a

COMMUNAL PRINCIPLE IN ABORIGINAL SOCIETY. 331

sequence of revenge I have illustrated in the case of Billy Blew (p. 218). It is, therefore, evident that in this case each "society" did concern itself with this crime affecting one of its members. This is brought out into strong relief by considering what would have been the case if Barney had been done to death; or, which is immaterial, supposed to have been, by an alien. In such a case no atonement, by submitting to the throwing of spears or other weapons "by all those who conceived themselves to have been aggrieved," would have been possible The blood feud would have been inexpiable but by blood, and would have been maintained, if necessary, by the whole body corporate to which the victim belonged, namely, the Kŭrnai tribe, against the whole body corporate to which the aggressor belonged; that is, the Brajerak (or alien) tribe. We may perceive how wide-spread such a feud might become from the case of Billy Blew, although here the white man had introduced disturbing elements. Thus, in the view now taken, the whole of "society" would have concerned itself as to the crime. Herein lies the fallacy of Sir John Lubbock's argument so far as it applies to the Australian aborigines, and probably, also, in its application to other savages. As his conclusion is also directed manifestly to that "first state of society" which may be supposed to be pictured in the present condition of savages, it necessarily also fails to apply to it.

Is it possible that there is in Sir John Lubbock's conclusions, perhaps, an unconscious survival of the belief in the original independent condition of each individual man; that is, of the "degradation theory" of man's primitive condition?

The evidence as to the corporate character of savage society finds its parallel in the universal evidence as to the corporate character of archaic society. All ancient institutions, and all ancient history, are full of this evidence. Two cases may be noted so far apart, both as to time and place, as to fully prove the universality of the principle. One is the Eric fine of the Brehon laws—a pecuniary fine levied on tribes, or on families, for the wrongs done by their members (Maine's "Early Institutions," 2nd ed., p. 23). The other from the Hebrews, being the case of Korah, Dathan, and Abiram (Numbers xvi.), and that of Achan (Joshua vii.). The sacred records of this people contain many instances in point; and it must be borne in mind that their earlier institutions had then been profoundly modified by their sojourn in the Nile valley.

It might have been expected that this principle of community of rights and community of liability, which is equally striking a feature both in archaic and savage societies, would have been recognized more generally than it seems to have been by writers on the condition of savages, and on the primitive state of society. Yet this does not seem to have been the case. A probable explanation of this may be found in the fact that civilized man is now an "individual." He is no longer a mere member of a corporate community. His whole life's training, his domestic and social relations, are strictly in accord with his individualized condition. It would, indeed, be strange if his mode of thought were not more or less, consciously or unconsciously, brought into relation therewith. It seems very general to writers on these subjects to argue from the stand-point of individual ideas, rights, and duties.

It is, I think, Sir Henry S. Maine who has first clearly pointed out the corporate character of archaic society ("Ancient Law," p. 125, *et infra*). He points out that the unit of ancient society was the family, of a modern society the individual, and that in ancient law we find all the consequences of this difference. It takes a view of life wholly unlike any which appears in developed jurisprudence. Corporations never die; and, accordingly, primitive law considers the entities with which it deals—*i.e*, the patriarchal or family groups—as perpetual and inextinguishable. These views, which he so justly states as to archaic society in the dawn of history, are true also as to the earlier form of society which has come down to us among the Australian savages. But they must be modified so far in detail as to become applicable to the far more rudimentary condition of the family as it exists with them. Sir Henry Maine regards the past from the stand-point of archaic law, and, therefore, cannot be expected to obtain a view into the depths beyond the development of that law. He, therefore, regards the patriarchal family as the original unit of society. But the view that this form of the family is the true and original instance of a corporate society is, I think, only superficially true. Sir Henry Maine says that legal antiquities disclose to us men distributed in perfectly isolated groups, held together by obedience to the parent; not a mere collection of individuals, but an aggregate of families. He regards the patriarchal family as "older, probably, than the state, the tribe, and the house (*op. cit.*, p. 134).

Here we see that the vista does not extend backwards beyond the period of individual marriage, yet the patriarch was no more than the "individual" surrounded by his wives, his children, and his slaves. His condition was a matured form of the pairing family, in which the restriction applied to the woman alone; and his corporate capacity was probably an inheritance from more ancient times, when communal society still existed.

The view which Sir Henry S. Maine advances, that the original unit of society was the family, is very general. It occurs, plainly formulated, even in recent works, such as

Professor Hearn's most learned and admirable "Aryan Household" (Melbourne, 1878). His view is this—" From the simple homogeneous household are evolved numerous distinct and related households, which in the aggregate form a whole, and the whole is the gens" (p 138).

Looking at this view from the stand-point of our investigations as to the class divisions of the Australian tribes, it seems necessary to dissent from the learned professor's conclusion, if it assumes the individual household as the unit, and as the commencement of social development. For that which represents the gens exists in those Australian tribes which have modified group marriage, and, therefore, not only no "household," but merely the germs of the individual family.* We have here again the same view as that stated by Sir Henry S. Maine, but in this case it is the monogamian family which is taken as the unit, and not the patriarchal. This view is, in fact, a modified form of the older views of the condition of primitive man as an independent individual.

It is possible that, in certain periods of the history of mankind, a household held together by domestic religion may, in accordance with the known laws of evolution, have developed into a larger body similarly constituted, for mankind loves to walk in old and accustomed paths. But, for this to be possible, the *Family* must have been in existence, either in its patriarchal or monogamian form. The investigations as to the status of savages such as the Australians afford grounds for the belief that the individual family only came into existence when descent through the father had become a possible belief, through the breaking up of the communal family, with its female line of descent. The

---

* Dr. Hearn, however, disclaims all attempts on his part to go beyond the monogamian family. "The Aryan Household," p. 153.

boundary line separating those two social conditions marks, I think, one of the most momentous stages in the progressive development of human society.*

According to the generally received view, the clan and the tribe would result from the natural expansion of the individual family. It seems to me that the most probable process of development has been by the segmentation of the expanding communal group into groups similarly constituted. This process would produce those aggregates which have been variously named clans, septs, or thums, and these tribal divisions have been held together by common descent, and the iron bonds of internal class rules.

Professor Hearn points out that the "clan" was an

---

* Dr Morgan seems to be of opinion ("Ancient Society," p 345) that the change from female to male descent, so far as the Greek or Roman gentes was concerned, may have been intentional, and, perhaps, brought about by "some motive sufficiently general and convincing to establish the injustice of the exclusion in the face of their changed condition" The probability of this suggestion is strengthened by what we know of the changes made in Roman law as to the law of inheritance affecting the cognates, and the effacement thereby of the distinctions in this respect existing between them and the agnates But such a motive could not arise until property had assumed a definite form through the change of hunting tribes to communities of graziers and agriculturists, with the concomitant settled homes and accumulation of moveable wealth Among the Kūrnai, as among other Australian tribes which have partially or wholly effected the change in the line of descent, there were no such motives, nor could there be; yet we see the change partially or wholly accomplished, and seemingly connected with the rise of individual marriage Neither can I hold, with Mr E B Tylor, at any rate so far as concerns the Australians, in the opinion stated in his most admirable work ("Early History of Mankind," third edition, p 285) I observe that he there states that savages "have had to elect which of the two lines, male or female, they will keep up by the family name or sign." This is as regards descent My objections are twofold :—1 In this view the idea of descent both in the male and female line must have been known to these savages 2. They must have deliberately elected which line they would follow. Descent in the male line could only be imagined on the breaking-up of the communal family by means of individual marriage Descent in the female line exists as a necessary consequence of the communal family. The inference drawn by Mr Tylor is not only not supported by our evidence as to the Australian aborigines, but is traversed by it.

original institution common to all the Aryan races. That which was common to these races must have been derived from their parent stock. Similarly, the "clan" system is common, in more or less well marked characters, to the Semitic races. It must have been derived from the Semitic stock. Were it possible to trace back both the Aryan and Semitic stocks to their common source, it is not unreasonable to suspect that we might find generalized in that community those peculiarities which we see in a specialized condition in them. That generalized form, for instance, of the monogamian and patriarchal families would certainly be some variety of the pairing family. The form of the family differed in each of the races I have instanced. In the Aryan races it was based upon individual marriage, with its restriction drawn closer by the requirements of domestic worship. It was necessary that an immediate and undoubted descendant should step into the position of the deceased Housefather, to render to him offerings and worship. In the Semitic races it was individual marriage as the Patriarchal family, with its restrictions applying to the woman alone. The domestic worship of the proximate deceased Housefather is here merged into the tribal (common) worship of the ultimate Allfather.

These considerations seem to me to harmonize the earliest historical institutions with those more rudimentary social states which we see still surviving amongst savages.

The degradation and progression theories. Closely connected with the views which I have now briefly considered is that as to the primitive condition of mankind. I may say a few words on this subject, more especially as the conclusions to which our investigations have led me differ somewhat on this point from those which Mr. Fison holds, and which he has already stated.*

Ante, p. 161.

DEGRADATION AND PROGRESSION THEORIES. 337

There are two views as to the primitive condition of man and of human society They may be described as the "degradation" and "progression" theories. The degradation theory implies a belief that mankind consisted at first of individuals who were independent of each other, and who subsequently coalesced as a society under a chief or head. It also implies that society was formed in consequence of an act of volition. This belief has been derived from two sources. One, being Semitic, is known to us through the Hebrews; the other, being Aryan, through the Romans and other nations. From the Hebrew source the theory derives the conception of man, created as an individual in an innocent and perfect state, afterwards becoming degraded; and it received a religious sanction through the Hebrew law-giver.

The Roman source itself received an accession from Greece. The Roman lawyers regarded "that law which natural reason appoints for all mankind as the law of nations." The Greek philosophers imagined that but for untoward accident the human race would have confined itself to simple rules of conduct, and a less tempestuous life. To live according to nature came to be considered the end for which man was created. On the subjugation of Greece, these two conceptions were amalgamated, and the Roman lawyers became enthusiastic disciples of the new school. Thus, at length, it became to be believed that the old *Jus Gentium* was indeed the lost law of nature which had governed man in his primitive state.* Through the conversion of the Romans to Christianity, these two lines of thought had a concurrent course, and, together, form the basis of the popular belief as to the primitive condition of man, and as to the origin of society. I think that this

---

* Sir Henry S. Maine, "Ancient Law," 6th edition, p. 46, *et infra*.

belief cannot be more generally indicated than by using the words of the learned commentator, Sir William Blackstone :—

"The earth and all things therein are the general property of mankind . . . And while the earth continued bare of inhabitants . . . all was in common among them, and everyone took from the common stock . . . such things as his immediate necessities required. These general notions . . . might perhaps still have answered . . . had it been possible for mankind to have remained in a state of primeval simplicity . . . Necessity begat property, and, in order to insure that property, recourse was had to civil society, which brought along with it states, governments, laws, punishments, and the public exercise of religious duties." *

The views advocated by Archbishop Whateley and the Duke of Argyll are somewhat similar, but infer, I think, a certain amount of primitive civilization. The statements which I have quoted suffice for my purpose, which is merely to indicate generally the two rival theories, and to point out what I conceive to be their present condition, and the bearing which our investigations may have upon them.

It is difficult to say which of the two conceptions forming the present degradation theory may ultimately be seen to have most profoundly influenced the social future of mankind. That portion of the belief which we owe to the Semitic source was indispensable to the successful dissemination of the Christian religion. The Aryan portion, in its form of the Law of Nature, became the parent of international law, and passed from the Roman lawyers to the French jurists. In the 18th century, this Law of Nature again passed from them to the French people, through Rousseau and the writers of whom he is the type. Utterly

---

* Blackstone's "Commentaries on the Laws of England," p. 3, 6th edition, 1775. Also, Stephen's "Commentaries on the Laws of England," p. 146, 2nd edition, 1848.

visionary as are Rousseau's theories, unreal as his representations of man in a state of nature are to us, his voice then spoke a language which thrilled society in its deepest chords. It seemed as if at length man's inmost yearnings after some higher and more perfect life had been answered by the sublimest words of truth. It was Rousseau's deep sympathy with the woe and anguish of down-trodden humanity that gave life and apparent reason to the visionary fallacies of his writings. The twofold conception of man in a state of nature and man degraded from a primeval condition of innocence, became in its new form and its fantastic dress a potent agent in bringing about the first French Revolution. In the conception of the primitive independent freedom and equality of mankind, Communism has its roots, and from these roots the future may see spring forth a growth that will perhaps cast a baleful shadow over the whole earth.

The progression theory, on the contrary, is of modern origin, and has arisen through the scientific investigation and comparison of the social condition and customs of savage and barbarous races, of the survivals of archaic customs still met with among civilized peoples, and of the most ancient written records left to us from the past. The evidence drawn from these sources is of the utmost weight, coming to us without previous intention as to its ultimate use, and its concurrent testimony is very strong. Such investigations disclose a remarkable conformity between the customs of existing savages and the customs of the ancestors of barbarous and of civilized peoples; also between the structure of savage and of archaic society. Such investigations raise more than a mere presumption that the social advance of mankind has been along similar lines of progress, or, rather, that the directions in which mankind may be supposed to have advanced socially are not merely parallel and independent, but are convergent and connected, when regarded in the direction of the past.

The development of society, as indicated by a study of the Australian class divisions, and the classificatory system of relationships connected therewith, seems to have been, as it were, by segmentation—that is, by the division of an original commune into two intermarrying communes. It is here, therefore, that we must expect to recognize the origin of marriage, in its form of group marriage, between the two exogamous segments of the commune. Subsequently, as is indicated for instance by the Kŭrnai system, arose individual marriage, bringing with it descent through the father, and the first indications of the disintegrations of the ancient communal society into individuals. These views imply that mankind in its earliest conceivable social condition consisted of independent communal groups, whose bond was common descent. The degradation theory, on the contrary, implies that mankind consisted of independent individuals.

The fundamental difference between the two rival theories, therefore, is, that in the older one the unit is an individual man, while, in the newer, the unit is a body corporate, formed by an undivided group of common descent. The social process indicated by the progression theory is strictly in accordance with the ordinary course of development; that is, it proceeded from the general to the special, and from the homogeneous to the heterogeneous.

The individual family has been developed out of restricted group marriage.
We have shown that in Australia group marriage is, in fact, based upon inherited marital rights, which one part of the contemporaneous generation has over the other part. But these rights have become more or less modified in various tribes, in so far that, subject to the class rules, the woman is given or exchanged. Perhaps the most frequent modification of group marriage is that in which the woman

RESTRICTED GROUP MARRIAGE. 341

is specially possessed by one man, with the co-existence of potential possession by all other men of the same class. Individual marriage is then but a further restriction of the communal rights, and out of individual marriage arises the family.

As the family—that is, the domestic group surrounding the individual, who is husband and father—is clearly established among such of the Australian tribes of whom the Kŭrnai community is a type, it becomes of interest to attempt to trace its germs in the more primitive tribal organizations. The rudiments of the family are discernible in those tribes where the women are more or less monopolized by the elder men, and more especially where, as in Western Australia, descent through the mother (which is characteristic of group marriage) is partially changed by the inheritance of the hunting grounds by the sons, who are yet of their mothers' class names. In comparing the structure of a number of tribes, I find that in those which are organized most nearly upon the old lines, the indications of individual marriage disappear, in looking backwards, in communal marriage.

The tribes which are discussed in this work may be placed in a series, in accordance with the peculiarities of their several social organizations. This series would commence with tribes such as the Dieri and the Kamilaroi, which have modified group marriage, the exogamous class divisions, descent in the female line, and the right to the female captive, controlled by the exogamous rule of marriage. It would proceed through such tribes as the Turra, having the exogamous class divisions, but with descent through the father; a usual state of individual marriage, but with occasional complete revival of the old communal rights of the intermarrying classes; and the exogamous rule still affecting the female captive The series would terminate with such tribes as the Kŭrnai, in which the class divisions survived only in a modified form; in which individual marriage was established, and the characteristics of group marriage are only discernible, more or less indistinctly, in surviving customs; but in which the female captive is still controlled by the modified class rules. That there are other tribes having a social organization higher than that of the Kŭrnai seems to me probable, not only from Mr. Stähle's positive statements, but also from those of other correspondents, such as Mr. J. Gibson, of Southern Queensland.*

Such a series of social organizations not only indicates the general character of the remainder of the evidence yet awaiting examination, but also is more than significant of the course which the social development of the Australian aborigines has followed. It must be remembered that in this continental area the savage tribes have been free from disturbing influences from without.

The monopoly of women by the older men is not probably the only cause tending to produce individual marriage. Mr. Fison has, in the case of the Kŭrnai, suggested a reasonable explanation as to its origin among them. There may have been, and there were probably, other causes not now apparent. Besides these causes, there are also the means by which individual marriage has been effected, such as gift, exchange, capture, and elopement.

<small>Lubbock's views as to marriage by capture.</small> It may be well to consider from the point of view now reached how far our evidence will, or will not, agree with the theories which have been formulated by Sir John Lubbock and Mr. M'Lennan, two writers whose works are regarded as being of great authority on the subject of savage and primitive society and of primitive marriage.

Sir John Lubbock's views, as I gather them from his

---

* The Gournditch-mara tribe, Appendix F; the Tŭrra tribe, Appendix H.

work, "The Origin of Civilization and Primitive Condition of Man,"* are as follows. He starts by assuming the former existence of communal marriage. On this, he thinks, followed marriage by capture, which led to female infanticide. He says, also, that he believes communal and individual marriage might exist side by side, as warriors would appropriate female captives, thus disregarding communal rights; and that "capture, and capture alone, could originally give a man the right to monopolize a woman to the exclusion of his fellow clansmen." I propose now to consider whether the facts before us justify the belief that in Australia individual marriage arose, in the first instance, out of communal marriage, by the monopoly of female captives in disregard of the common tribal right, and that it could have arisen in no other way, which is what Sir John Lubbock's statements amount to.

That marriage is brought about throughout Australia by capture is quite certain. A few examples will illustrate the conditions under which this practice exists. Among the Kŭrnai, marriages were brought about most frequently by elopement, less frequently by capture, and least frequently by exchange or by gift. Marriage by capture was as follows:—

1. Women were stolen from kindred divisions or kindred clans, as by the Tatūngolūng from the Braiakolūng. That is, they made raids upon those communities with which they intermarried.

2. Women were captured in wars between the clans, as in the case of the battle of Bushy Park, at which the Brt Britta woman became a captive to men who were held by the elders to be too near to her, and she was therefore given to Bŭndawal, whose division and hers intermarried.

* 3rd edition, 1875, p. 95, *et infra*.

3. Women were captured from alien tribes, as in the case of the Omeo Brajerak, who were killed at the Top Plain by the Kŭrnai (p. 222); and in the case of the night attack by Brūthen Mŭnji (p. 214) on the Brajerak, at the Upper Tambo River.

In these cases the wives of the slain Brajerak were taken. The Kŭrnai and the Brajerak were not intermarrying tribes, unless by capture, and in this case each man took the woman whose husband he had been the first to spear. It must be remembered that the Kŭrnai had no classes to which those of the Omeo Brajerak were analogous. Had it been so, it is quite certain that, supposing the woman and her captor had been of two analogous classes, she would have been forbidden to him by public opinion, based upon the ancestral class laws as enunciated by the elders of both sexes.

The conclusion to be drawn from these instances is that, among the Kŭrnai, marriage by capture came under those same rules which regulated marriage by elopement, exchange, or gift.

Our correspondents in various parts of Australia have sent statements to us entirely supporting the assertion that female war captives are dealt with under the class rules. I need not quote those again which have been already given, but refer the reader to them in the earlier part of this work (p. 65). In addition to these I may now note some further statements lately received.

Among the Kamilaroi (Gwydir River, N.S.W.) "it was customary that a female prisoner became the wife of the man who captured her, and, if he did not care about her, he would hand her over to some of his friends. But this proviso must be made, that the men of the tribe would not permit one of their number, say a Hippi, to keep a woman as a wife if she were of a forbidden class. Should a man persist in keeping a woman who is denied to him by their

laws, the penalty is that he should be driven out from the society of his friends, and quite ignored. If that does not cure his fondness for the woman, his male relatives follow him and kill him, as a disgrace to their tribe, and the female relatives of the woman kill her for the same reason."
—(Mr. Cyrus E Doyle, Kunopia, N S.W.)

I learn by inquiry from a man of the Mūk-jarawaint, which was apparently a clan of a large tribe occupying, at least, the country from the Wimmera to the Avoca River, and from the Grampians to the Mallee Scrub, north of Lakes Hindmarsh and Tyrrell, that the female war captive was at first common to the men present at her capture, and then only became the property of her captor if she were of a class from which he might take a wife. In some cases the head man of the party took her.

The tribe of aborigines at Eucla, W A. (Great Australian Bight), is divided into four classes—Būdera, Būdū, Kūra, and Wenŭng. "If a female is made captive, she is common first to all the Booderah, and then to all the Coorah; that is, if taken captive by a Booderah or Coorah. If by a Wenung or Boodoo, either can then claim her as a slave-wife, if they are without a wife; if not, she is used as before-mentioned, and allowed to go home. She has always the choice of remaining as a slave-wife, instead of returning to her friends, and she generally prefers remaining, as she is afraid of being killed by Kokittah menang (wild men). None but a Boodoo or a Wenung may marry her, and he only with a majority of votes from the 'doctors' and old Booderahs. The 'doctors' must also guarantee that no evil will happen to the tribe, as they are such firm believers in Mobung (magic)."—(Mr. D. E. Roe, Eucla, W.A.)

In the Wonghi tribe (sometimes called Wonghibon), whose territory was situated on the north side of the Lachlan River, for about eighty miles above Whealbah, "a woman was the property of her captor when she was not of a class forbidden to him. I do not think a blackfellow would persist in retaining a female captive of a forbidden class; indeed, I feel sure he would not, as he would incur the contempt of every member of his tribe, but whether he would be killed or not I cannot say."—(Mr. A. S. P. Cameron, Conoble, Mossgiel, N S W.)

In the Dieri tribe, Lake Hope, "he who captures a woman, in war or otherwise, of the same class (Mŭrdū) as himself, exchanges her with someone for a woman of the proper class."—(The Rev. H. Vogelsang, Kopperamana Mission, S.A.)

At the last moment I have learned the following from one of the three last surviving Brataua Kŭrnai:—About the time when the whites settled in Gippsland, a large war party went across the mountains to the north, to attack the Brajerak. On their return they brought with them five female captives.* These became respectively the wives of head men (one a Dinna Birraark) of the divisions Būnjil Kraura, Mūnjū, Dairgo, and Yowŭng, from which I have no doubt contingents of the war party had gone. My informant made this significant statement, in speaking of one of the five Lauajerak whom he knew personally—"Before she was the wife of Tankli she belonged to all the Yowŭng men." For further evidence I refer to appendices F, G, H, and I.

These statements amply prove the proposition that, among the Australian savages, marriage by capture was only permitted when the captor and the captive were of some classes which might legally intermarry. The exceptional case of the Gournditch-mara tribe of Western Victoria goes to show that in that community, which had four classes which were not exogamous, the female captive was

* Called Lauajerak, as the men were called Brajerak. Laua=woman *e.g.*, Laua-yak = western woman, as Bra-yak (Braiaka) = western man.

not retained by the captor, but was given to someone else by him, under the sanction of the tribal council, and of the head man, or chief.

As I have already pointed out, the Gournditch-mara seem to have been exceptionally advanced in their social arrangements, but it appears to me that they were not the only such exceptions Mr. Fredk. W. Taplin, who has been intimately acquainted with the Narrinyeri for the last twenty-two years, knows of no instances where female captives were taken by them from their fellow clans.

It may, I think, be assumed with safety that marriage by capture existed so far back as the time when the class divisions originated—that is, at the segmentation of the commune—and that it was controlled by those deeply seated rules of conduct which are based upon common descent, and upon the class divisions.

We find it now existing as one of the means by which communal marriage is brought about, and affected by the rules which restrict the latter, and its practice amounts merely to a violent extension of the marital rights over a class in one tribe to captured members of the corresponding class in another tribe.

In this view marriage by capture might exist in an undivided commune, and the female captive would, in that case, be incorporated with it. We cannot suppose that men of such a commune would refrain from capturing women of other communal groups We may, on the contrary, feel assured that, when opportunity offered, captives would be made. The question, then, is, would the individual warrior retain his captive in defiance of communal rights? If he resembled his descendant, the Australian savage, I should say he assuredly would not, unless in accordance with the tribal laws. There is no reason to believe that a warrior of an undivided commune of the past would any more disregard custom than would a man of the modified divided commune of to-day. If he did, it would mean, to him, the severance of all ties. He would become an Ishmaelite against whom all men's hands would be raised, and this would mean far more in a society having a corporate character than it would in one more highly developed and individualized.*

Marriage by elopement. The existence of elopement as a means of bringing about marriage among the Australian savages has not hitherto been suspected. I was long aware of its occurrence among the Kŭrnai, but it was only on carefully working out and weighing the details given in previous pages that I became aware that, in so far as they are concerned, elopement was the principal form of marriage. Suspecting that it might be common elsewhere in Australia, but confounded by observers with the kindred form of marriage by capture, I instituted inquiries, and I now give a few extracts from communications made to me by correspondents, from which it will be evident that elopement is and has been a recognized institution with at least some of the aboriginal tribes. The presumption arises that it will be found to prevail generally, and I am now

---

* I desire to guard myself against being supposed to assert that breaches of the communal laws, and of the present customs of the Australian savage, did not and do not occur That they did and do occur is quite certain. The penalties provided against such infractions of the law prove this. The exceptions prove the rule For instance, among the Kŭrnai marriage within the forbidden degrees is a heinous offence Before the settlement of Gippsland by the white man, I am told that a Brabrolŭng eloped with his brother's daughter, who counted, under the classificatory system of relationship, as his own daughter. They escaped pursuit, and were not seen again until years after, when, the country having been settled, the native police came over from Melbourne. The Kŭrnai tell me that the delinquents then reappeared, and, under the protection of the native police, left the district, and were never again seen or heard of. Such instances might occur even under an "undivided commune." But they could never have been more than exceptions

preparing to trace and to record its mode of occurrence elsewhere on the Australian continent *

Among the Kamilaroi (Gwydir River, N. S. W.) "although it was not customary for a young man to run off with his future wife, it was sometimes done. It was usual for a man to get the consent of the girl's parents, but it does not seem to have been absolutely necessary, as in many cases the man would take the girl away without consulting them."—(Mr. Cyrus E. Doyle, Kunopia, N S W.)

In the Wimmera tribe (North-Western Victoria) "cases were of very frequent occurrence, and might be said to be customary, where a young man eloped with his future wife."

---

* I anticipate that much unexpected evidence will turn up as to marriage by elopement. For instance, I observe, in Mr. M'Lennan's "Studies in Ancient History," &c , p 316, the following as to marriage among the Turkomans :—"A youth becomes acquainted with a girl, they are mutually attached, and agree to marry, but the young man does not dare to breathe his wishes to the parents of his beloved, for such is not etiquette, and would be resented as an insult What does he do? He elopes with the girl, and carries her to some neighbouring Obah, where, such is the custom, there is no doubt of a kind reception, and there the young couple live for some six weeks, when the Reish-suffeeds, or elders, of the protecting Obah deem it time to talk over the matter with the parents "—" Frazer's Journey, 1830," vol. ii , p. 372. Also, at p 317 of "Studies in Ancient History," this :—"Among the Soligas (India) when a girl consents to marry, the man runs away with her to some neighbouring village, and they live there until the honeymoon is over. Then they return home and give a feast to the people of their village."—"Buchanan's Journey from Madras," vol ii , p. 178.

Mr. M'Lennan gives these examples in support of his theory of marriage by capture; but, on the contrary, they are clearly evidence of the existence among the Turkomans and the Soligas of marriage by elopement Mr. M'Lennan supposes these cases to illustrate a state of transition from the symbol of actual capture to a symbolism of which traces remained in Sparta in historic times. According to Xenophon ("Rep Lac ," 1, 5) the young wife was not, immediately after the marriage, domiciled in her husband's house, but cohabited with him for some time clandestinely, till he brought her, and frequently her mother, to his home The same custom also prevailed in Crete (Strabo x., p. 432). If these ancient customs symbolize anything, it is, I submit, elopement, and not capture

Another instance quoted by Mr M'Lennan (p. 81) from Bell's "Journal of a Residence in Circassia," looks to me precisely like a case of elopement.

—(The Rev. C. W. Kramer, Ebenezer Mission, Lake Hindmarsh.)

In the Dieri tribe (Lake Hope), "if a man to whom a girl has been refused then elopes with her, her relations make up a party to recover her. If the man makes no resistance, nothing is done to him; otherwise, violence is used towards him."—(The Rev. H. Vogelsang, Kopperamana Mission, S.A.)

In the far north, South Australia, "it is customary for a young man to run off with his future wife without her parents' consent."—(Mr. W. Gow, Blanchewater, S A.)

Among the Narrinyeri, at the mouth of the Murray River, "it was sometimes the case that, where parents refused their consent, a young man would elope with their daughter. If caught, he would be thrashed with clubs, and, in some instances, the offender has been put to death. The girl would ever bear the reproach of having lived with a man without being given away."—(Mr. Fredk. W. Taplin, Point Macleay, S.A.)*

In the now almost extinct "Ya-it-mathang"† tribe, of Omeo, "where a man eloped with an unmarried woman, he was beaten by her relatives, who, however, frequently permitted him to retain her. In cases, however, where a man persisted in keeping a woman when the tribe was against it, the people would most likely kill him."—(Informant, Jenny Cooper, the last survivor of the tribe, *per* the Rev. J. Bulmer, Lake Tyers.)

In the Port Essington tribe, "girls are betrothed when

---

* The late Rev. Geo Taplin informed me, with respect to marriage by elopement, that "in past times a woman who ran away with a young man without being given by her relations, was called 'Kanauwurle,' or 'theirs,' and looked upon as a 'strumpet'" He also mentioned a custom attending elopement, which is precisely that which I have noted (p 202) among the Kŭrnai, namely, the *jus primæ noctis* of the comrades of the "young Lochinvar"

† Ya yau = yes.

quite infants. Sometimes elopements of unmarried girls take place, but the betrothal is not thereby cancelled, unless by consent of the *fiancé*. The woman is therefore still regarded as belonging to him, unless, as occasionally happens, he gives up his right to her. The girl, if caught, is severely punished."—(Mr. D. Morgan, Coburg cattle station, Port Essington.)

It will be well to point out that, in addressing my correspondents, I did so simultaneously both as to marriage by capture and marriage by elopement, so that any misunderstanding should be avoided. The quotations just made apply to elopement only, as those pieviously given applied to capture only.

The time has, I think, now arrived for a careful review and consideration of the statements made by travellers and by other writers as to the Australian savage. I feel convinced that, when regarded by the light of present knowledge as to the actual structure of their society, those statements will not only be found to have an unexpected bearing upon the conclusions generally held as to their social development, but also that those statements will be found to support the views advanced in this work. At some future time I hope to undertake this examination. At present I shall merely point out one instance which I have at hand.

William Buckley, the so-called "wild white man," who lived thirty-two years among the tribes of Port Phillip, has left a narrative through which are scattered many interesting particulars as to those aborigines.* At first sight, his statements seem to record merely a series of duels and battles about women who were stolen, speared, and slaughtered. The whole seems to be a picture of lawless

* "Life and Adventures of William Buckley," &c , by John Morgan. Tasmania, 1852.

violence. On further examination, however, there are statements which, when regarded by the light of present knowledge of the Australian savage, lead to somewhat different conclusions.

Those social aggregates, which Buckley calls tribes, are evidently analogous to those which, for want of a more precise term, I have called "divisions" and "clans." He describes them as more or less freely mingling with and visiting each other, as speaking the same language, and as consisting of from twenty to sixty families. He says, moreover, that "they are very averse to marrying one of their own relations, even of a distant degree" (p. 51), "and will not . . knowingly marry a relation . . except when two brothers happened to be married and one dies; in that case the survivor claims the widow" (p. 66). He distinctly states (p. 51) that "the first thing preparatory to marriage is to get the parents' consent;" and that "often a girl is promised to a man as soon as she is born" (p. 89). On the other hand, there are many statements which prove that marriage by capture existed in the Port Phillip tribes, and also others which point to marriage by elopement having been common among them (pp. 61, 64, 68). These statements pointedly indicate a community recognizing common descent, a common language, and a common country, and divided into exogamous groups.

I now quote an incident related by Buckley, which is very characteristic (p. 62):—"A young woman was speared through the thigh. As she belonged to our tribe, she was brought into our huts, from whence, it seems, she had absconded with a man of the other party, without her parents' knowledge. . . The quarrel being over, and all quiet, the men went to the lake fishing, leaving the women to their usual occupations, and the poor girl lay by herself in one of the huts. The man she had eloped with, knowing all this, went to her and carried her off; so that when the tribe returned they discovered the flight of the fugitives, on whom they vowed vengeance."

Buckley here proceeds to narrate other occurrences. His party shortly afterwards started to meet another "tribe," by appointment, and there found the eloped couple. The meeting seems, from his narrative, to have been pre-arranged. He then goes on to say—" In the first place, they seated themselves on their rugs, in groups. . . The young man already mentioned advanced towards us . . and challenged our men to fight. . . A spear was thrown, but he warded it off cleverly with his shield. . . One of our men advanced very near to him, with only a shield and a waddy, and then the two went to work in good earnest . . until the first had his shield split. . . His opponent struck him a tremendous blow on one side of his head, and knocked him down. . . His friends cried out 'Enough!' . . They soon after separated quietly."

This narrative, as well as the other statements I have quoted, might be applied almost word for word to describe similar occurrences and customs with the Kŭrnai. I think we may feel assured that the Port Phillip aborigines had individual marriage, with survivals of group marriage and the class divisions, and that with them marriage was brought about by gift, capture, and elopement; but in which degree either of these three preponderated over the others I cannot determine.

I have now shown the prevalence of capture and the existence of elopement as means of bringing about marriage, and I have pointed out that both are under the direction of the class rules, which regulate all marriage. As to the Kŭrnai, Mr. Fison has, I think, suggested a very probable explanation of the prevalence of marriage by elopement with them. But it seems to me, judging from the frequency of elopement elsewhere in Australia, that it must have been known to the ancestors of the Kŭrnai, and have merely with them assumed a preponderance in consequence of the peculiar circumstances of their condition.

Marriage by elopement and marriage by capture differ only in one essential—namely, the presence or absence of the woman's consent. We find that both these forms occur not only as producing individual marriage where the class rules have become much weakened, but also group marriage where the class rules are still full of vitality. It is not probable that either elopement or capture has been able by itself alone to produce individual marriage, except, perhaps, in such exceptional cases as that of the Kŭrnai. But there is another institution in the Australian tribes which, together with the custom of betrothal, I consider quite sufficient; especially when aided by elopement and by capture, which, being at first completely under the control of the class laws, afterwards received greater prominence as these class laws became weakened.

Individual marriage caused by monopoly of women by the older men.

The institution to which I refer is the monopoly, more or less, of women by the older men of the tribe. This is very common all over Australia, especially where group marriage is still in the ascendant. But this monopoly is not exclusive; at certain times and on certain occasions the old communal right revives in favour of the younger men, or of friendly strangers visiting the tribe.* Yet this revival of communal rights takes place in accordance with the class rules. This practice of partial monopoly produces a scarcity of women available as wives, and will inevitably compel the men who are without wives to capture women, if it is

* It may be even more correct to say that the old communal rights have never ceased to exist, but that the older men claim the right of withholding them from the younger ones and granting them at intervals.

possible to do so; or else to induce them to elope, if there is any chance of eluding the penalties thereby incurred. Women so captured are, as we have shown in this work, only to be retained by their captors if of the corresponding class, and will then rank with the other women of the tribe. In elopement the class rules must be followed. If they are disregarded, then the offence often becomes capital.

It is worth while to consider what is the nature of the monopoly and by whom exercised. It is the monopoly of women in partial exclusion of the other clansmen. It is exercised by the elder men to the exclusion of the younger men. These elder men are those who wield authority in the tribe. They are the repositories and expounders of ancestral custom, and they are supposed to possess not only wisdom, but also secret and deadly powers of sorcery, by which they can destroy their enemies. Their dicta are therefore charged with authority, and they bear the means of making that authority obeyed. It is universally true that man, as an individual or as a class, will, if he have the power, appropriate to himself privileges and advantages, to the exclusion of others. All history and experience is full of instances. This is precisely that which the elder men of such tribes as those I have mentioned do when they monopolize women to the exclusion of their fellow-clansmen.

The perpetuation of this monopoly is encouraged by those interested in it having sisters or daughters to exchange with each other for wives, and is aided by the custom of betrothal when girls are even mere infants. This betrothal occurs all over Australia, in tribes whose customs prove them to stand low down as regards other tribes in social development. I meet with it, for instance, in full force in a central Australian tribe (Kūnandabūri) whose customs attending marriage smack strongly of an undivided commune.* The exigencies of life attending the spread of the aborigines over the Australian continent would necessarily cause a communal group—say organized upon the class system—to break up, during its expansion, into other groups of a character similar to and governed by the same organic laws as the parent unit. The structure of existing tribes shows me that these segmented groups, while spreading over and settling the country, would still recognize the bonds of class connecting each with the other. The communal rights would still bind the whole, and would be exercised whenever the scattered groups re-united on ceremonial or festive occasions; while, in fact, there would arise, through mere distance, a restriction upon the full exercise of the communal rights when the several groups returned to their proper localities. The betrothal of a girl belonging to one group to a man of suitable class and degree in some other and distant group, would, I think, tend to raise a feeling of special relation between the two when marriage took place, even when the common marital rights of the group were admitted. That which I have stated as probable in the early stages of the divided commune, is, in fact, that which can be clearly recognized in the structure of the various tribes of to-day, whether organized upon the Kamilaroi or the Kŭrnai type. I am thus led to suspect that betrothal dates back to an early period of the divided commune, and to associate it with monopoly of women. Such a practice of monopoly, aided by betrothal, would in itself tend to bring about the pairing family as we see it here, namely,

* I am in receipt, while seeing this work through the press, of very full and important particulars as to this tribe, for which I am indebted to the courtesy of an old brother explorer, Mr J. W O'Donnell, whose aid in gathering information I now gladly avail myself of an opportunity to acknowledge.

the monopoly by one man of one or more women.* The practice of capture and elopement would easily and naturally fall into the path thus struck out, and individual marriage would result. Exceptional cases, such as that of the Kŭrnai, would accelerate the process and confirm the habit. This explanation of the origin of individual marriage is, I submit, entirely in accord with what we know of the Australian aborigines. It is therefore in accordance with general probability, and it also renders unnecessary Sir John Lubbock's assumption that "capture, and capture alone, could originally give a man the right to monopolize a woman to the exclusion of his fellow-clansmen."

Sir John Lubbock, as it seems to me, regards capture as the root of all, and that from it sprang individual marriage, exogamy, and female infanticide.

Mr. M'Lennan, on the other hand, believes that the practice of female infanticide in the tribe (primary horde), and the scarcity of women thereby produced, led to the capture of women for wives and to those habits which established exogamy.† He says also, when taking the Australians as an example, "Owing to exogamy, the mothers in each horde were foreigners, and, owing to the system of kinship, the children born to them were esteemed foreigners also." ‡

<small>M'Lennan's views as to marriage by capture</small>

Three propositions contained in these statements, and in his work generally, are worth considering.

1. In the primitive hordes, female infanticide prevailed, as it does now among savages.

2. The scarcity of women thus produced led to the practice of capturing wives—resulting in exogamy.

---

* Monandry of Mr. J. F. M'Lennan.
† "Studies in Ancient History," &c., by John Ferguson M'Lennan. London, 1876, p. 132, *et infra.*
‡ P. 186.

358   SUMMARY AND GENERAL CONCLUSIONS.

3. The wives so captured, and the children born to them, were regarded as "foreigners."

As there are now no "primitive hordes" known to exist, the Australian savages may serve me for an illustration, as they serve Mr. M'Lennan.

I am not aware of any satisfactory evidence that among them female children were as a rule more frequently killed than male children. From my own knowledge, I can see no reason that such should be the case. Infanticide has been practised by them—

1. Where children increased so rapidly in numbers as to become a burden.

2. Where children were born imperfect or deformed, or were twins.

3. Where children were regarded as being illegitimate— *e.g.*, where the parents both belonged to the same class, or were too nearly related to each other.

I do not think that among the Australians there were, beside these, any peculiar inducements to destroy female children. The Australian women are not a burden to the tribe.* They gather their full share of the food supply. They are the beasts of burden on a march. They fight desperately, when occasion calls for it, in defence of their kindred. When married they are not an expense to their kin in the shape of dower, but bring to him who has the disposal of them an equivalent. It is by exchange of a daughter or a sister that in many tribes a man most easily obtains a wife. Among the Kŭrnai a man with several daughters was rich in so far that their husbands were bound to find him in food ("neborak"†). So far as the Australians are concerned, the evidence is against the conclusion drawn by Mr. M'Lennan.

---

* See Mr Fison's remarks, and the foot-note, *ante, p. 134.*
† As to *neborak, see p. 207.*

The second proposition finds its chief support in the first. In speaking of Sir John Lubbock's views, I have fully stated my own as to the origin of marriage by capture, and the views I advance render it unnecessary to call in the aid of female infanticide to produce it, together with those habits which are supposed to have established exogamy.

In the third proposition, the Australian tribes are distinctly implied, and hence our evidence is peculiarly adapted to serve as a test of the soundness of the conclusions drawn. We have certainly no "primitive hordes," but the class division of an Australian tribe will well serve for the purpose of illustration. It is composed of two groups complementary to each other. One group is a brotherhood, and the other is a sisterhood. It is saturated by principles of corporate rights and obligations, and it may well serve as the modern type of the ancient homogeneous groups postulated by Mr. M'Lennan, and in which he conceives that captured women and their children were regarded as "foreigners."

As a test, we may take the Eaglehawk class of a Maneroo (Brajerak) tribe, and the Crow class of a second such tribe, each tribe having both classes Each class may then serve our purpose as representing a "primitive horde." We will suppose that a man of the Eaglehawk class of the first tribe captures a Crow woman of the second tribe. Although alien born as to her captor's *tribe*, she is yet a sister to all the Crow women in it, and her children will not be "foreigners," but Crows, of that particular tribe. This principle is, I think, brought out in an equally striking manner by taking two tribes which have no class divisions in common. I have given an instance when Briakolŭng Kŭrnai killed some Brajerak men, and, in this case, they also captured their women.* Here there were not any

* P. 222.

class divisions common to both tribes, and it is, therefore, on all fours with a capture of women by one "primitive horde" from another. The women would be spoken of as Brajerak women, but their sons would be Yeerŭng, and their daughters Djeetgŭn; that is, they would belong to the Kŭrnai, and not to the Brajerak. In other words, they would not be regarded as "foreigners." These conclusions are also confirmed by the case of the five Lauajerak women.* The children of the one married to Tankli were Kŭrnai. I do not know whether the other four had children or not.

The evidence contained in this work, and Mr. Fison's discussions of that evidence, suggest that exogamy was the natural consequence of the segmentation of an original commune into two intermarrying communes, and the institution thereby of class divisions embracing both. It has been said that these class divisions are based upon sex. They are; but each class has necessarily members of both sexes, and the prominence which has been given to their sexual arrangements by the existence of descent through the mother is due, not, as it seems to me, so much to the fact that those classes are based upon sex, as that the idea of descent in the female line is the only one possible under a communal system of marriage. The undivided commune, assuming one to have existed, was probably endogamous. The two resulting communes were exogamous as to each segment, but endogamous as to the whole. The community of wives among brothers (own and tribal) was, and is still, a necessary part of a society governed by class rules, and the Levirate is a consequence of such community. These institutions have not, as Mr. M'Lennan conceives, led to exogamy, but have survived from the communal times,

* P. 346.

which, I doubt not, preceded that division into classes which gave rise to exogamy.

These considerations raise a strong presumption that there is a fatal error in Mr. M'Lennan's premises as to female infanticide, the relations of "primitive hordes" to female captives, and the origin of exogamy. If such is the case, then many of the principal conclusions throughout his work will be vitiated.

It is on these grounds that Mr. M'Lennan's views as to the origin of marriage by capture and exogamy are unsatisfactory to me, and I anticipate that they will be found equally unsatisfactory by those who prosecute this branch of anthropology in the field rather than in the study. It seems to me probable that had Mr. M'Lennan been in possession of fuller facts as to the actual condition of the Australian and other savages, his logical mind would have inevitably led him to somewhat different conclusions to those he holds.

Although I feel myself called upon to dissent from Mr. M'Lennan's conclusions as to the development of man's social condition, I do so fully appreciating the learning and research shown by his "Studies in Ancient History and Primitive Marriage," which will always be land-marks in anthropological science.*

For my part I think that marriage by capture probably

[* I gladly take the opportunity of expressing my hearty concurrence with this remark of Mr Howitt's Though the facts which have come under our observation compel us to dissent from Mr M'Lennan's theories, we fully appreciate the distinguished ability which his work displays His suggestion, which seems not to have attracted the attention it deserves, that the old legends of conflicts of heroes with animals may refer to battles with tribes who bore those animals as their totems, appears to me to be equally acute and valuable. It is so amply borne out by what we know of present day savages, that it may almost be said to amount to a discovery which has taken many an ancient legend out of the region of myth into that of history.—L. F.]

had its origin as far back as the undivided commune, and that it then fell under the communal rule. That it existed also in the exogamous communes, and that then, perhaps, arose marriage by elopement. Further, that these two means of bringing about marriage have continued until the present day, yielding obedience, perhaps reluctantly, to the ancient class rules, but gathering strength of resistance to them from the monopoly of women which was practised by those wielding tribal authority. Thus, in the case of the Kŭrnai, elopement has become the recognized means of effecting marriage, and the former monopoly has become established as the pairing family.

Analogies between the Kurnai society and primitive society as disclosed to us by history. Whether the pairing family of the Kŭrnai would ever have undergone a further development into the monogamian family, it is not possible to say; any such changes are now effectually arrested and rendered impossible, but some reflections suggest themselves, which I may note briefly.

It seems to me that among such archaic conditions as those described, the domestic and social systems of the progenitors of the civilized races may have originated. It seems quite conceivable that a "pairing family," as I have described it among the Kŭrnai, might, under favourable conditions, develop into a monogamian family.*

A parallel may be drawn with the Aryan race. Under such a process of evolution the Mŭngan might become the

* Dr. Morgan has clearly seen this and pointed it out in his great work, "Ancient Society." He says (p. 17):—"The ancestors of the Grecian, Roman, and German tribes passed through the stages we have indicated, in the midst of the last of which the light of history fell upon them. . . . Commencing then with the Australians and Polynesians, following with the American Indian tribes, and concluding with the Romans and Germans, who afford the highest exemplification respectively of the six great stages of human progress, the sum of their united experiences may be supposed fairly to represent that of the human family from the middle status of savagery to the end of ancient civilization. Consequently, the Aryan nations will find the types of the condition of their ancestors when in savagery in that of the Australians and Polynesians."

Housefather, with complete power of life and death as regarded the members of his family. The wandering ghost of the ancestor, instead of visiting his descendant in dreams, and teaching him forms of incantation to guard the Mūngan and his family from the evil machinations of sorcerers within and without the tribe, or against the malignant Brewin, might become the house-spirit, ever guarding those clustered round the sacred hearth; and the veneration which is now paid to age and to the elders take the form of worship by the visible members of the family of the invisible members. Thus, while each family would have its peculiar worship, the ceremonies of initiation might become modified into the tribal worship of their eponym Yeerŭng, and Djeetgŭn under such conditions be a survival as a female deity.

Under such hypothetical conditions, descent, which carried the common right to procure food over the territory claimed by the division or the clan, might develop into the common right to depasture or to cultivate it. Under such changed conditions, the division, the clan, and the tribe would claim an actual and common right in the soil.

The Birraark, instead of deriving his corrobboree songs and dances from the "ghosts" of the ancestors of his tribe, or instead of calling them back to the presence of the living in the dim evening, might become the bard, the soothsayer, or, as the prophet, deliver the oracles of the gods.

It is not possible to surmise how long a period of time might be required for a tribe such as the Kŭrnai to slowly progress from that point at which their primitive social history terminates, for them as well as for us, to an analogous position to that in which our Aryan ancestors first become visible to us in the dim and distant past. But, as regards any Australian aborigines, I think it is highly improbable that such a progress could ever have been made. From the state of a tribe of hunters having the pairing family to the state of a tribe of graziers and agriculturists having the monogamian family, the distance is vast, and implies not only a potentiality of intellectual progress (which I neither admit nor deny for the Australian aborigines), but also those favourable surrounding conditions which could make it alone possible for that change to take place. Whatever the sum of these favourable conditions might have been, this is certain, that it must have included, as a necessary factor, the existence for food supply of indigenous animals capable of domestication, and of plants capable of successful cultivation. As Dr. Morgan has shown reason to believe, it is thereupon that the passage from savagery to barbarism depends.* The Australian continent has, I think, no indigenous animals suitable for such domestication, nor any plants which could be to the Australians that which the cereals have been to the Asiatic, or that which maize has been to the American race. Such an advance by Australian aborigines would, therefore, have been in the highest degree improbable; but I think it is legitimately open to conjecture whether we may not perceive in the domestic and social state of the Kŭrnai, conditions analogous to those from which it may be reasonably supposed the domestic and social state of our archaic progenitors were developed at a time before they became visible to us in the misty past, in the border land between the visible and the invisible.

<small>General conclusions.</small> The general conclusions to which the consideration of the evidence contained in this work has led me may be briefly formulated so far as they relate to the course of social development of the Australian aborigines. The following stages of progress may be broadly stated:—

I.—*An Undivided Commune.*—(Consanguine Family of

---

* "Ancient Society," p. 18, *et infra*.

Morgan; Hetairism, or Communal Marriage, of M'Lennan; Communal Marriage of Lubbock.)

In this there was, probably, more or less promiscuous cohabitation, at least between those of the contemporaneous generation. It may be that marriage by capture co-existed, by which female captives would be incorporated into the commune.*

II.—*A Segmented Commune*, consisting of two or more exogamous intermarrying communes.—(Punaluan Family of Morgan, Marriage in which brothers have their wives in common of M'Lennan, Communal Marriage of Lubbock.)

This would arise by the segmentation of an original commune. Each of these exogamous communes would be built upon the old lines. A theoretical right of promiscuous cohabitation would still exist in each segment; but, in the course of time, there would arise various forms of group marriage, the evidence of which is universal. Marriage by capture would still exist, side by side with various forms of communal marriage, and female captives be incorporated with the class analogous to their own. The still existing uncertainty as to paternity, and the action of the class rules, would give greater prominence to the idea of descent through the mother.

III.—*Individual Marriage*—(Syndyasmian, or Pairing Family, of Morgan; Monandry of M'Lennan.)

This arises through the breaking up of the communes, but traces of the communal rights still survive. Marriage takes place by gift, by exchange, by capture, and by elopement, one or other of these predominating. Female captives are, in this stage, still subject to the class rules. Descent changes from the female to the male line.

---

* This is my own view, and herein alone I differ from Mr. Fison in any material point He has distinctly pointed out in his part of this work that he stops short of the undivided commune.

This stage lands us not only in existing custom, but also in the realm of history. The patriarchal and monogamian families have been developed from the pairing family. The first stage in the sequence given no longer exists, so far as is known, either in Australia or elsewhere. The other stages are nowhere, probably, existing with hard and sharp lines of separation from each other, but the groups representing them are distinct.

I submit with some confidence that these conclusions may be accepted by advocates either of the degradation or progression theories indifferently. As the former hold that man has become degraded from a once perfect and innocent state, and from perhaps a civilized condition, the two views may have a concurrent course backwards to the undivided commune, beyond which it is difficult to conceive of any society as existing. It is therefore at that stage that the two rival theories may be held to take divergent courses. It can be of little moment whether the degradation theory stops short at the divided commune, which still exists in modified forms, or at the undivided commune, which, though not known to exist now, is to be inferred as having once existed.

What further evidence future researches may afford cannot be foretold, but this is certain, that the evidence so far obtained discountenances the conclusion that existing savages are the degraded descendants of once civilized races.

INDEX.

Aborigines, cause of their decrease, 182; of Gippsland, 227; present social condition of, 317, 326; primitive condition of, 327; communal principle among, 327.
Adoption, 104, 112.
Ahts, 143.
Ancestral worship not the basis of relationship, 111; why offered to males only by males only, 112
Ancient gens, the, 108.
Antakerinya tribe, 36, 65.
Appendix A, 95; Appendix B, 165; Appendix C, 171; Appendix D 261; Appendix E, 267; Appendix F, 274; Appendix G, 279; Appendix H, 284; Appendix I, 288; Appendix K, 292.
Aunt, my father's sister only, 77; is my mother-in-law, 84, 93.
Australian dialects, wide divergence of, 63, *note*.
Auziles, 154.
Avenger of blood, 124.

Bachofen, Mutterrecht, 127.
Balearic islanders, 154.
Battle of clans, 217.
Barn, magic, 252.
Baukan, 254.
Bedouin, 116.
Betrothal among Australians, effect of, 354.
Bible account of early society, 163.
Bidwelli tribe, 322.
Birraark, 253; Appendix K, 292.
Birth of a child, 204
Blood feud, 156, 216, 221.
Brajerak, 109
Brett, the dead hand, 244.
Brewin, 250, 254.
Brewit, 199.
Bridgeman, Mr G. F., 31, 38, 40, 53, 61, 167.
Brothers' children, 78, 79.
Brother and sister, tribal, defined, 91.
Brother-in-law, 92
Brown, R. G., 32, 33, 34, 205, *note*.
Buckley, William, 55, *note*; 136, *note*; 190, *note*; "the wild white man," 351.
Bulk, magic, 247, 251, *note*.
Bullumdut, 254.
Bulmer, Rev. J., 179, 200, *note*; 204, *note*; 223, 288, 350.

Bunjil, 210, 323, 324, *note*.
Bygars, Gonds and, 154.

Cameron, Mr A. S. P , 40, 47, 346.
Camps, regulations of, 208.
Cannibalism, 214, 224
Capture, marriage by. See *Marriage by Capture*.
Carew, Mr. Walter, 143
Clan, 215, 224; battle of, 217; of Kurnai, 227.
Class divisions, 31; two classes, 33; four classes, 35; conjecture as to formation of, 70 ; of the Kurnai, 320.
Change of descent, 74
Chatfield, Mr W, jun , 41, 66, *note*.
Codrington, Rev. R., 32, 33, 62, 68, 147, 312, *note*.
Communal rights, 53, 155.
Cousin defined, 77, 87.

Darling River tribe, two divisions of, 34 ; totems of, 41.
Dead, reluctance to name, 249
Degradation theory, 161, 336
Descent, the line of, does not affect personal relationship, 119 ; through male, 158 ; uterine precedes agnatic, 165 ; change of line, 312
Descent through females is the rule of the classes, 68 ; necessary result of the marriage relations, 73
Dieri tribe, legend of Murdu, 25; marriage by capture in, 346 ; marriage by elopement in, 350.
Disease, belief as to, 250.
Disruption of a tribe, 305.
Distribution of food, 261.
Divergence of Australian dialects, 63, *note*.
Djeetgun, 194.
Doyle, Mr. C. E , 53, *note* ; 180, 205, *note* ; 326, 345, 349.
Du Vè, Mr. C. J., 247.

Eggs of swan, property in, 226, 252, *note*.
Elders, authority of, 211.
Ellis, Polynesian researches, 100.
Elopement, marriage by, 200; prevalence of, 348, 349, 350, 351 ; among Turkomans and Soligas, 349, *note* ; in Sparta, Crete, and Circassia, 349, *note*
Emberson, Mr H , 173
Endogamy. See *Exogamy*
Eponyms, 232.
Erinyes, their functions, 123.
Evil-eye, 248.
Exogamy, the rule of Australian divisions, 63 ; breach of, punished, 65, 66, *note* ; overrides marriage by capture, 65, 344 ; defined, 117, 138, 321, *note* ; M'Lennan's views as to, considered, 357.
Expiation for marriage, 151.
Eyre, discoveries in central Australia, 52.
Eucla tribe, 345

Falconer, Mr A , 62
Family, duties of, 206 ; of the Kurnai, 203 ; developed out of group marriage, 310
Father-in-law, 86 ; son-in-law's duty towards, 105, 207
Father's brothers, 61, 83
Father's sisters, 84

Female infanticide   See *Infanticide*.
Females no incumbrance of savages, 136, 358.
Florida Island Kema, 37, *note*.
Food, common right to, 207 ; distribution of, Appendix D, 261 ; provision of, 206 ; forethought in providing, 208 ; plentiful, 208.
Forethought, instance of, 208
Fraser, Rev. J G , 125, *note*
Friend, Mr. P S , 65, *note*
Fuller, Rev. E , 62.
Funeral ceremonies, 243.

Ganowanian system, diagram showing, 96.
Gason, Mr S., 25, 55, 61.
Geawagal tribe, Appendix G, 279.
General conclusions, 364.
Gens, the ancient, 108, 158.
Gentes, exogamous, 63 ; intermarrying, 113.
Gentile relationship, 121.
Gesture language, 55
Ghosts, 246 ; white men thought to be, 248.
Gibson, Mr. J , 180, 204, *note ;* 205, *note ;* 269.
Giles, Mr. C., jun , 36, 65
Gippsland, first settlement of, 181 ; aboriginal population of, 227.
Gonds and Bygars, 154
Gould, Mr Lionel H., 31.
Gournditch-mara tribe, 204, *note ;* 232, *note ;* 246, *note ;* 253, *note ;* Appendix F, 274, 327, *note ;* 347.
Gow, Mr W , 350
Grandchildren, 81, 82, 94.
Group relationship, 56, 99, 102 ; is a real relationship, 102.

Hagenauer, Rev. F. A., 204, *note ;* 230, *note*.
Half-sister marriage, Kamilaroi, 45, 115 ; does not affect descent, 47 ; a local peculiarity, 48 ; authority for, 48, *note*.
Hand of a corpse, 244
Hawaiian sister marriage, 100.
Hearn, Professor, his theory of the gens, 109, 334 ; of ancestral worship, 110 ; his statement as to uterine succession, 120 ; theory of agnation, 126.
Herbert River tribe, 32, 36, 65.
Homan, Rev W , 61.
Homicide, distinction between simple and impious, 123.
Husband and wife, 92.

Individual marriage, 340.
Infanticide not effected by violence, 175 ; female, 67, 135 ; male, 138 ; Appendix C, 171 ; among the Kurnai, 190, 357.
Inheritance, 245 ; of sister's son, 129.
Initiation, ceremonies of, 192.
Intaphermes' wife, choice of, 125, *note*.
Isolation of Kurnai, 233.

Kalmuks, 140.
Kamilaroi, 47, *note*
Khonds, 141.
Kinship, terms of, 318 ; development of, 318 ; M'Lennan's views as to, 318,
Kocchs and Hos, 141.

INDEX.

Kramer, Rev. C. W , 320, *note*; 350.
Kroatungolung, the, 227, 308.
Kubitha, 37, *note*.
Kühn, Rev. Julius, 179, 210, *note*; 241, *note*; 253, *note*; Appendix H, 284.
Kunandaburi tribe, 328, 355.
Kurnai, their present numbers, 181; meaning of name, 187; isolation of, 233; their character and intelligence, 255; their numerals, 255, *note*; their life one of dread, 259; their present social condition, 317; whence they probably migrated, 323; marriage by elopement among, 200; marriage by capture among, 343.
Kurnai system, theory of, stated, 297; peculiarities of, 298; objections to theory, 308; importance of, 311

Lance, Mr. T. E , 37, *note*; 48, *note*; 53, 326.
Larakia tribe, 64.
Laws of marriage, &c., chapter iii, Kamilaroi marriage.
Levirate, law of, 146.
Lewin, 192
Little, Mr J. A. G , 64
Lockhart, Mr. C. G. N , 41, 66.
Lubbock, Sir John, his theory as to war captives, 65, 149, 342; of the four classes, 107; his argument against Morgan's theory, 115; confusion as to exogamy, 116; mistake as to American Indian system, 83, *note*; 118; explanation of Orestes' plea, 126; basis of marriage, 127; of individual marriage, 149, 342; of expiation for marriage, 151; theory of totemism, 165; that, among savages, society does not concern itself with individual wrongs, 329.
Lyon, Mr. G. O., 61

Mackay tribe, 34, 167.
Magic, various forms of, 251
Maine, Sir H S , 332, 337.
Malayan system of kinship, 99.
Male infanticide, 138.
Marriage, with sister, 99; with half-sister, 45, 115; marriage is a status, not a contract, 127; expiation for, 151: customs of, 200; obligations of, 205; by capture, 343; by capture cannot be a complete system, 141; by elopement, 200, 348; regulations of, 200, 227.
M'Gregor, Dr., 185, *note*; and 205, *note*.
Maori, 105, 153; genealogies, 105, *note*.
M'Lennan, Mr. J. F., 26; his theory of kinship terms, 101; his use of terms exogamy and endogamy, 321, *note*; misleading, 117, 139; his view of Orestes' plea, 123, *note*; his theory of the rise of kinship, 131; of female infanticide, 133, 357; of exogamous tribes and marriage by capture, 138, 357; of polyandry, 144; of the Levirate, 146; his objections to the theory of expiation by marriage, 151.
Monopoly of women in Australian tribes, 354.
Moral feeling, 257.
Morality of savages, 102.
Morgan, Hon. Lewis H , objections to his nomenclature, 26, 76, 81; his theory of the reformatory movement, 99, 115, 160, and *passim*; definitions quoted from, 236, *note*.
Mota, 34, 62; male infanticide, 138; polyandry of, 147.
Mother's brothers, 77, 85, 93.
Mother's sisters, 86.
Mothers-in-law, 93; avoidance of son-in-law, 103, 203, 291, *note*; reason of, 104.

Mukjarawaint tribe, 324, *note*; 345.
Murdu, legend of, 25.

Nair polyandry, 145.
Names, 190, 210.
Naming the dead, reluctance to, 249.
Narrinyeri, 307, 350.
Nasamones, 154
Naudowessies, 154
Navitilevu hill tribes, statistics of, 172.
Neborak, 207.
Nephew and niece defined, 77-79.
New Britain tribes, 33.
Ngariego tribe, 34, 324
Ngrung, nose piercing, 191.
Numerals, the Kurnai, 255, *note*.

Obligation of marriage, 205.
O'Donnell, Mr. J. W, 356, *note*.
Old age, reverence for, 211.
Orestes, plea of, 122.

Polyandry, M'Lennan's theory of, 144.
Property in swan's eggs, 226, 232, *note*.
Punjil, 210, *note*; 324, *note*.

Reeve, Mr. W, jun., 32, 66.
Relationship, chapter iv.; as between group and group, 56, 90; summary of, 90; group relationship is a real relationship, 101; line of descent does not affect personal relationship, 119; gentile relationship, 121; relationship to the father does not include relationship to the mother, and *vice versa*, 120; terms of, defined, 236.
Ridley, Rev. W., 37, 43, 45, 48, *note*.
Robinson, H. C., diary of, 157, *note*.
Roe, Mr. D. E., 345.
Rooney, Rev. J, 176.
Rusden, Mr G. W., Appendix G., 279.

Savages, their method of reasoning, 70, 132; morality of, 102; not descended from civilized ancestors, 162.
Scars, ornamental, 192.
Sister-marriage, 99.
Sister-in-law, 92.
Sister's children, 78, 80.
Sister's son, inheritance of, 129.
Sister, tribal, defined, 92
Social unit, the, 90, 128, 340.
Spirits of ancestors, 246.
Spirit séance, 254.
Stähle, Rev. J. H, 179, 193, *note*; 205, *note*; 246, *note*; 253, *note*; Appendix F, 274.
Suppliants and friendly aliens, protection of, 222; punishment of offending, 222.
Swan's eggs, property in, 226, 232, *note*.

Table A, 34; B, 36; C, 39; D, 43; E, 45; F, 61, 62; A, 227; B, 236; C, 241.
Taplin, Mr. F. W., 350.

INDEX.

Taplin, Rev. G., 61, 307, *note;* 350, *note.*
Taylor, Rev. R., 153.
Terms of kinship, 236 ; table of, 61 ; anomalous terms, 167, *note;* of the Turanian system proceed from the class divisions, 76.
Thibetan polyandry, 146.
Totemic subdivisions, 40.
Totems, evidence as to totemism, 165 ; of the Mackay tribe, 167 ; of the Mount Gambier tribe, 168.
Tribe defined, 29 ; M'Lennan's use of, 139 ; an aggregate of clans, 224.
Turra tribe, 210, *note;* 241, *note;* 253, *note;* Appendix H, 284.
Turndun, 197 ; Appendix E, 267.
Turanian system, 26, *note;* diagrams showing, 96.
Tylor, Mr. E. B., 269, 335, *note.*

Umbilicus, 204, *note*
Uncle, is the mother's brother, 77 ; the father-in-law, 85
Undivided commune, 99, 150, 160, 327.

Vogelsang, Rev. H., 52, *note;* 179, 346, 350.

War, leadership in, 212 ; a night attack, 212 ; battle of the clans, 217.
West Australian tribes, 31, 36.
Wife's mother, taboo of, 203, 291.
Wild dog, superstition as to, 218, *note.*
Williams, Rev. John, 161.
Witchcraft, disease caused by, 216, 250 ; bulk, 247, 251, *note;* barn, 252
Women, capture of, 224, 343 ; no encumbrance to savages, 136, 358.
Wonghi tribe, 345.
World props, 55, *note.*
Worship, ancestral. See *Ancestral Worship.*

Walker, May, and Co., Printers, 9 Mackillop-street, Melbourne.